Global Public Square

Identity & Action in the 21st Century

Francis Sealey

chipmunkapublishing
the mental health publisher

Published by
Chipmunkapublishing
PO Box 6872
Brentwood
Essex CM13 1ZT
United Kingdom

http://www.chipmunkapublishing.com

Chipmunkapublishing gratefully acknowledge the support of Arts Council England.

Author Biography

Francis Sealey was born in 1944 and was a Producer and Executive Producer for many years working for both the BBC Open University and the Community Programmes Unit. He has been active in politics and community action for most of his life, being a Parliamentary Candidate in 1974 and founder and activist in a number of social & community networks. Since 1993 he has been a freelance producer working with a number of training, public and voluntary organisations. In 2007 he founded 21st Century Network (now GlobalNet21) to help recreate public space and bring genuine debate back to public life.

In four years GlobalNet21 has grown significantly and now hosts many meetings, webinars and podcasts and uses social networks as an important way to publically engage. Francis Sealey is now Chairman of GlobalNet21 and with others is now responsible for its activities and development.

Francis Sealey

Acknowledgements

This book has been the result of many years of active life in both politics and community. There are many people to thank for the progress of this book. There is my family who have helped with the development of ideas and structure, including my wife Lois who has helped with suggestions and contacts my son Mark who helped design the cover, and my son-in-law Dominic who has been a constant presence of debate and discussion.

I would also like to thank Christina Wiltshire who first made contact with Chipmunk and has helped with photos and research as well as the ideas arising from 21st Century Network. Without her initial contact with Chipmunk this book would not have been possible. Of course the growing members of the 21st Century Network (now GlobalNet21) have helped immensely through months of discussion around the central ideas of this turbulent and uncertain century. Their contribution is still continuing and will help the ideas in this book develop further as the years go by.

Francis Sealey

CHAPTER 1 - Muddling Through

Surviving Our Future

The 21st Century is perhaps the most critical time facing the human race and how we manage our way through the decades of this century may well determine if we survive it at all. This is a century where we need to get below the superficial froth of life that gives us constant pleasure and distraction and somehow focus on the underlying tensions that are making our life on this planet unsustainable. That means knowing what these tensions are and what are the fault lines of our planetary existence. It also means understanding our own identity within that environment and creating within us both the potency and the power to make a difference. We have to more clearly distinguish between illusion and reality and forge our character on the real essence of our existence - the planet that exists rather than the planet we conjure up in our mind.

This book is about the journey to find meaning beyond the froth of our surface lives that we create from generation to generation and to relate it to a fast and dangerous real world that is in danger of imploding. It is an attempt to find authentic meaning when all around us no meaning seems to exist at all. Rather than hiding in the social structures of escape we look at how we can change our environment and ourselves together and try to make a difference so that it matters.

But this is easier said than done. Our lives often float on a shallow surface and it is that we often consider reality. We fail to see beneath or try to understand the total system of which we are but part. Our ego has led us too often to believe that we can have dominion over this world and hence we have built our lives on foundations of sand. When the winds blow as they have in this century then that foundation shakes and our ego is never strong enough to survive the storm. So we retreat into a private world of isolation, or pleasure or indifference rather than create a future based upon common purpose.

To create such a future, we need debate and discussion and yet all too often, the opportunities for such are few or non existent. Our churches and political parties are no longer the forums they once were and are more concerned with public relations, power or comfort rather than ideas. The public space where people can exchange ideas and discover the nature of their own reality and that of their environment has been severely restricted. The ancient Greek idea of the agora or Public Square where people gathered and exercised their citizenship has largely gone from public life and been replaced by the notion of citizenship as a means of control, cohesion and conformity rather than an expression of diversity and exploration.

This book is written on the belief that we need to recreate that public space once again and to do so in a global age where issues increasingly cross national boundaries. We have to find a way of using global public space to forge some sense of direction in a century when the old maps that created understanding in the last two centuries have been torn up or found wanting. It is only if we find new ways of connecting and ensuring that those connections are meaningful that we can create a true synergy between our character and the environment around us. That is the real challenge of our age and one on which our survival may well depend.

Imaginative Worlds

As we move through the years from youth to maturity and then old age, most of us like to think we make sense out of life. When we look back after many years, it is reassuring to know that there is some sort of pattern in the way we have led our life. For most of us, life without purpose is a life that is meaningless and so to give purpose to our lives; we often create it our imagination. The problem with a life lead in our imagination is that we live a constant delusion or we come face to face with that delusion as reality checks our fantasy and changes it. And for some of us, we have moments in our life when our fantasy has had that reality check; but that does not necessarily mean we have discovered life in its objective reality: It usually means that we substitute one imaginative fantasy for another.

There must be times in all our lives when suddenly there is a shift in our perception of reality - when the world no longer appears as we once thought it was. Many people ignore those moments and carry on as usual. But perhaps two or three times in my life I have had such moments when it seemed almost impossible to carry on as usual.

One of these moments was in February 1974. I was addressing an eve of poll meeting in the February General Election of that year in the United Kingdom as a Parliamentary candidate. It had been a very active campaign and the controversy of that period together with the excitement that it generated made meetings well attended and well informed. I remember standing before a packed audience and making my eve of poll speech with what I hoped would be a passion and enthusiasm that could be transferred to the critical yet listening audience. But as I was speaking, I almost had an "out of body experience" and for a few seconds or maybe more, it felt as if I were an observer of my own performance and of the audience surrounding me. And as I observed, I imagined I was watching a game rather than a real exercise in democratic choice between competing ideas. Suddenly, the whole exercise became unreal. Those few seconds of reality check made me deeply disturbed. My mind was in turmoil because I began questioning in those few seconds the relevance of what I was doing. Most of us at times during our life question the relevance of what we do, but we carry on regardless. For me it became difficult to carry on as usual after looking almost surreally at the ritual performance that evening because what I observed made me doubt that it would change the world and make a difference. I knew at that moment I had to rethink my attitude towards personal and social change because the "game" was no longer sufficient. Enjoyable it might have been, but effective it certainly was not.

At that time, I was 30 years old and full of ambition and hope for the future. I had become a Parliamentary candidate for the Labour Party and was fighting an election during the time of the coal miner's strike and the three-day week. In many ways, it was the last campaign of the old industrial age. It was a classic confrontation in the minds of many of us between capital and labour. And it was a classic confrontation at a time when the world was fast changing and when the old industrial world was gradually collapsing before our eyes. All around us were signs of the New World that was beginning to emerge. We had just gone through the cultural revolution of the 1960s when all seemed possible. Suddenly the world began to appear small as young people developed their own ideas across the globe and those ideas seem to have more similarity than those held by a parent generation. The economy was changing fast from an industrial production to a service based one and economic growth was making a working class increasingly prosperous. And a year before in 1973 an oil crisis saw oil prices rise worldwide because of the power of the oil producers in the Middle East. In a way, this was a sign of the times to come when resource shortages and the predictions of those shortages in the future would make our seemingly abundant planet suddenly become finite. Scarcity in a world of plenty now became a future possibility in the modern world.

And yet here I was fighting an election as if the old world was still upon us. Of course I knew it wasn't because I had been part of the Cultural Revolution in the 1960s; but my teenage years had been brought up in the atmosphere of the Post War world where normality meant going back to that period before the war but without the economic depression that had then swept the world. I had been brought up in a childhood world of people who wanted to return to "normalcy," and that meant not only forgetting the old world of war and depression but also ignoring the new world of change and uncertainty. The decade or so following the Second World War was a period caught in a time warp. That was understandable for those people who went through the war and whose formative years were in that period between the two world wars. But some of us, who were brought up after the war, then somehow that concept of "normalcy" did not ring true. All of us, at that time, and in our own way must have experienced the sensation of somehow moving from one world to the next as the years following the War progressed into the 1960s and beyond.

However it was strange that that should happen when I was on a public platform fighting the battles of the past and trying to make them relevant to the present. When the realisation and understanding of change confronts you in such a dramatic way, then it can shake the ground of all your being and from there on in your imagination, you have to create a different world. I suppose since that time, I have spent my life trying to create that different world and, in doing so, hoping that it would be possible to make a difference. However as time goes by every world you create in your imagination to effect change comes under question, as you wonder if you have had any effect at all; or whether at every step of your life you have still been playing an imaginable game and simply muddling through.

Making Sense Of Our World

Many of us spend our lives trying to make sense of history. We find it almost impossible to think that the past is just an unconnected series of moments. We have to interlace those moments with meaning in order to make sense of our lives. Most of us spend our time trying to create links between the moments that make up our lives in order that it has some shape and pattern. When in 2001 John Gray published his book Straw Dogs[1], then that book both inspired and infuriated people at the same time. In that book he dared to suggest that there is no meaning in history and all of us live from moment to moment. 20, 30 or 40 years ago have very little significance to us today. What matters is what happens now, the people we know today and the relationships we have. The important thing is to take advantage of each and every moment.

Yet all of us at times pause to reflect. We look back on the times we have experienced and hope that there are moments where we've made a difference. For many that difference is making a difference to society and changing the collective around us but for others it is making a difference to one or two individuals. However most of us sometimes doubt whether we have made any difference at all. We look back at all the plans we have had and all the ambitions when we were young and wonder if at the end of the day those ambitions have come to very little. The problem is if we cannot make a difference in our lives and if we cannot take action that is meaningful in a world of turbulence there seems little hope. If life has been just a chain of pleasure and personal events then the future at a time of great change seems more uncertain than ever. The here and now is not sufficient. We want the future to exist so that the here and now can have significance for our children too. Somehow we have to make sense of this world and live in it in a meaningful way. If we feel that everything around us is out of control there is

---

[1] Straw Dogs: Thoughts on Humans and Other Animals by John Gray, Farrar, Straus and Giroux, Published: October 2007 ISBN: 978-0-374-27093-3

little we can do except exist and the message of Straw Dogs is that just to exist is probably our fate. The art of living is learning to live with the moment.

Those of us though who believe that we can use our reason, for better off or worse, to change events find this difficult to accept. Whether we are being deluded into the believing that we can make a difference when all the time what we do has very little effect is one of the most important questions for each and every one of us. But those of us who believe this are faced with a dilemma. We want to believe that reason is important and yet we know that it has failed time and again. In the 21st century that recognition of failure has been faced with stark brutality. After several centuries where progress had become the religion of the day, we suddenly came face-to-face with the fact that progress could not go on indefinitely into the future. Reason that we once thought infallible and that would engine progress from generation to generation was now seriously under threat. It seemed as if the modern world was falling apart as our planet was faced with unprecedented challenges. The challenge in the 21st century was to combine with reason an intuitive understanding of the world around us and only from that base to take the right sort of action. But how can we possibly do that?

Recently a group of us invited a 95-year-old man talk about his life. He was born in Germany and opposed the growing Hitler movement. Indeed his father was responsible for getting a number of Jews out of Germany including Einstein. It was clear that as Hitler became more powerful that the life of this 95 year old man then a teenager, would be in danger. So one day, just before the War, as storm troopers ransacked his house, he found himself approaching his house from a distance on his bicycle. He immediately and discretely turned his bike around and cycled to safety through France and into Spain. He then came to England and joined the British army becoming a major by 1946. So much had happened to him in his life and I asked him what he regretted and he said,

"As you grow older you realise that life is never as you expect it. You never achieve your ambitions and aims as you once thought. It is difficult to regret as we never know what life would have been like had we taken a different path. But when I look back on my life with all the events, its joys and tragedies then I know I have led a good life. Whatever happens to us in life both tragic or happy, the one thing I do know is that when life offers us opportunities then we must grab them and make the best we can. That is the only way we can live."

I thought that put life in perspective better than most other statements I have heard both before and since. But how do we know how to seize opportunities and which ones are important for us at any point in time? This book is written in the belief that we all need to grasp at opportunities throughout our life in order to make a difference and especially when the world is increasingly in turmoil. It is written because I know I have done that all my life and seized the moment; but as I get older I begin to wonder what opportunities got lost, what ones offered false paths and what others have born fruit. I have always been conscious of muddling through with enthusiasm and have often wondered whether this is the road to sanity.

Living By Chance

One of the most difficult ideas for most of us to accept is that in life we just muddle through. Of course we have the illusion often that we have plans, the grand design, the blueprint for a successful life but really all that we do is muddle through. Most if not all of us are faced with the absence of long term planning in our lives and realise that chance has overwhelmed purpose in influencing the choices we have made. Most planning has been short term and if we are lucky then we just about get one step ahead of ourselves at every stage.

Realising that we all muddle through was difficult for me as from a very early age I was always on a mission, or I thought, to make a better world. Now if your ambition in life is to do just that how can you possibly admit to yourself that you are mudding through? Does not muddling through end up with a muddled world and how can that be a better one by any stretch of the imagination?

And anyhow I was a human being; a rational creature of the modern age and our modern age was full of blueprints and maps that told us exactly where we were going. One blueprint told us we were going to heaven if we followed a creed or belief as our life long map. Well no muddling through there. Another told us that history was full of meaning and progressed in a series of dialectic jumps to a certain future – so no confusion there either. Another told us that by inductive reasoning we could solve the mysteries of the universe and ahead of us lay abundance for all. Well that seemed like a good plan. This was the 20th Century and nearly three centuries of enlightened thinking had produced a series of blueprints for us to choose from. We could even pick and mix from the many maps as modernism gave way to post modernism – but we had direction and purpose – and for those of us on a mission well who could ask for anything more.

But of course in our everyday life we followed the flow of fate and chance, we made mistake after mistake, we were impulsive and often absurd and when such behaviour was pinned on the maps of our enlightened age then chaos resulted more often than purpose. Our blueprints then became dreams or illusions that gave us a semblance of meaning when all around us confusion reigned as we muddled through.

In the 1970's I travelled to Yale University in the United States to do a radio interview for the British Open University with Professor C.E. Lindblom because he had turned muddling through into an art – or at least thought he had and wrote extensively about it. He called muddling through "incrementalism" and argued that in life we all took small or even "baby steps" in our approach to decision making. This he referred to as muddling through as often these steps did not relate to one another in any grand design or purpose.

As I attended his garden party before the day of the interview, surrounded by young attractive men and women, all seeking his attention, I wondered if they considered themselves ambitious there in one of America's ivory tower universities as they looked to their futures with aspiration and design. And were they like the rest of us just muddling through? Around me were men and women with plans for their futures and many with their lives mapped out in their minds whilst at the same time they were arguing academically that what we all really do is muddle! That it seemed to me was the ultimate confusion between ideas and practice; but then it was a confusion that we all share.

Fading Blueprints

We are after all more creatures of rationalisation than reason and our acts of rationalising are often vulnerable attempts to put meaning into our muddled existence. We call it reason or design but it is little more than illusion. The 21st century has come on us like a shock and issues like fundamentalism, resource shortage, expanding population and global warming have shot through the certainties of the ideas of the late 20th century. Indeed the 20th Century blueprints were rationalisations but they were so on a grand scale. The humanistic religions, socialism, liberalism and even conservatism did provide for us a framework to understand what was happening in the world around us and most of us signed up to one blueprint or the other. Today those blueprints have gone or appear wanting and we are muddling through without those usual maps.

On 9/11 2001 the world was brought to a shocking halt as two planes crashed into the Twin Towers in New York and another hit the Pentagon in Washington. The sudden horror of the new world and the underlying anger and confusion contained within it immediately hit us all. It was one of those defining moments when we all realised that the 20th century was over but what was being heralded in we just did not know. Some felt it was a new dark age where the values of the Enlightenment and human reason were being undermined by reactionary forces. Others saw it as the beginning of the end of the world and the advent of the second coming. Yet others saw it as an opportunity to reshape our values at a time when the old world and its ideological structure was no longer relevant to the world we lived in. I belonged to this last group who knew that our old maps had gone and wanted some sense to emerge out of the ensuing chaos that the collapse of the Twin Towers had highlighted.

I remember on the day that happened that my overwhelming feeling was that we were all one world and if we did not behave that way then our world will probably not have changed fundamentally but will have finished completely. My hope was that the global dimension of our lives would remain somehow in tact and that we would not descend into some hopeless parochialism. Talking to friends we all felt that we needed to do what we could to enhance the international consensus that had developed around the horror of

9/11 and try to help ensure that no precipitous action would result from the fallout. Some of us formed a local United Nations Association Branch and invited our MPs to be accountable on an MP Watch website that we set up. We wanted to use the UN to bring together the nations of the world around some basic humanistic principles but were frustrated in that when the USA and the UK led a war on Iraq in search of weapons of mass destruction that were not there and links with Al Quaida that did not exist.

Despite world wide opposition and unprecedented protest marches all over the world including up to 2 million people on the streets of London, politicians cowered before their Governments and voted for and supported an invasion that has made the world more like a powder keg than a place safe from strife. Democracy had failed and that led to our increasing frustration. It reminded us of the Cuban missile Crisis in 1962 when the world seemed on the brink of nuclear war and most people felt helpless faced with that stark reality.

Ten years on from the 9/11 event and Osama bin Laden is dead, there is a revolution of expectation on the streets of Tunisia and Egypt with violent supression in Libya and Syria and we still are left in confusion as to the direction our century is travelling. Bin Laden represented the the force that many demanded of travelling back to an imagined Islamic tradition and enforcing it on us all with whatever means possible. But the demonstrations on the streets of Middle Eastern and North African countries were often inspired by young secular Moslems who represented the spirit of modernity. The new world suddenly had become a strange cauldron of tradition and modernity and much else as well.

We have seen democracy fail whilst others still demand it. We see the spectre of terrorism still writ large despite wars to suppress it and the assissination of leaders like bin Laden. It is difficult to know how to handle our domestic politics or wonder if it has any meaning and it is even more difficult to make sense of the changing international world where the forces of modernity, tradition and survival come face to face with an unsustainable planet.

Running Out Of Time

Trying to support and enhance internationalism was important in a growing age of conflict that was taking on new dimensions; but it was not enough. The problems facing us needed a paradigm shift in attitude as well as structure and it was important to work on both.

It was suggested that this book be written because some of us had created "21st Century Network[2]" as one way to provide a forum where these issues could be discussed on a global scale. It was an attempt to involve people as widely as possible as well as politicians in discussing the changes necessary and then taking whatever social action was appropriate as events unfolded.

21st Century Network (now GlobalNet21) was set up in the spring of 2007 to discuss some of the issues that confront us on a daily basis when we did not have the maps and blueprints that provided ready answers for us in the 20th century. This was clearly filling a need as the organisation grew rapidly and meetings became popular and well attended. It was clear that there was a growing need to try and understand the world around us and to involve as many people as possible. The advantage of having maps of understanding is that they offered cohesion and without those in the 21st Century we seem to be descending into chaos. Fragmentation was everywhere and instead of the globalisation of cosmopolitanism we were beginning to experience increasing tribal and parochial resurgence. Religious fundamentalism was again raising its intolerant head not just in the Middle East but also in Middle America, on the Indian Sub continent and elsewhere. Political parties were everywhere losing their relevance as interest groups in a variety of fragmented forms gained citizens allegiance. It seemed that chaos was the order of the day and somehow we had to live with it and make it work for us.

The danger of course is that this would take time and in that time much turmoil would reign. Yet this was a dangerous world with fast increasing populations, spreading migrations and the growing availability of weapons of mass destruction. The proliferation of the opportunities to be totally destructive on a scale unknown before

---

[2] For more information on 21st century Network see the meetup site at http://www.meetup.com/21stCenturyNetwork/

was now very real. On top of this the planet was in danger as our industrial world became day by day unsustainable. The stakes for our very survival were high.

And yet although adjustment to this new world would take time, it seemed as if time was the last gift on offer. When in the late 18th and early 19th centuries some key countries of Europe led by the United Kingdom began to move away from an agricultural community to an industrial one then it seemed as if the blueprints of the past had been torn up then. For half a century or more it was difficult to make any sense over what was happening and for meaning to emerge. The early 19th century was one of romantic illusions, utopian dreams and hard-nosed utilitarianism as usefulness rather than human worth became the cry of the day. It was not until the middle of that century that the new blueprints for understanding emerged as modern day conservatism, liberalism and socialism took shape.

Today we do not have that amount of time to play with as we make sense of the changing world around us. We have ten to 20 years to bridge the resource gap that will result from oil drying up, the same amount of time or less to slow the rising temperatures of the world that will change the face of the earth and bring death and suffering to many. We have probably the same amount of time to tackle both the inequalities of wealth that exist on a global scale and the humiliation that the poor feel at the expense of the wealthy. If we fail in that then the possibility of increasing conflict fought through modern technological warfare will be upon us with a vengeance. And we have to face these issues at a time when conventional politics is facing a crisis of paralysis. The reputation of politicians is today probably lower than it has ever been and people's faith in them delivering solutions is very low. It is not just the fault of politicians as they have become increasingly powerless faced with the growing scale of globalisation with huge capital movements across the globe and a growing burden of debt in both the developed and under developed world.

Our Well Being Endangered

There is a vacuum in both vision for change and in faith that the necessary changes can take place. This creates a vicious circle. The more there is confusion then the worse it gets because society becomes dysfunctional, as do the individuals that make it up. Our essential well being rests with us being able to adapt to our environment as autonomous human beings. If we are unable to do this then the incidence of mental illness increases as our coping mechanisms suffer. It is difficult enough to adapt to a world with the certainty of maps to guide us through complexity. When that complexity increases and there are no longer maps then our ability to adapt diminishes.

And in that vacuum the Western world has put the goal of affluence as the path to salvation. We have created within our societies a structured status environment to satisfy our need for being recognised. After the First World War many people sought refuge in the twin ideologies of Fascism and Communism as "action" antidotes to the decline of the liberal capitalism of the 19th century. After the Second World War that antidote became the pursuit of wealth and status. Vance Packard documented that in his sociological books "The Status Seekers[3]" and "The Hidden Persuaders[4]." These books were written at the time that Richard Yates published his novel (later made into a film directed by Sam Mendes and starring Leonardo DiCaprio and Kate Winslet) "Revolutionary Road[5]." The book is centred on the life of the Wheelers who are initially drawn together because they believe that each represents the uninhibited glamour that is essential to success. After several years of marriage however they are wearied by the mundane aspects of domesticity, their ambitions and intellectual attitudes now appear flimsy and shallow.

Their suburban life and circle of friends makes Frank Wheeler crave for self worth and eventually they decide to leave Suburbia and escape to France. But Frank gets frightened over leaving his cosy existence. To do that would be to escape a life style that he has always admired. His fear is that in escaping to find him self then he will find nothing.

---

[3] The Status Seekers, Vance Packard. First published in April 1959, Publisher: David McKay **ISBN:** 0671771620
[4] The Hidden Persuaders, Vance Packard, first published in 1957, [Harmondsworth] : Penguin Books, [1961]. ISBN 097884310X
[5] Revolutionary Road by Richard Yates, Vintage Contemporaries ISBN 0375708448

The story ends tragically with the death of Frank's wife in a botched up self-abortion and the naked existence of their life becomes exposed. Although the book was written in the 1950's it has become popular again as many of us question the emptiness of a life of possession and status. Yates successfully represented in his book another nail in the American Dream as Scotts Fitzgerald had already done before him in his book "The Great Gatsby." Both showed that the pioneering spirit in America and the blind optimism it engendered resulted in alienation and insecurity that impacted on sanity itself. Today it has more relevance than ever.

In 2007, Oliver James published his book "Affluenza[6]" to illustrate that the constant goal of affluence in the Western world and especially the English-speaking world has led to a contagion of mental illness.[7] James has pointed out that in the English-speaking nations people are twice as likely to suffer mental illness as those from mainland Western Europe. An average 23% of Americans, Britons, Australians, New Zealanders and Canadians suffered in the last 12 months, but only 11.5% of Germans, Italians, French, Belgians, Spaniards and Dutch.

James believes that it is the combination of inequality in those societies (this not having changed substantially over time) with the widespread relative materialism (or as he calls it "Affluenza") that is the problem. Placing a high value on money, possessions, appearances and fame when there is already enough to satisfy fundamental needs creates an unhealthy society and mental illness.

Such an acquisitive society creates unrealistic aspirations and the expectation that they can be fulfilled. It does so to stimulate consumerism in order to increase profits and promote short-term economic growth. James goes further and suggests that high levels of mental illness are essential in these societies as "miserable people make greedy consumers and can be more easily suckered into perfectionist workaholism."

---

[6] Affluenza by Oliver James Publisher: Vermilion (September 2, 2008); *ISBN*-10: 0091900115
[7] Affluenza by Oliver James and published in 2007 by Vermillion.

Our society is centred on fame, celebrity and false dreams that we can all become celebrities or successful and we crave this in our status society where recognition is like a drug for many of us. And yet the planet itself is telling us that this is a fool's paradise. We have come to the end of the road but are too blind to see it. Somehow we have to learn to see again – both our selves and the world we live in. We need to have an image of ourselves that is not based upon false expectations but one that reflects who we are. We also have to see the world for what it is in the 21st century with all its fragile nature and finite capacity. Until we do both our mental state and our planet itself will suffer illness that after time maybe irreparable.

Muddling To A Purpose

Today we are faced with a growingly complex world, with the absence of maps or frameworks for us to make sense of that world and therefore often an inability to cope and adapt. Somehow we have to create both an understandable world whilst at the same time trying to understand ourselves more.

Somehow we have to try and make sense of a world as we ourselves muddle through. How do we create meaning for what we do and an attachment to our environment when the world itself seems in a muddle? How can we create coherence for the world we live in and for ourselves when all seems chaos and we understand that chaos is now the nature of things? In the 19th and 20th centuries we developed blueprints that often turned out to be illusory. Life has enough illusions so in the 21st century we have to avoid the grand design illusions of the previous two centuries and yet we have to do it sufficiently and adequately so that we can function in a meaningful universe and a sustainable planet.

That is the challenge of the 21st century and one that we are only just beginning. 21st Century Network was created to try to begin that process in a small way and this book is about the changes in society and in ourselves that we need to consider if we are to survive through the chaos of the fast changing world. It is not about creating new certainties as that is creating new illusions. It is rather about learning how we muddle through whilst at the same time making sense of our world and our own lives. It is also about the need for networks like 21st century to grow and expand so that more and more people engage in the discussions about our world and our survival in it. We need to create new global public squares where people are connected and engaged in helping us to navigate our way through this present century. It is a discussion that has to involve everyone and at all levels and that includes ordinary citizens as well as decision makers on a global scale. The question though is this a step too far beyond our reach as humankind or is there still the hope that change can take place this way – with synchronicity – both top down and bottom up.

So in Part 1 there are three chapters that look at the missions and ideals we have held in the past and how adequate they are for the 21st Century if well being is to be preserved and increasing mental illness prevented. We also look at the "change dilemma" – that is the dilemma of making people good before you get a good society or creating a good society in order that people can be good.

Part 2 look at the illusions that are a part of our lives and how we have to develop self-knowledge as part of the process of changing both our environment and ourselves in the modern world.

Part 3 considers global issues and the changes that are necessary there and whether our conventional democratic models are sufficient to deliver that to us.

The final Part 4 discusses how change can take place in the 21st century and how we can make a difference through networks like 21st century and others. It looks at our well being as citizens – a well being that has to be both local and global at the same time.

Redefining Our Values

21st Century Network is not a solution but one of the many pathways that we have to develop in the 21st century in order to adapt to the changing world order. It is difficult for us and we will often find ourselves regressing to old ways of thinking and behaving. When Alvin Toffler wrote his book "The Third Wave[8]" he explained in a postindustrial society, we need to adopt postindustrial attitudes. The first Wave he argued was our agricultural past, the second our industrial past and present. The third wave was our growing postindustrial future. As with many futurists his work had many a canvas of fantasy and imagination. However one point he made is relevant for any period of great change. When change takes place then our attitudes are confused. As Toffler explained many people thrust from an agricultural setting into an industrial one about to go post industrial and service based will hold attitudes that reflect all of these three different paradigms. Sometimes we will think in one mode and at other times in another and yet at others we will create hybrids in our imagination as we deal with conflicting thoughts and events. Rationality will not necessarily be the order of the day.

In setting up 21st Century Network that became very clear from the start. We said of the network

"This is a group for those who believe that we need to develop a new form of humanism that includes people of all religions and none but who embrace humanistic values as the basis of their actions. These are values of global compassion, personal self-discovery, shared development, planetary concern and a love of community.

We would love you to join us if you believe in these principles and wish to strengthen the humanist philosophy contained here. We want to bring those together who want to sustain a new world where diversity is valued."

What we were trying to do was bring together people who shared common humanist values and who believed that human beings should not be treated as "things." We were against the slavery of people through their use as a commodity or as an object. We wanted each human to be able to reach their full potential within society and that meant not only having a society that would facilitate that but also empowering individuals to demand that. At a time of great

---

[8] The Third Wave, Alvin Toffler, Publisher: Bantam (May 1, 1984) ISBN-10: 0553246984

change we felt it necessary to redefine these values and make them appropriate to a world without blueprints where people had to make an art of muddling through.

It was clear that those with or without a religion could hold these values. However those who globalised the world economy to the extent that the cheapest labour could be exploited including the use of children could not hold them. Nor could these values be held by fundamentalists who imposed creeds on people in such a way that their human choices were constrained by dogma. But most religious people did not share such views and were in the humanist embrace. We felt it was important to involve all who shared this and try to forge anew such basic values for a new age.

But it was clear that some humanists who joined did not feel this way and felt that all religion was illogical and the root of most of the problems in the world and some had got stuck in the 19th and 20th century humanism that defined religion as illogical and human reason as sacred. What a contradiction there! They had become secular fundamentalists in their attitudes and had not opened their minds to creating a broad alliance of diversity across the many divides necessary for survival in post 9/11 era. Some – few that is true – came on the site looking for religious people to just have a go.

Crossing The Barriers

So there was a learning process there for all of us. How do we create new alliances that cross barriers and boundaries and still keep our values in tact? Somehow the new millennium has to find a way to network our movements rather than to put them into ideological straight jackets so that we end up at each other's throats. This is one of our biggest challenges and means not only a change in society but also a change in us. Change now is total and cannot be compartmentalised any longer. But it will take time and our attitudes will reflect both the past century as well as the present for some time.

And yet as we said earlier we have little time. It was the famous 20th Century economist John Maynard Keynes who once said "in the long run we are all dead." Behind that statement was the view that we do not have to worry about the long run in economics because we will be long gone by that time; and anyhow, the long run will take care of itself. The problem is today that the long run is getting ever closer to the short and medium term. Time is being concertinaed up as global problems like population growth and climate change impact on us. Those who are young today will be faced with the consequences of these problems long before their life is over.

So it is imperative that we begin to face up to that total change earlier rather than later and creating 21st Century Network was one way of attempting to do this. It is initiatives like this that are important and that link personal with global change as part of the same process. So this book explores some of these issues. It does not pretend to have answers but it does raise the problems and suggest a number of avenues for revitalising our culture and political life so that together we can make a difference. We may still muddle through but we will know that we are doing it rather than have the illusion that we are not and we will incrementally make changes in ourselves and our environment that reflect a shared future. That is the challenge and it is a challenge for our survival.

Part 1 – Making A Difference

How to achieve happiness in society has been one of the great quests of history. It has been debated certainly from the time of the ancient Greek and today it has almost become a Holy Grail. But for large parts of history, all over the world, many people have understood that happiness only comes in small doses. It is only since the 17th century that humans have considered it a basic human right to pursue the goal of happiness.

This section of the book looks at that pursuit of happiness and the different ways people have tried to achieve it. We have particularly looked at a modern western society where happiness has been often confused with the acquisition of wealth and status. That longing for recognition, for fame and acceptance is as strong as ever despite the fact that the condition of our planet is making it more difficult to achieve.

Because of that, the other age old debate about whether you need to create a good society in order to create good people or whether you need to create a good person in order that society can itself be good has become more relevant. In a way, this dichotomy sets the scene for the rest of the book. Not only does it relate to the question of happiness and whether that can be achieved, it also relates to whether in our short life on this planet, we can actually make a difference. Is life about making a difference or is it merely about enjoying ourselves regardless of the consequences?

So in the first chapters of this book we look first at how we view ourselves and the world, and how that is often based upon illusion rather than reality, and also how that can impact on our own society and on the world in which we live. We consider whether we need to become empowered individuals as well as trying to create a sane society and to do so simultaneously rather than believe that one is the cause of the other. Finally we relate this to the whole question of happiness and whether real happiness can be found in having a goal in life that does make a difference to ourselves and our planet rather than merely following the pursuit of pleasure.

In a way these chapters help us think and set the scene for considering the whole area of self-knowledge and knowledge about our planet - both subjects we consider later in the book. At a time of unprecedented change in a world that seems turned upside down and where our values are questioned probably as never before, then addressing these questions becomes an important prerequisite for considering our own role in achieving social change that matters to our selves and others.

CHAPTER 2 - Mission Driven Illusions

Reuniting Germany

I have suffered the illusion all my life that I could make a difference. From a very early age I was always interested in politics and had dreams of a better world and indeed thought that we were driving progressively towards that better future. I always wanted to play my part. Long before my age reached double figures I was sitting down writing a paper on how to reunite Germany whilst my friends were out getting their knees dirty and their faces covered in mud. Not that I never joined in that childish play, as I did, but I felt it equally important for reasons that escape me now that Germany should be reunited. Those adults around me who had just experienced the war thought me plain mad but excused me, as I was a child still. But for me I was on a mission and it was the mission that drove me rather than the issue itself.

In reading the book by Kazuo Ishiguro "When We Were Orphans[9]" I was struck by the quote on the very last page of the novel where Sarah writes to Christopher about their lives and the love that they could never quite get together. She says,

"...for those like us, our fate is to face the world as orphans. Chasing through long years the shadows of vanished parents. There is nothing for it but to try and see through our missions to the end, as best we can, for until we do so, we will be permitted no calm."

The more I thought about it the more I thought there was the something of the orphan in me as I was brought up by grandmother, my mother long gone and my father unknown. Well I was never technically an orphan but near enough in my mind to occasionally think that. So maybe I was driven like many I know to find my vanished parents in the continual missions of my life. At 9 years of age uniting Germany had become those lost parents but other ideas

---

[9] When We Were Orphans by Kazuo Ishiguro, Faber and Faber; New edition edition (5 Mar 2001) ISBN-10: 057120516X

and goals adopted me as I progressed through life permitting me no respite.

By the time I was eleven years and on my way to Grammar school I had convinced my headmaster and his secretary (goodness knows why she was on the interviewing panel) that I wanted to be a missionary. I had by that time joined what was called Christian Junior Endeavour at my local Methodist chapel and we were used to getting a small pamphlet from the Methodist Missionary Society telling us about the exploits of white male missionaries in far off lands. Fed on a diet of television that had just invaded our homes with small black and white screens, I suddenly saw myself a mixture of the Lone Ranger and a crusader for God converting heathens with a wave of the hand. With a Hi Ho Lord, my zeal was directed towards the Mau Mau who was daily in the news. In later in life I found that they came from Kenya though I did not know that at the time. I only knew that they did not believe in the God of my missionary society and thus were fair game for the wave of my hand. In my mind I had scores of them falling to their knees in prayer as I passed over them with a blessing.

The Mau Mau uprising, as it was called, took place between 1952 and 1960 and was really an insurgency against what was then British colonial rule. British forces and the Kenyan police ruthlessly suppressed it with thousands of causalities resulting. Recently lawyers acting for Mau veterans have documented 6,000 cases of human rights abuse that allegedly took place. At the time all of this passed over me as I deluded myself with the belief that my mission driven passion could right all wrongs and bring God given harmony to the troubled scene.

Within a couple of years I had moved from reuniting Germany to converting the entire Mau Mau to the chosen path and I had not yet even reached the tender age of 12 when Jesus was reputed to have entered the Temple in Jerusalem and openly challenged the Pharisees. Suffer little children even when they are insufferable.

Well that was some start. Since then my life has been a series of missions concocted in my mind to somehow save the world in one way or another in wave after wave of idealism. It was Carl Jung who questioned idealism and what often lay behind it. In discussing idealism and the power of the ideal to achieve social justice, he says in "The Undiscovered Self[10]"

" Who is making the idealist demand? Is it, perchance someone who jumps over his own shadow in order to hurl himself avidly on an idealistic program that promises him a welcome alibi? How much responsibility and apparent morality is there, cloaking with deceptive colours a very different inner world of darkness?"

Every form of addiction is bad," Jung later said, "no matter whether the narcotic be alcohol or morphine or idealism." Whatever one thinks of Jung, and like many thinkers he had his fair share of strange beliefs and notions, that should not stop us looking at some of the insights on "being" that he highlighted. And the fact that he looked on idealism as an addiction – a way that we organise our lives to cover over the shadows of our past is something I could identify with, as that is probably what I did together with most idealists.

And if idealism can be a mechanism that helps us through the struggles of life as narcotics and alcohol can for others calling it substance abuse then cannot idealism at times be reality abuse too? Yet we look at substance abuse as a dysfunction that often reflects mental illness. Idealism we look upon much more positively and often with admiration – yet that idealism is often driven by mission to hide so many shadows in our lives. And if our idealism is often a coping mechanism in our lives then it raises the question of what is illusion and what reality. In order to survive do we not all create illusions that we somehow mistake for reality?

Reality & Illusion

Idealists of course are not the only ones to experience illusion. We all weave meaning into what we do and we all need to feel there is purpose somewhere hidden in our endeavours. But could all this be an illusion too that drives us as human beings and gives us the motivation to survive? The reality could be that we fool ourselves

---

[10] The Undiscovered Self by Carl Jung, Signet Book; Reissue edition (7 Feb 2006) ISBN-10: 0451217322

into thinking this is actual consciousness and that this somehow elevates us above other species on this earth. That way we feel both better and meaningful. Maybe we are living the constant illusion that action means purpose and as long as the adrenaline of action runs through our veins then we are drugged into the comfort zone of feeling that we have achieved. But rather than achieving we have merely kept in motion, feeling the constant wind of excitement but never arriving at any satisfactory destination.

So it is not surprising that from a very early age I had severe doubts about what difference I was actually making and my motive behind wanting to do so. Not that ever stopped me as the locomotive of action compelled me to continue. But the faster it went the more doubts I had. Periods of activity were followed by short periods of contemplation as I reassessed the world and my place in it. From becoming a Methodist local preacher at the age of 15 wanting to convert elderly village ladies to the lure of socialism to then renouncing all and becoming an agnostic at 17 and then looking for secular and political goals for salvation, the missions continued unabated.

In doing that I realised that in facing the conundrum of the world and how I fitted into it is what we all do and the way we cope with that affects whether society defines us as mentally ill or not.

The World Health Organization (WHO) report from 2001 estimated that one person in four people will suffer from a mental health problem globally at some point in their life and that according to a 2003 WHO fact sheet on "Mental Health in the European Region, " mental health problems account for up to a third of all GP consultations in Europe.

That is an awful lot of people and I began to wonder how many of them had tried to reunite Germany when they were only 9 years of age and wanted to be a missionary when they were only eleven! Was their demise that they failed in their mission and that the drug of idealism had lost its magic charm? Well maybe reuniting Germany at that time was out of their league as it clearly was mine but somehow they had failed to adapt to the world that they were in and that troubled their being. Adapting is crucial to mental health.

In "The Picture Of Dorian Gray " Oscar Wilde paints a picture of a man who wants the illusion to be the reality. In that novel the beauty and youth of Dorian Gray, captured by the painter Basil Hallward, is the truth that Dorian Gray wants sustained – but it is an illusion resulting in a series of debauched acts. Dorian Gray adapted to his environment dysfunctionally and made his fantasy a reality to himself. Oscar Wilde always thought people more interesting from the illusions people had and the masks they wore and once famously said,

"Man is least himself when he talks in his own person. Give him a mask, and he will tell you the truth[11]."

Wilde believed that to obtain the essential detaching from life it is necessary to invent, to lie and to wear a mask. So he deliberately creates a mask as a shield from the shadow of his imperfect nature. But the mask is a product of man's intellect created by the mind to hide irrational imperfections. And it is the mask that eventually dominates man's image of himself and becomes the reality.

In his book "To Have Or To Be[12], " Erich Fromm talks about the condition of "having" where our life is dominated by our possessions and what we have is what we are and contrasts it with the state of "being" – where what we are comes from inside us through our own self knowledge and engagement with the world. However in the book he also talks about "appearance" too. Sometimes we create the appearance of "being" rather than expressing it in any spontaneous way. It is a superficial state that is about pretence or illusion. Appearance becomes our mask; but Fromm does not look upon it with the lighthearted approval of Oscar Wilde. Our mask to Fromm is the conscious state we are in and that consists of " a blend of false information, biases, irrational passions, rationalizations, prejudices in which morsels of truth swim

---

[11] The Critic As Artist, by Oscar Wilde Green Integer (October 1, 1997) ISBN-10: 1557133689

[12] To Have or to Be by Eric Fromm Continuum Publishing Group; Rev. Ed edition (1 Dec 2005) ISBN-10: 0826417388

around and give the reassurance, albeit false, that the whole mixture is real and true."

This level of consciousness, which is supposed to be reality and that, we normally accept, as being is often our mask – the appearance we give to the world. To Fromm what he calls our character structure is what constitutes our real being and may partly reflect our behaviour but he argues it is usually a mask that we wear for our own purposes. Our mask may tell people that we want to change the world but the reality of our character structure maybe for example that we really want to be liked. The mask is our illusion to the world that hides the real motivation both from ourselves and from others.

Fromm believes that the repressed reality within us is basically determined by society through irrational pressures that creates a sort of fiction that we rationalise and thus keep the truth about ourselves a prisoner. However when society changes and the environment becomes alien to us then the fiction that we have created and believe is under attack and our mental well being depends on whether we can adapt or not.

In another of his books, "The Sane Society[13], Fromm writes, "Mental health, in the humanistic sense, is characterized by the ability to love and to create, by the emergence from the incestuous ties to family and nature, by a sense of identity based on one's experience of self as the subject and agent of one's powers, by the grasp of reality inside and outside of ourselves, that is, by the development of objectivity and reason."

Bur society does not often provide that sanity and Fromm felt that neurotic conflicts arise from needs and desires created by society. For him neurosis represented a number of psychiatric conditions in which emotional distress is reflected in physical, psychological and mental disturbance all evidenced by anxiety. This often takes the form of acute or chronic anxiety, depression, phobias, obsessive-compulsive tendencies, and even personality disorders, such as borderline personality disorder or obsessive-compulsive personality

---

[13] The Sane Society by Eric Fromm Routledge; 2 edition (11 Oct 2001) ISBN-10: 0415270987

disorder. For Fromm this happens because an individual has a "poor ability to adapt to one's environment, an inability to change one's life patterns, and the inability to develop a richer, more complex, more satisfying personality."

Crucially it is how we handle or cope with our illusions that are critical and whether we can adapt to a changing world.

Handling Illusions

For modern man and woman it has become increasingly difficult to handle our illusions. I guess I handled mine by believing in them. I really thought my missions were real and that my efforts reflected how I saw the real world. Any deep and sub conscious drives caused by the shadows of lost parents were dismissed - hidden passions and irrationality submerged under the cloak of a false sense of reason that propelled me on my way. In that sense I was an heir to the Enlightenment. For three hundred years or more our conscious reason has been everything. The age of science has made us all think that we are rational creatures and that by an act of will we can shape the world. The romantic poets cry that the "child is father of the man" went unheeded as we rushed into premature adulthood.

Somehow in our rush to grow up to the age of reason where all things are rational and clear and every problem solvable through an act of human will we forget the now famous allegory of Plato's Cave.

In the allegory, prisoners are chained in a cave, unable to turn their heads. All they can see is the wall of the cave whilst behind them burns a fire. Between the fire and the prisoners there is a parapet, along which puppeteers can walk. The puppeteers, who are behind the prisoners, hold up puppets that cast shadows on the wall of the cave. The prisoners are unable to see these puppets. Instead of the real objects that pass behind them, the prisoners see and hear nothing but shadows. "The Allegory of the Cave" symbolizes the illusion that we all face everyday in life. Plato is saying that humans are all prisoners and the cave our world. What we perceive as real are actually just shadows on a wall.

In the pre modern world the division between illusion and reality was managed by what Plato called "mythos" and "logos." They represented two different aspects of every day life and there was a balance that made them complimentary. Logos was rational, pragmatic, and scientific thought that enabled men and women to function in the world but it was insufficient for individuals to make sense of their environment. As Jung pointed out for individual human beings rational argument can only be successful if emotionality does not exceed a critical point. If it does then the reason diminishes and in it's place are "slogans and chimerical wish-fantasies." For Jung these can sometimes get out of control leading to "collective passions" that can develop into a psychic epidemic.

Before the age of Enlightenment this dichotomy of reason being shaped by emotion was handled by the concept of "mythos, which is concerned with wisdom, inspiration, intuition and value— knowledge in a metaphysical sense. Mythos was concerned with what was timeless and constant in our lives and looked back to the origins of life and the depth of our culture. Mythos was not empirical but was concerned with meaning in life and thus avoids the despair that can come in its absence. It was concerned with the eternal and universal and was deeply rooted in the unconscious mind.

Barbara Armstrong in her book "Battle For God[14]" argues that mythos was a strong and ever present existence in the pre modern world. It was celebrated in festivals and ceremony and was about behaviour rather than belief. No one felt a possession of a myth as they do modern monotheistic religions. Myths were but tools for understanding the unknown. Myths were not creeds written in stone but flexible constructs from our imagination that helped us to have meaning and was manifest in behaviour.

The Enlightenment of the 18th century and beyond began to discount mythos as illogical and superstitious as all around it appeared that logos was winning out with the success of science and technology. In fact Barbara Armstrong went further and argued that what we

---

[14] Battle For God by Barbara Armstrong HarperCollins Publishers Ltd; New edition edition (2 April 2001) ISBN-10: 0006383483

once called mythos, we now tried to explain through logos – that is in rational terms. She even postulates that fundamentalism in religion is a result of this – as it is a system that uses reason to justify myth. Once this happens then the myth becomes dangerous because it becomes a matter of belief rather than behaviour and people are willing to fight and die over their beliefs. Emotionality takes over in the Jungian sense and clouds our reason with passion even though we claim that reason still rules. We haven't "outgrown" myth; we just call it by a different name: ideology or revealed truth.

So our modern world has left us bereft of the tools to distinguish reality and illusion and we sometimes see the shadows on Plato's cave as reality. Mythos gave us those tools and although they were a constant in the pre modern world they were never taken as gospel truth and there were a diversity of myths to give meaning to life. Today we have turned myth into truth and used logos to justify them when reason is inadequate to do so. So there is a vacuum at the heart of our existence that plays heavily on our sanity.

The Sane Society

Brought up in the post war period of the 1940's it was easy to believe that we could create a sane society for ourselves by social reconstruction. That became my faith well into my teenage years. It was not just that Germany could be reunited by a rational argument on a piece of paper but I thought that poverty could be abolished at a stroke and happiness would be in sight for all. I remember when I had just given up on religion at 17 years of age having a discussion with my former Methodist minister and trying to convince him that when the Welfare State was perfected that religion would vanish, as there would be no need for it. Given the right economic and social conditions human nature would respond positively.

But I soon learnt that not everyone felt that way. The great individualists often negate the effect of society on us and a former Prime Minster of the UK, Margaret Thatcher, was once famous for stating there is no such thing as society! One of her favourite influences was Frederick Hayek who in his "Road To Serfdom[15]"

---

[15] Road To Serfdom by Frederick Hayek **Publisher:** Routledge; 2 edition (17 May 2001) ISBN-10: 0415253896

saw society as a form of collectivism and believed that all forms of collectivism including those based on voluntary cooperation could only be maintained by a central authority. For him the individual was supreme and the market the mechanism through which individuals should operate. It is through the market that individuals make an impact and society is but the mere collection of individuals interacting through that mechanism. The market was the language of social intercourse and was also the limit of society.

Although I had much admiration for Hayek, (though little for Thatcher), I could never accept the view that society was neutral. I always felt that our nature and the limits of our freedom were often determined by the constraints that society placed on us. Since the Enlightenment our freedom has often been expressed through possessive individualism[16] where an individual is conceived as the sole proprietor of his or her skills and nothing is owed to society for them. Our skills in the world of the possessive individual are looked upon as commodities that can be bought or sold in the open market in a society that has a never-ending quest for consumption. It is this culture of possessive individualism that prevents people developing their powers of being – of moral judgement, reflective thought and indeed even spontaneous friendship and love. This framework of acquisitive behaviour then shapes our capacity for rational thought and that determines our actions and relationships. In that sense we are not free but are the victims of forces that shape us.

Max Stirner[17] in the 19th century argued that religion and ideology often constrained our freedom, as did the institutions of a growing industrial society. He saw people being transformed into things and their relations with each other dominated by ownership that acted like chains. Although his advocacy of a selfish egoism to transcend this is not a path we would follow now, his criticisms of how social forces and institutions affect our freedom and our capacity for rational thought still has an important ring to it.

---

[16] See The Political Theory of Possessive Individualism: Hobbes to Locke (Oxford Paperbacks) by CB Macpherson for a full discussion of possessive individualism.
[17] The Ego And Its Own; The Case Of the Individual Against Authority (Dover Books ON Western Philosophy) by Max Stirner

And of course, it has always been the view of the left that society shapes character. In Marx's view of alienation modern industrial production under capitalist conditions meant workers would inevitably lose control of their lives by losing control over their work. For the worker this *"mortifies his flesh and ruins his spirit[18]."* So the worker is alienated from his work and this leads to his alienation from fellow workers. It is only by acting on the external world and changing it that man can change himself.

Freud's studies on "the pathology of civilized communities" stresses the idea that civilization breeds inner and interpersonal conflict. It is this that compels us to renounce instinctual satisfactions that are incompatible with social harmony. This he considers necessary because those instinctual urges can be destructive.

Many Post Freudians like Fromm and Reich did not consider our instinctual self destructive in the way that Freud did and this caused a rift with him. Rather they saw our basic instincts distorted by the "mask" or "appearance" that society forced upon us. Fromm believed that our basic passions that give form to our appearance are rooted in the conditions of human existence rather than our instincts. Rather than our instincts being destructive as Freud thought, Fromm felt that our loneliness and isolation resulted from being separated from other human beings and also from our own basic nature. Society he characterises as sick when it fails to satisfy our basic human needs.

The mentally healthy person, in his view, "is the productive and unalienated person . . . who relates to the world lovingly, and who uses his reason to grasp reality objectively; who expresses himself as a unique individual entity, and at the same time feels one with his fellow man[19]"

Perhaps a sane society is one where there is not only community and a sense of belonging and identity but also one where we feel that we can contribute in some way however small and make a difference. The more this feeling escapes us then the more we become alienated

[18] *Economic and Philosophical Manuscripts of 1844*
[19] The Sane Society by Eric Fromm Routledge; 2 edition (11 Oct 2001) ISBN-10: 0415270987

from that society and the more we become alienated from ourselves. When that happens we hang onto false images of our freedom and in our illusion of freedom make the smallest of happenings in our lives the cause of feeling free whilst we are still basically in chains. Our illusions become pathological and our sanity based upon insecure foundations.

To relate to the world lovingly then we need a society that empowers engagement and to have a sane society then we need to be engaged ourselves. It is the complex relationship between the individual and society that creates engagement. To want to contribute we need to be free of our illusions and this means both understanding ourselves and having some idea about the world in which we live.

Coping With Change

The problem is that the world we live in has suddenly become more complex for all of us. When I was busily changing the world as a child in my small home in a West Country town I also lived under the illusion that shops like Liptons and the then Timothy Whites were local shops and that a win by Labour in the local elections would be the beginning of the revolution. My parochial world somehow translated to the globe and there was an illusory logic in it all. The world seemed somehow manageable and ready for post war reconstruction step by step and in a rational way. Even the Cold War gave it some structure that made sense whatever side you were on. But as the 20th century came to a close all that changed.

As the 21st Century begins it is easy to see our freedoms wane and the belief that we can make a difference suffer. The world is alight with the collective passions of those who feel that they are dissatisfied or disowned. Rationality is shaped by destructive emotions as the world spins into turmoil. At a global level passions run so high that violence is brought to the door of the USA through the destruction of the Twin towers, there are bombings in Madrid and London, war in Iraq and Afghanistan and Darfur saw genocide repeated only a decade after Rwanda saw the very same. Western societies are rife with disgruntled youth as gangs form focal points of loyalty as the attractions of the acquisitive society loses its form and any discipline it may have had. Banks crash and economies fly into recession and a cloud hangs over the future. Governments often feel powerless and individuals often more so. Societies are not only faced with a democratic deficit as electorates struggle to make their governments accountable but individuals suffer a deficit of potency in coping with an ever changing and sometimes chaotic world.

The illusion that we are free and that our behaviour is determined by our own will is being challenged as never before and maybe because it was an illusion then that is no bad thing. This illusion is one that has dominated the Western world since the Enlightenment, which saw the dawn of the age of reason. By applying human reason, most problems seem to have a solution or it set in motion the process to find one.

And yet today that Enlightenment thinking has come under challenge as never before. We have suddenly realised that after decades of so called progress our main achievement is to create an unsustainable planet that might end up destroying us all. The sanity that led to rational progress has finally made the prospect of an insane outcome very real. Suddenly sanity and insanity are terms that have lost their meaning in any conventional sense. What was once considered sane thought has resulted in insane outcomes and those who "madly" riled against the conventional wisdom of progress now appear strangely sane.

In a world that is so turned upside down then how do we cope? What is the changing relationship between individual and society and how does one impact on the other? Somehow we have to divorce the intelligence that has been used in the pursuit of scientific knowledge and the intelligence that is used in running our own lives and forming interpersonal and social relationships. In the first we have succeeded at a huge pace in the last century but in the second we have seen a century of turmoil and carnage and we are left now with our future as a human race in doubt. We need more than intelligence to survive the problems now facing us. We need to somehow reconstruct what it is to be human and what our relationship is with other species that share our planet and with the actual planet itself.

New Frameworks

In *The Sane Society*[20], Erich Fromm writes, "The aim of life is to live it intensely, to be fully born, to be fully awake. To emerge from the ideas of infantile grandiosity into the conviction of one's real though limited strength: to be able to accept the paradox that everyone of us is the most important thing there is in the universe and at the same time no more important than a fly or a blade of grass."

Fromm used the word "progressive" to describe our striving to be more fully human and that is a different sense of the word to that usually used in the West where it is used to describe the process of modernisation. By more fully human Fromm meant the shared goal of directing people to a solution of achieving unity with nature through individuation, love of the stranger and reverence for life. Achieving this also achieved a stronger sense of community as well as a greater awareness of consciousness. For much of his life Fromm had seen the opposite where regressive behaviour had been the norm leading to individual psychopathology (symbiosis, narcissism and destructiveness) or group narcissism and hostility to people outside the tribe.

Psychoanalysts like Fromm and Reich were writing in the period between the two world wars or just after and these were turbulent times as the boot of Nazism stamped over Europe and the Gulags of Siberia were being filled by Soviet kulaks waiting a slow death. To them too the world was turned upside down and it appeared as if the scar of irrationality had descended on the human race. They sought to understand it and to explain the dark and hidden forces that lay hidden beneath the surface of nearly three centuries of a supposedly rational and enlightened age. They desperately wanted an age of humanity to be restored.

It seemed as if rationality had returned in the post war period and the world made safe again for progressive thought. It was the time of the New deal, the Marshall Plan, the post War Labour government in the UK, John Maynard Keynes and the great

---

[20] The Sane Society by Eric Fromm Routledge; 2 edition (11 Oct 2001) ISBN-10: 0415270987

experiment in social engineering. Whether it was Soviet Communism, the path of Social Democracy or capitalism with a human face, all movements had a blueprint for reconstruction once again through the reason of science and technological advance.

When the Berlin Wall fell there were cries of the "end of history" and the dawn of a new age of human enterprise. There was a spirit of optimism in the air that material progress would be the driving force of the global economy and that all would ultimately benefit. The age of social engineering had gone amidst the globalisation of corporate advance and free movements of capital across national borders.

Yet this way of optimism became the global illusion and beneath the surface lay hidden the dark shadows of reality. The passions in those shadows were those of inequality and humiliation as countless peoples felt that the world of material progress and optimism had passed them by and their reality was one of desperation and despair.

And with the fall of the Berlin Wall, there was also the fall of the ideologies of the 19th and 20th centuries that had given the "character" to the conflicts and battles of those two centuries. The world was faced with a chasm of structure through which people could try to understand what was unfolding before their eyes. There were no blueprints or maps any longer that gave meaning and direction to the future.

Bereft of meaning, religion once cast off to the private sphere was again becoming a major issue as fundamentalists were influencing the government in Washington and some Islamists were advocating the adoption of Sharia law through the state. Theocracies once banished in a new secular world were again frightening possibilities. Fragmentation seemed to be everywhere as tribal loyalties emerged again to fill the yawning gaps of community and belonging.

As mentioned earlier Fromm refers to what he calls "social character" and describes it as the cement that holds society together. Individuals develop a social character so that they can adapt to their environment so that they can function. When an individual fails to develop a social character that is adaptive then their emotions often fail to adapt to changing conditions. Alternatively a social character may develop that clashes with an individual's environment because the world they once knew was disappearing.

So in the 21st century not only has society lost those frameworks or blueprints that gave character to the world – the ideologies of the 19th and 20th centuries but individuals are finding it increasingly difficult to develop a social character that is adaptive to the ever changing environment because the changes are often beyond conscious comprehension. So we are developing dysfunctional societies and dysfunctional individuals as well and the well being of both is at stake in a turbulent world.

It is little wonder if in the midst of all this books like John Gray's "Straw Dogs[21]" appear to question whether human life has any meaning at all and to also suggest there is no theme in history and that it is but a mere sequence of moments unrelated over time. He questions the whole ethos of the Enlightenment and like Nietze before him looks upon the growth of Post Enlightenment humanism as no more than "secular theism," seeking salvation on earth rather than in heaven.

We are he argues no higher than animals and certainly not qualitatively different. The main force within is those basic animal drives to survive and have food and shelter. Without that we are in danger of an early death. Gray in his book argues that as our global population grows to unsustainable numbers then those survival instincts will become paramount and it will shape our rationality and behaviour. Rational thought will serve need and emotion rather than anything nobler and in an acquisitive and competitive society; rational thoughts soon turn to dangerous passions.

And he also shares the view of James Lovelock who in his book "Gaia: A New Look at Life on Earth [22]" looks upon our planet as a self regulating mechanism that will deal harshly with any threat to it's sustainability. For Lovelock as with Gray that threat is now

---

[21] Straw Dogs by John Gray Granta Books; New edition edition (1 Sep 2003) ISBN-10: 1862075964

[22] Gaia: A New Look at Life on Earth by James Lovelock Oxford Paperbacks; New edition edition (28 Sep 2000) ISBN-10: 0192862189

coming from the human species that have harnessed science and technology to plunder the earth and make life unsustainable and placed the planet's support systems on high alert. Our rational approach to the world has given birth to an irrational future.

Reconstructing our place in the world is a major task and perhaps the most critical one facing us in the 21st century. It means reassessing how we see our planet and how we think we relate to it as well as to other living creatures that inhabit it. It will mean understanding both ourselves more acutely and how that understanding affects our behaviour rather than just our beliefs. It is only by doing this that will allow us to break the chains that tie us to anxiety about our life and make us free to be autonomous human beings. To change our world we have to change ourselves but to change ourselves then our world must change too.

Somehow we have to learn to accept that as Fromm said "everyone of us is the most important thing there is in the universe and at the same time no more important than a fly or a blade of grass." We need to develop new blueprints or maps to understand the world that places the human being on our planet with more humility and wisdom than we have had for several centuries with decades of ever assertive and ascending notions of rationality. We need to understand that rationality is often clouded in all of us with emotion and passion and that those "shadows" can stand in the way of a sustainable world.

To make our world more sustainable is the challenge of our age but to change the world we also have to change ourselves, as one will not happen without the other.

CHAPTER 3 - The Change Dilemma

Seeking The Good Society

Those of us who are driven with a mission usually want to change the world in one-way or the other. It may be as fanciful as reuniting Germany or converting the Mau Mau or it may just be making life better for a single person or a group – and helping to change their world.

I always thought it was easy to change the world and thus my interest in religion and politics. As a religious person I first thought that converting people to the faith would be the answer to all human suffering but later I combined religion with politics and argued that the Sermon On The Mount was a revolutionary Socialist declaration and Christians needed to be aware of it.

Religion was all about changing ourselves and then through changed behaviour convincing others to do the same and before you knew it the whole world would be happy. I am not sure I really believed that so simply. Indeed, my experience of most religious people was that they had a belief system but it rarely affected their behaviour. It was more of a comfort zone for themselves or finding others as friends and creating community rather than setting the world to rights by enlightened behaviour. However the thought was there – the thought that good people would make a good society.

It was not long before my religion took on a political form and I developed the belief that the good society was all about political action that produced an environment that brings out the best in human nature. Eventually I renounced religious dogma but kept the politics and worked towards making the good society in the belief it was that that formed good people. And in that change I was faced with the dilemma that all social change agents have felt in their lives. Do you have to make people good before you get a good society or do you have to create a good society in order that people can be good?

By 1966 and at the age of 22 the second Labour Government of that decade was elected after less than two years of struggling through on a wafer thin majority in the British House of Commons. Now with a much more comfortable majority, I felt that political change could really begin in earnest. Not that I saw it as I was off to Canada for two years.

Changing Attitudes

A few months after I arrived in Canada the BBC screened one of its most famous "drama-documentaries." On December 16th that year the programme "Cathy Come Home" was broadcast across the network (12 million people watched it) and it concerned homelessness and its effect upon families. Written by Jeremy Sandford, produced by Tony Garnett and directed by Ken Loach, the programme has become a British TV "classic."

Very few programmes had the impact on people that this one did and it was not long before the issue of homelessness became more prominent on the public and political agenda. Shortly after the housing charity "Shelter" was formed.

"Cathy Come Home" radically changed the nature of the debate about homelessness. It challenged the conventional wisdom that Britain in the 1960s was moving towards total prosperity and that poverty was the fault of the poor. But did it change anything fundamentally?

Ken Loach (the programme's director) pointed out, "The film portrayed an injustice but, of course, homelessness is worse now than when that film was made."

For Ken Loach and some of his colleagues it changed them from being social democrats to Marxists as in making the film they realised that nothing was going to change through conventional politics. Just as making a programme on resource scarcity (see chapter 8) had made me reassess the world and what the driving forces of change were so Ken Loach and his colleagues were driven to reassess those forces when he made "Cathy Come Home."

The programme had a great effect on people's attitudes but it did not change them enough to translate into political action that came up with solutions. Nor did the political system respond itself and homelessness still blights the country. So for Loach and friends a more confrontational approach to politics was needed. The film one of the most successful and important ever to be shown to a British audience did not change people nor did it result in political solutions. Change had not taken place by either making people good or effecting a change in the political environment.

Good Society Maketh Man

Political revolutionaries tend to believe that we should first change the political and economic structure around us before substantial change will take place, as only then will people be free to change their minds. The chains will be unlocked. "False consciousness" can only be changed to "real consciousness" when economic change ensures we are no longer alienated human beings. Marx put it succinctly when he said, " it is not the consciousness of men that determines their existence, but, on the contrary, their social existence that determines their consciousness.[23] " This is the very base idea of historical materialism.

However we only have to look at both the French and Russian revolutions to see that revolution did not change people and old ways soon began to emerge undermining the very revolutions themselves. The French Revolution turned into the "terror" and the Russian Revolution into the mass executions under Stalin. The easy explanation for this is to exclaim these were not real revolutions or that they were revolutions betrayed. The other explanation is to suggest that they were flawed in the first place.

The argument that such revolutions were flawed is based upon the belief that although the revolutions did make significant economic and political change they failed to change human beings themselves because they failed to understand or take account of human nature and thought it could change only too easily. Wilhelm Reich illustrated this in his book "The Mass Psychology Of Fascism."

---

[23] —Karl Marx, Preface to Critique of Political Economy

Wilhelm Reich wrote his "The Mass Psychology of Fascism[24] " in 1933 and it was published in that year. Reich experienced the German crisis years, 1930-33 and the rise of Hitler. The Nazis eventually banned the book when they came to power and Reich was expelled from the International Psychological Association in 1934 for political militancy. German newspapers started attacking him as a womaniser, a communist, and a Jew who advocated free love. Seeing the danger he was in, he left Germany and eventually went to the United States in 1939. On August 23, 1956, six tons of the printed works of Wilhelm Reich were burned, by court order, in a New York incinerator. One of the books burned in New York was The Mass Psychology of Fascism, Reich's psychosocial analysis of the rise of Hitler.

What made this book so dangerous to both Hitler's Germany and the 1950's United States of the McCarthy era – one of persecution and victimisation for dissidents in American society? Well the book itself examined many of the unconscious forces that lay beneath our conscious being – the shadows that we carry with us. It was because both Hitler Germany and 1950's America found the libertarian impulses in human nature a dark force that needed to be suppressed. Yet for Reich it was these free and libertarian impulses that formed the basis of individual freedom and a free society – something that neither Hitler nor McCarthy could tolerate.The accusatorial atmosphere of 1950's America nor the brutality of the German Nazi regime could stomach a view that provided a map to free expression.. In such regimes then books get banned or burned.

Class Is In Our Mind

What lay at the heart of "The Mass Psychology Of Fascism" was the intriguing question of how Hitler managed to impose himself on Germany – a country with 70 million people and a radical tradition. It was a mystery as to how a nation of hardworking individuals could let themselves be enticed by what we later came to know as a psychopath.

---

[24] The Mass Psychology of Fascism by Wilhelm Reich Farrar, Straus and Giroux; 3 edition (November 1, 1980) ISBN-10: 0374508844

When economic crisis struck Germany in the 1920's then hyperinflation hit the middle classes hard. At the height of the crisis prices doubled in Germany every 49 hours wiping out the savings and future of individuals and families. It was almost a classic crisis that Marxist theory would consider as a trigger point for revolution. As middle class (bourgeoisie) families saw their wealth vanish then objectively they became working class (or proletariat) and according to Marxist theory their new objective class would change their consciousness into proletariat revolutionaries. But that just did not happen.

Reich made a distinction between "subjective class" and objective class." Although the German petty bourgeoisie had lost all their wealth and had objectively become proletariat they did not see it that way. Subjectively they still felt different. Reich wanted to illuminate the state of mind of the middle classes - their frustrations, resentments, fears, envies, and hatreds that went together to form what Reich called an "emotional plague," which found release in the themes and imagery displayed by Nazi ideology.

Of course Reich has his theory for understanding the reaction of the German middle classes. He asserted that the German middle class had an authoritarian family structure. He suggests that severe parental repression of infantile sexuality creates character armour that makes a middle class child conducive to state authoritarian structures and political authority figures. It is the patriarchal family that adversely impacts on a child's emotional needs. Sexually repressed individuals Reich argues accept duty and obedience. Reich defines fascism as "the organized political expression of the structure of the average man's character.[25]" For Reich the Fascist mentality is that of the "little man" who both craves authority and is at the same time rebellious. Hitler's Fascism gave the opportunity for the worship of both authority and rebellion – a powerful attraction to the German petty bourgeoisie who on no account wanted to be perceived as proletariat.

What Reich did in his "The Mass Psychology of Fascism" was to provide a dramatic and important example of why mere economic

---

[25] 17. *The Mass Psychology of Fascism*, trans. V. Carfagno (New York, 1970), pp. xiii, xv.

change was not enough to create the good society. Without understanding the individual and the unconscious forces that lay within that individual and the family then it would be impossible to effect change by a simple materialistic model of social change. We have to understand both the mind and the body, and our failure to do that, Reich believed resulted in us destroying each other and our planet.

Transforming Ourselves.

Of course the other side of the equation is that of creating the good man and hoping that will have the cumulative effect of making a good society. Whatever the problems and dysfunctions in the material make up of any society if human kind can change then all will be well with society. Change is the collective weight of our individual acts.

Of course individual live's can be changed through personal transformation and if a life is transformed then for that person their world has changed as well. One fine example of this is Alcoholics Anonymous. For those joining, it is about admitting that there is a problem and then seeking a path to change. The 12 steps programme offered is about personal transformation entirely and are,

- We admitted we were powerless over alcohol--that our lives had become unmanageable.
- Came to believe that a Power greater than ourselves could restore us to sanity.
- Made a decision to turn our will and our lives over to the care of God as we understood Him.
- Made a searching and fearless moral inventory of ourselves.
- Admitted to God, to ourselves and to another human being the exact nature of our wrongs.
- Were entirely ready to have God remove all these defects of character.
- Humbly asked Him to remove our shortcomings.
- Made a list of all persons we had harmed, and became willing to make amends to them all.

- Made direct amends to such people wherever possible, except when to do so would injure them or others.
- Continued to take personal inventory and when we were wrong promptly admitted it.
- Sought through prayer and meditation to improve our conscious contact with God, as we understood Him, praying only for knowledge of His will for us and the power to carry that out.
- Having had a spiritual awakening as the result of these steps, we tried to carry this message to alcoholics, and to practice these principles in all our affairs.

God is often used as a term to mean a "greater power than ourselves" and can for many be a spiritual rather than a religious term and could mean no more than fate. But it is a programme to change lives.

Meditation is also a method to change one's life so that a person is relaxed and can give up the negative passions of wanting and possessing in life. The hope is that if that happens then an individual is better able to cope with life and the suffering that goes with being human. It is a personal coping mechanism that can help individuals to view their total life in a manageable form.

But programmes and methods like the two mentioned above are individual programmes for people to make their own life better and change their own world. It is not about believing that such transformation can change the world for others and thus make the good society. The belief that change in one individual can have an impact on collective change is something very different. Some religions believe that and hence their missionary character; but other movements also share this view. For example, this approach to change is seen quite often in the Green movement and in some of the personal growth and transformation movements as well.

Being Green

There are large elements in the global green movement that believe that the earth can be saved by the individual actions of people as citizens or as consumers. Many Greens argue that most of the world's environmental problems are caused by the fact that there are too many of us consuming too much. The solution is to change our consumer behaviour. When Julia Hailes and John Elkington wrote the best-selling "Green Consumer Guide" it was to do just that – to change the pattern of consumption in society. They claim that if people buy Green then companies will reflect this and produce and distribute Green! Julia Hayes gives an example of this in a Daily Telegraph article in May 2007 when she says,

Take Wal-Mart, for example, one of the world's largest companies. They've started using their huge purchasing power to force their 61,000 suppliers to change practices. And you can be sure that companies wanting to sell their products to this super-store are taking notice - fast.[26]

Her argument is that as individuals we get few chances to vote but we spend money most days of our lives and if we spend green then we are virtually voting green through our purse. This will change the behaviour of the retail market and they will force change on their suppliers.

Others think the world will change by individuals adopting a "green way of living" and then persuading others to do the same. David Pollard has a wonderful Blog called "How To Save The World" and there is a wealth of information there. He suggests many ways that we can help save our planet by personal behaviour. Here are four examples below.

Stop at One: *Consider the virtues of a single-child family. Learn why children in such families are the happiest and most successful.* *Better* *yet,* *adopt.*

Become Less Dependent: *Learn how to fix things and make things instead of always having to buy replacements. Cut your own lawn, and perform other services yourself, even if you can afford someone else to do it. Self-sufficiency is good for your*

---

[26]

http://www.telegraph.co.uk/earth/main.jhtml?xml=/earth/2007/05/0 4/eadebate04.xml *self-esteem, reduces consumption and waste, helps the environment, and is good exercise.*

Be a Role Model: *Talk to others about, and show others, what you're doing, not just what you're thinking. People are far more inspired by a good role model than a good speech. And if people tell you you're a good role model, get out there and flaunt it in the right places -- if you're a woman engineer, go out to the schools and tell girls what a great career it is. If you're doing half the things on this list, you're a great role model -- inspire others to follow your example.*

Be a Pioneer: *If you have the time and the passion for it, pick a new cause, use the Internet to find like minds, do your homework, organize, and do something completely new. Start a community energy co-op. Set up a 'virtual' market for local crafts, organic or free-range foods, or whatever needs better local distribution. Establish a community-based business. Or create a whole community, self-selected, self-organized, self-sufficient, with people you love, and show the world how much more sense this makes than living in a community of strangers and driving long distances to work for someone you dislike so you can buy stuff you don't need made by other strangers even unhappier with their lives than you are. The new culture will be built bottom-up, one community at a time, and the sooner we start finding a community model that works well in a post-civilization society, the better.*[27]

The hope is that by adopting a green life style that people will join with others and the movement will escalate. David Pollard here refers to setting up community-based organisations and he goes on later to talk about "Intentional Communities." This is the new in word for communities with intent. The early nineteenth century was a period when such communities were set up and one community in the United States, New Harmony, founded by Robert Owen was set up with the intent of developing a co-operative life style. Some Greens talk about communities like this in the 21st century based on green life

---

[27] http://blogs.salon.com/0002007/

styles. David Pollard in his Blog sets out the steps needed to create an "intentional community."

1. **Find Members:** *Select the people who you would love to have in your community, and live and/or work with. Just as in any other activity that involves social networking, this is by far the hardest step. We desperately need better social networking tools and processes.*

2. **Set Intentions & Principles:** *Collectively, the members decide what the objectives of the community will be, and what principles it will live by. These may include principles that define its responsibilities and values, how new members are admitted, a size limit for the community, how resources will be owned and 'profits' distributed, the decision-making process, required contribution and participation from members, and many others. Like the membership itself, these principles may be fluid, at least until the community has been operating for a while.*

3. **Design the Community:** *Now collaboratively the members design what the community will look like and how it will operate.*

4. **Obtain Needed Resources:** *Acquire what the community needs to achieve its intentions*

5. **Create the Community:** *Together, make it happen.*

6. **Connect & Outreach:** *Connect with other communities, with the outside, and with schools and other organizations and people looking for models of a better way to live.*[28]

Behind the view that individual changes of behaviour and the formation of communities of people with intent is the belief that this can change society as a whole and create the type of world that those who advocate this think is good. It is a people led rather than an economic or political environment led approach to social change.

Personal Growth & Transformation

There are countless examples of personal growth and transformation movements where we are told that through individual prayer, meditation or simple compassion we can change the world without

---

[28] http://blogs.salon.com/0002007/2004/08/16.html#a843

any other intervention. But there are others that do not quite make such exaggerated claims but still believe that personal example and innovation will help to change the world we live in step by step. One example of this is Debra Schweiger Berg in her book "The Power of One: The Unsung Everyday Heroes Rescuing America's Cities.[29]" In it she advocates citizen and personal action through a letter, a phone call or through personal sacrifice and by it "taking back our society." As she says,

"Political Science professors had convinced me that well-designed, top down government programs could produce the most "efficient" and "effective" results. Never did I entertain the thought that the private sector might be able to do it too. Now, however, I was forced to reassess my view of the world and the capabilities of ordinary people."

In it she looks at the private, non-profit and charitable sectors and illustrates the work of some of the most outstanding - several people who have helped change the face of society one person at a time. She cites examples such as one woman who was a catalyst for Amber Alert, how a group of people tackled street graffiti and how business areas were revitalised and new jobs created. Her frustration with government action is clear and there is a strong bias that such action causes welfare dependency. However she also genuinely believes in the potential of individuals to shape their own lives.

The greatest power is not think tanks, government funding or political action but what is inside us that empowers us to effect change and that is central to Debra Schweiger Berg's argument that if more people were encouraged to act this way then the world would change and by the actions of many the good society would be created. We cannot wait for the political and economic environment to change. We must get on with the job right away.

One Dimensional Failure

---

[29] The Power of One: The Unsung Everyday Heroes Rescuing America's Cities (Paperback) by Debra Schweiger Berg, Trafford Publishing.

The problem with both approaches – either making people good before you get a good society or creating a good society in order that people can be good – is that it is one-dimensional. It relies to heavily on a single approach to change. Those who believe that making people good is the answer tends to think that all effort must be based on changing human nature and the values that people hold. Until this has happened then a truly good society is impossible. This is the ultimate in the personal is political approach to change. And yet there is no example of the long-term effects of such an approach being successful. Change in the psychic sphere has always remained private or restricted to small groups often because it underestimates the magnitude of the problem that needs social change.

For example green living may have an influence but the scale of the problem is huge if global warming is to be contained. According to the World Wildlife Foundation's Living Planet report, as of 2003, the demands of humanity as a whole exceeded Earth's capacity by 25 percent. Americans, the biggest consumers, consume at a rate that's twice what the planet can sustain.

Saving the planet means much more than the cumulative change of individual behaviour; it also requires significant and fundamental change in the infrastructure of our energy system and this will mean rethinking almost everything around us, how we live, our transport, the way our cities work and our agricultural system. It will mean changing the very behaviour and goals of government and corporations. This is a bridge far beyond the assault of changed individual behaviour.

And yet there again those changes cannot take place at governmental level unless it has the support of people who understand the scale of the problem. To allow government the freedom to take action then the consciousness issue has to be tackled as well. As we discovered in the French and Russian Revolutions it is no good imposing political change through some sort of citizens committee or vanguard of the proletariat if attitudes do not change as well. Cultural attitudes have to change to reflect new realities otherwise the illusive world in which we live becomes rigid and inflexible.

And it is living in an inflexible illusion that causes our well being to suffer and the paralysis of neurosis sets in. Mental distress can often be seen as psychological consequences of demoralisation, despair and discrimination experienced by individuals and communities. When we fail to adapt to a changing world either within our own psyche or through the bankruptcy of our political actions then our well-being is threatened. Somehow we have to cease being one-dimensional and adopt a total approach to change that enhances well being and takes us closer to reality both within ourselves and on our planet.

CHAPTER 4 - Well Being & Happiness

Signs Of Times To Come

In the mid 1970's I went to Sweden with an academic colleague from the Open University to make a programmes for the OU Comparative Government Course. He was a good friend but we found ourselves differing on what we saw going on in Sweden at that time. He was an unrepentant Social Democrat who believed that Sweden was the model state of social democracy that provided security for all and hence happiness. We interviewed for the programme Alva Myrdal who together with her husband, Gunnar Myrdal, had made a major contribution in the 1930s to the work of promoting social welfare. In many ways this man and wife team were the Beatrice & Sydney Webbs of Sweden. In 1943 Alva Myrdal was appointed to the Social Democratic party's committee and given the task of drafting a post-war programme. In 1982 she received the Nobel Peace Prize.

For my colleague the programme of Social Democracy advocated by the Mydals was the key to the good society – one that was fair and provided security for all. We visited Sandviken to do much of our filming. Sandviken is an industrial town (pop. 24,000) in Gästrikland, and was totally controlled in the municipality by the Social Democrats. It was a planned industrial city with ironworks and steelworks (founded 1862) that produce high-quality steel.

The idea was to show how a social welfare economy provided a fair and just society and that the implementation of welfare polices provided a social base for that fair society – the assumption being that social welfare meant happiness. And yet that is not what I saw all around me. It was true that social welfare measures had created a more egalitarian and fairer society but it had not created a happy one. Around me was alienation with bored youngsters on the streets, high rates of drug taking and alcohol consumption and a distinct lack of purpose particularly amongst the young. In this vacuum religious fundamentalism was on the ascent as it tried to fill that void with certainty and direction. True it was not a large movement and was dismissed as part of the lunatic fringe by the establishment locally but it was growing and a sign of times to come.

In this sense Sweden did represent the future but not in the way that my Open University colleague imagined. He thought Swedish Social Democracy represented the model for the future of other states and particularly the United Kingdom. What it really represented is the alienation and lack of direction of people who although socially secure had lost a sense of purpose. For them there were no maps to guide them, no social movements to give them meaning and there was merely the hedonistic pleasure of existing. This was the world that all of us were beginning to face as the twentieth century turned into the 21st but Sweden had got there before any of us.

Happiness & The Good Life

What I observed in Sweden highlighted for me an essential question that had been the topic of debate in my mind since my interest in politics was embryonic – what is the purpose of government. Is it to create a good society or is it to maximise happiness. It was always a difficult debate, as defining both what happiness was and what the good society meant was difficult. Equally difficult was the topic of "resilience" – why some individuals are able to maintain their well-being and health even in the face of significant life challenges whilst others found it more difficult.

What was central to this discussion was the question - is there a form of "good life" that is more conducive to human happiness than others? There are a number of views that have developed about the relationship between the good society and happiness and these can be summed up in four sub headings.

The Ideal View

First there is the view advocated by Plato when he looked upon life as a shadow of what is perfect and that our goal was to seek the perfect society – a society that was an ideal.

The original Platonic view of the world is that it is a dual place. The upper state is the world of perfection and the lower state is the world of reality. The theory is that the state of reality is an imperfect copy of the state of perfection. According to the Platonic view, humans only see glimpses of the good while existing in the state of reality. Ordinary mortals find it difficult to reached the state of perfection and live forever in the shadows. What is needed are "philosopher kings" to help shape a society so that it reflects the state of perfection as far as possible. It is this view that made the historian Karl Popper describe Plato's view as totalitarian.

To Plato the good life is one where we chase after the ideal and individuals can only do that if they exhibit perfect virtue. They can only do this by understanding that true happiness means being satisfied to the point one does not have desires. Happiness is giving up present pleasure for the sake of a utopian ideal.

The Eudaimonic View

In the Eudaimonic view, well being consists of fulfilling or realizing one's true nature through the actualisation of human potentials. Plato's student Aristotle articulated this view. Aristotle argued that the good life is different for each individual because it comes from living one's life according to one's virtues, and each person has different virtues. When Aristotle speaks of the good life as the happy life, he does not mean that the good life is merely one of feeling happy or amused but the good life for a person is the active life of functioning well and being successful as citizens.

Happiness is an activity, not something passive. It is not something that happens to you or comes to you from without. It is an activity rooted in human choices. Aristotle believed that citizens must actively participate in politics if they are to be happy and virtuous – or should engage in action to improve the general welfare. In this view, happiness is concerned with factors such as having purpose in life, continued personal growth and development, and good relationships with others.

Happiness is thus closely related to the concept of the good society because happiness was truly found in having a purpose and for Aristotle that was taking part in civic society. It was not about chasing an ideal as with Plato but following a purpose to make a better world and doing so with moderation. For Aristotle contemplation was also important and he considered contemplation to also be action.

The Hedonistic View

The hedonic view focuses on happiness and defines well-being in terms of pleasure attainment and pain avoidance. Equating well-being with hedonic pleasure or happiness has a long history. The fourth century Greek philosopher Aristippus taught that life's goal is to experience the maximum amount of pleasure, and that happiness is the totality of one's hedonic moments. The 17th century philosopher Thomas Hobbes asserted that happiness is the successful pursuit of our human appetites and the infamous DeSade believed the seeking of pleasure to be the ultimate aim of life.

However it was Jeremy Bentham who turned the pain/pleasure principle into a systematic political philosophy. He is famous as having said,

"...it is the greatest happiness of the greatest number that is the measure of right and wrong...[30]."

This became known as the doctrine of Utilitarianism and was the starting point of a radical critique of society aimed at putting institutions of the 19th century together with practices and beliefs to the test of this "objective" standard. The pleasure pain account is what governs us as Bentham said,

" Nature has placed mankind under the governance of two sovereign masters, pain and pleasure. It is for them alone to point out what we ought to do, as well as to determine what we shall do. On the one hand the standard of right and wrong, on the other the

---

[30] Jeremy Bentham: A Fragment on Government (Preface) Cambridge University Press (October 28, 1988) ISBN-10: 0521359295

chain of causes and effects, are fastened to their throne. They govern us in all we do, in all we say, in all we think..[31]."

It has often been said Bentham's theory, unlike that of John Stuart Mill's, faces the problem of lacking a principle of fairness and opens the door to a laissez faire approach to social justice where everyone must fend for themselves. It was criticised by Charles Dickens in his novel "Hard Times " which depicted the utilitarian state as one that lacked compassion and any sense of fun! It was left to John Stuart Mill later in the 19th Century to add some sense of social justice to the theory when he qualifies the pleasure/pain principle adding - as long is it does not inflict "harm to others." This then became the guiding liberal principle of the 19th century.

The Instinctual View

There is another view of the relationship between the good society and happiness and this is the instinctive view. This view holds that we are not happy because we have divorced ourselves as human beings from our basic instincts by creating self-awareness and over exaggerating our "consciousness."

This view is seen in the ancient Chinese religion Taoism that advocates the merits of "non action" or "right action." The Taoist view sees action in the world around us as activity and change that happens naturally and that self-awareness by individuals can be self-defeating unless that awareness goes beyond mere self. Conscious action can often be destructive of the planet and the person. A key principle in Taoism is that of *wu-wei*, or "*non-doing*." *Wu-wei* refers to behaviour arising from a sense of oneself but connected to others and to one's environment. It is not to be considered inertia or mere passivity. Rather, it is the experience of going with the grain or the flow. Some of the "new age" religions and philosophies also take the view that the ego is what prevents humans evolving beyond their present state. Andrew Cohen, spiritual teacher, and Ken Wilber, spiritual philosopher, are two such thinkers. Mapping the evolving

---

[31] Jeremy Bentham , *The Principles of Morals and Legislation* (1789) Oxford University Press, USA (January 11, 1996) ISBN-10: 0198205163

edge of human potential and exploring the states and stages of consciousness they attempt to go beyond the ego.

John Gray in his book Straw Dogs argues that it is in living with our instincts in this way that we can survive as a human race. As he says,

"The good life is not found in dreams of progress, but in coping with tragic contingencies[32]."

He believes that the human capacity to elevate consciousness to an almost transcendental level has resulted in us living out of harmony with nature because we do not follow our instincts to cope. We concoct the grand designs rather than dealing every moment with the suffering of people.

John Gray is often looked upon as an anti humanist but in many ways he is not as his message is how to find the best way to alleviate suffering. Erich Fromm who certainly was a radical humanist also considered this. He felt that man's need to destroy came from an "unlived life," that is, the frustration of the life instinct. He maintained that true happiness could be achieved through empathy with others. For him the life instinct resulted in behaviours associated with love, cooperation, and other social actions. These instincts are based on human needs not just animal needs but are deep rooted and emanate from life instincts within human kind.

So the instinctual view is about understanding our totality through our instincts rather than our reason as this brings us closer to nature and our planetary environment. It is only then that we can achieve happiness as it is rooted in our being.

Being Happy

These four models of happiness are signposts to help us think through what it is that makes us happy and how that relates to the

---

[32] Straw Dogs by John Grey, Granta Books; New edition edition (1 Sep 2003) ISBN-10: 1862075964

good society and our well being within it. However it does not answer all. In Richard Laylard's book "Happiness[33]" he cites Scandinavia as being one area of the world where there is greater trust between people and happiness because of it. And yet my filming in Sweden had highlighted to me that although there was a high degree of economic well being, there was also alienation and no small degree of disenchantment.

Sweden was a country whose economic growth was rapid as it industrialised late and the move from an agricultural to an industrial economy took place in the 20th rather than the 19th century. During this period of rapid expansion it was the social democrats that helped plan that expansion ensuring that Sweden became a fair and egalitarian society and in that they were highly successful. They followed the Aristotlean model with the purpose to make a better world and doing so with moderation. That sense of purpose gave a direction at a time of change and turmoil and people could be happy in the knowledge that there was fairness and security as change took place – very unlike the industrialisation of much of the rest of Western Europe a century earlier.

But once that had been achieved for the vast majority of the population then that sense of purpose went and happiness was no longer based upon achieving a better society in the here and now. Instead it was directed to the international arena and Sweden became one of the internationalist nations of the world and this gave an ideal to be chased and hoped for (Platonic model) whilst others sought pleasure in the world of alcohol, drugs and sex and became hedonistic.

My overall feeling when filming there was that there was a deep sense of boredom as Sweden found it difficult to adapt to a full economy with basic securities guaranteed. And about the time when I was filming this it so happened that Tibor Scitovsky published his book "The Joyless Economy: The Psychology of Human Satisfaction.[34]" In the book Scitovsky argues that welfare has been confused with consumption and economic growth in our developing

---

[33] Happiness by Richard Laylard published by Allen Lane 2005
[34] **The Joyless Economy: The Psychology of Human Satisfaction** Tibor Scitovsky , Oxford University Press.

western economies and in the USA in particular. He felt that human progress cannot be measured by quantative means alone but measurement should be qualitative as well.

Scitovsky sets out to analyse the failures of our consumerist societies and points to the fact that in them constant stimulation is always needed for people to have satisfaction. And stimulation is often the novelty of fashion, art, the latest gadget, the fast car, new and challenging work and even scandal! If that need for stimulation is frustrated then violence can occur. The book challenges the foundation of contemporary economics and liberal political theory that all choice is rational. Instead he argues that human need is based on a balance between stimulation and the need for the right measure of comfort in our lives. Too much stimulation produces pain, too much comfort produces boredom.

It seemed to me that Sweden had chosen the path of comfort instead of stimulation and what I was seeing in the young was high degrees of boredom. This contrasted with the Thatcher years of the 1980's in the UK when there was constant stimulation and for large sections of the population not enough comfort. Instead of boredom, this produced pain. Neither society seemed happy, as they had not got the balance right. Economic well being was just as able to produce boredom or pain as it was satisfaction and the model "good society" was not necessarily a happy one.

Happiness & Economic Well Being

It may seem strange that economic well being sought through "comfort economies" like Sweden or "stimulant economies" like Thatcher's Britain could not produce happiness for significant sections of the population. But it seems that economics is not enough.. Economic growth does not bring happiness.

There have been studies of the relationship between economic growth as measured by GDP and personal levels of happiness and these show that happiness increases as GDP does but only up to a certain level. Once this level has past then increases in wealth as measured by GDP do not lead to increases in personal happiness. It seems that there are psychological limits to any happiness that results from the consumption of material goods[35].

Essentially happiness has not generally increased for people in Western economies since the 1950's where in some cases living standards have doubled or at the very least happiness has not risen commiserate with the rise in living standards. Why this is the case is partly answered by Scitovsky's work mentioned above. Too much comfort results in boredom and too much stimulation ends up in pain; but that is only partly the answer.

In Richard Laylard's book "Happiness[36]" he attempts to explain why he considers this the case. His argument is that it is the relative income levels between people and groups that result in happiness or unhappiness. In his book Laylard refers to a question put to a group of Harvard students

- In the first world you get $50thousand dollars a year, while other people get $25 thousand (average.)
- In the second world, you get £100 thousand a year, while other people get $250 thousand (average)

What was surprising was that a majority of students voted for the first type of world. They valued having a relatively higher income than others even though the absolute income was less than the second world option. They value relative income over absolute income. It seems that happiness is a result of how people perceive themselves relative to others. Happiness has to do with self esteem rather than income levels. If people have high income but their self-esteem is low then happiness suffers too. High self esteem comes from having one's needs fulfilled, being satisfied with one's level of education and self worth. It results from being optimistic and not feeling hopeless in life and also being around other people and friends and enjoying good health.

---

[35] Lane, R.E., The Loss of Happiness in Market Democracies. Yale University Press, New Haven, 2000.
[36] Happiness by Richard Laylard published by Allen Lane 2005

But it is more than just self-esteem. In one study from the University of California[37] in 2004 a sample of older employees were asked to fill out a questionnaire on what made them happy and gave them self worth. Some answered that they were happy but had a low value of self worth. Those who did the experiment suggest that those who sometimes have high self-esteem feel that they have not reached their goals in life despite being assertive, smart, skilled and attractive. So although having a high value of self worth they are unhappy because they feel that they have not reached the goals in life that they thought necessary for recognition. It is the recognition of themselves as being successful that is important and having the recognition of others. If recognition is not there then people can suffer problems of mental health.

Well Being & Mental Health

Recognition from others is often essential to the development of self worth. To be denied recognition is to suffer a distortion to one's concept of self and an injury to one's identity. A lack of recognition can lead to alienation of humans from each other and Marx elaborated on this in his work. Much of Marx's view was derived from Hegel who emphasised the importance of recognition in his philosophy and it became integral to his understanding of the concept of self-consciousness.

Self-consciousness is different from self-awareness. When we perceive that we exist then we have a degree of self-awareness as an individual separate from others with our own personality and private thoughts. However when we feel self-conscious then we are not just aware of ourselves as existing separate beings, we are conscious of much more including the smallest of our actions. Such intense focus on ourselves can often cause shyness and embarrassment, and can affect self-esteem. For our self-consciousness to be fed we often need the food of recognition. But the essential question for our well being is what is it that we want to be recognised for? How is it we value our self worth?

---

[37] This can be found on the website
http://www.apa.org/releases/selfesteem_happy.html

In the 1950's Vance Packard produced a clear answer to that question when he put forward the view that it was status that we most sought after. In his book "The Status Seekers" he questioned the then prevailing view that increases in wealth produced a classless society. He says,

The recent experience of the people of the United States is instructive. In the early 1940's an era of abundance began which by 1959 had reached proportions fantastic by any past standards. Nearly a half-trillion dollars' worth of goods and services -- including television, miracle fibers, and vichyssoise -- were being produced.

Before this era of fabled plenty began, it was widely assumed that prosperity would eliminate, or greatly reduce, class differences. If everybody could enjoy the good things of life -- as defined by mass merchandisers -- the meanness of class distinctions would disappear.

But that did not happen. Packard argued that Americans were replacing or refining the class system with "a fascinating variety of status systems within it." He says that the status system is based on how we rate others and how they rate us. In where we live, what we buy and even how we worship most people rate each other and according to the results of that a our status is defined. This though has not produced a society of well being. Packard contends that people are badly stressed and indeed scared by anxieties and inferiority feelings that result from the unending process of rating and status striving.

Indeed it seems that status is genetically programmes into us. In Richard Layard's book "Happiness[38]" he cites Michael McGuire's research at UCLA where moving monkeys from one social group to another affected their sense of well-being. The higher a monkey's position in the hierarchy of a group, the better the monkey feels. The higher the status the more reward a monkey gets. He showed that when a monkey is placed in a different group where rank changes then that monkey's coronary arteries clog up more rapidly than those with higher status. Layard quotes that those who win Oscars

---

[38] Happiness by Richard Laylard published by Allen Lane 2005

in the film industry live on average four years longer than those who are only nominated. Status position can thus affect physical and mental health.

In Erich Fromm's book "The Sane Society" he argued that a society in which consumption becomes the de facto goal in life is essentially a sick society. It produces a social character that finds adaptive behaviour difficult. The social character, which Fromm considers that part of us that forms the link between our environment and our inner instinctual self can also be the base of our neurosis. In consumption based society the social character "adapts to the market economy by becoming detached from authentic emotions, truth and conviction". It produces a marketing character as the social character where "everything is transformed into a commodity, not only things, but the person himself, his physical energy, his skills, his knowledge, his opinions, his feelings, even his smiles." People find care and compassion difficult "not because they are selfish, but because their relationship to each other and to themselves is so thin".

Materialistic values often detract from happiness and the feelings of insecurity generated, adversely affect well being. The "unending process of rating and status striving" produces a treadmill that is characterised by unhappiness and insecurity that can only be appeased by more acquisition and more status cravings. It is a catch 22 situation. So a sense of well being that is the result of a syndrome of essential positive feelings is replaced by negative drives that can cause mental illness and depression.

Societies are repressive when they do not allow the full expression of human needs but channel those needs into the narrow strivings of consumption and status. Fromm argued in "Man For Himself" that such a society results in "the failure of man to achieve maturity and an integrated personality." When there is that failure then there is widespread neurosis and that limits human kinds capacity for freedom and love.

So the socio-economic conditions in which we find ourselves can often determine mental health and there is clearly a need to find ways of raising us above destructive and negative emotions that endanger not only our well being but also our mental health. Two ways of rising above the constant quest for status through material goods and status position is through having "goals" to live for on one hand and reflection on the other.

Happiness & Purpose

It has often been said that if a person has a project then he or she is happy. If there is no project then there is despair and maybe even depression. When I worked at the BBC we used to joke how good our pension scheme was and we would laughingly attribute that to our view that once retired BBC people died earlier than most as they appeared to lose their role in life. I am not sure if this was true or not but it did underline the belief that there was a correlation between depression and early death on one hand and retirement without purpose on the other.

Many people associate "retirement" with relaxation, holidays and leisure activities; but for some, it can be the start of depression. Depression after retirement is a common problem especially for those dedicated solely to their past career and without other interests to fill the vacuum. People whose sense of self esteem and worth is dependent on the work they do are particularly at risk. With no further role to play, they have a sense of being worthless and without a goal.

A 1999 study by Cornell University psychologists has found that retirement can cause marital discord and depression. Jungmeen Kim and Phyllis Moen[39] studied 534 married men and women between the ages of 50 and 74 and found that men who retired while their wives were still working showed a higher level of marital stress then newly retired men whose wives did not work. The happiest men were the ones who found another job and whose wives were not working.

The links between positive mental and physical health was one of the concerns of Carol Ryff, the Director of the Institute on Aging

---

[39] Presentation: "Couples' Work Status and Psychological Well-Being in Older Adults" by Jungmeen E. Kim, Ph.D., and Phyllis Moen, Ph.D., Cornell University, Session 4639, 3:00 PM - 4:50 PM, August 23, 1999.

and Professor of Psychology at the University of Wisconsin-Madison. It was her work that illustrated the fact that people who achieved a sense of meaning in their lives are happier that those who live from one pleasure to another. Her explanatory studies have focused on individuals' life experiences and their interpretations of them and how this accounts for variations in well-being. She has also examined midlife development and old age and the processes of resilience and vulnerability that individuals cumulate through adversity and advantages in their lifetime.

In her work Carol Ryff has assessed sense of purpose, which she describes as "having goals to live for," and autonomy, "the ability to follow one's own convictions," as well as the degree to which a person feels he or she is growing over time. "

It's caring about more than just us," she says. "It's the way in which we contribute positively to the social order.[40]" Yet she also says that it goes beyond how good we feel when we reach out beyond ourselves; it also has a positive effect on one's physical health. Through her research she has shown that qualities like mastery, autonomy and the strength of our relationships – are the buffers to midlife stress. Although financial resources and educational background gives an advantage, those with those benefits fare badly if there are poor social relationships or a self-defeating outlook. On the other hand studies show that many of those lacking these resources can still enjoy a great sense of well being if they have a sense of purpose and a positive outlook, good relationships or spirituality.

Happiness & Reflection

If action that provides us with goals in our life is important to our health then so is reflection. Indeed Aristotle always considered reflection to be "action." Aristotle held that there were three basic activities of man: theoria, poiesis and praxis. Theoria is about contemplation – the act of detaching from an object and observing it as a spectator. Poiesis is from the root "to make" and is about an

---

[40] *How Healthy Are We? A National Study of Well-Being at Midlife*, edited by Orville Gilbert Brim, Carol D. Ryff and Ronald C. Kessler, University of Chicago Press, due out February 2004.

action transforming and sustaining the world. It represents that moment when activity branches out of thought and takes on a life of its own. Praxis was about the process of putting theoretical knowledge into practice. So how can action that starts as contemplation become a process where it can actually effect change?

Paul Freire applied these terms to liberation politics and argued that education had to be liberating if it was to be meaningful. Liberation was the process that translated contemplation into action. He say is his book "The Pedagogy Of the Oppressed[41],

"Liberation is a praxis: the action and reflection of men and women upon their world in order to transform it."

Today we have divorced ourselves from understanding that reflection is a part of understanding our selves and our goals more clearly and is thus an integral part of action. Plato thought the end of life was contemplation as this was the only way to understand values that our senses hid from us by illusion. Freire saw contemplation as a means to understand both the world and us and then change both.

So if the work of Carol Ryff and those following the Aristotelian model that having a goal in life, a project is important for happiness then the Freire view of contemplation leading to action through a process or praxis is important. Happiness is not just doing something. It is about how what we do affects the image we have of our self worth and ourselves. Often the image we have ourselves is influenced by the image that others have of us. This is why status is important to so many and the status that we seek can often be based upon the shifting sands of the society we are in and it's over arching values. Reflection has to take us beyond those chains.

---

[41] Pedagogy of the Oppressed by Paulo Freire, Penguin; 2nd Revised edition edition (25 Jan 1996) ISBN-10: 014025403X

In his book "Straw Dogs[42]" John Gray says that

"Contemplation is not the willed stillness of the mystics but a willing surrender to never returning moments."

What distorts reflection is the yearning for past moments and glory, the destructive emotions of "old unhappy far off things and battles long ago" Reflection or contemplation should free us from those past moments to create present ones that help us relieve suffering and follow present goals. The praxis or the process here has to be compassion and this must be the driving force that turns our thoughts into meaningful actions.

Resilience

At the end of my teens I was invited to join a local book group in my small West country town. It was a strange request as all the other members were middle age or beyond, youth workers, teachers and librarians. I felt strangely honoured and went to just one meeting. However that meeting did introduce me to Bruno Bettelheim and his book "The Informed Heart." Bettelheim was imprisoned in 1938 to 1939 in the concentration camps of Dachau and Buchenwald. Here he began to study not only his own behaviour but also those who where imprisoned with him.

He became interested in "extreme behaviour." What he discovered is that in some ways there was exceptional responses by some individuals to being faced with the crisis of loss of liberty and possible death in the most inhuman conditions. What interested Bettleheim were those who coped best were not always the ones that might be identified as survivors and those who sometimes collapsed in such circumstances were sometimes those who had been identified as survivors.

He transferred what he had learnt from his study of extreme behaviour in such extraordinary situations to mass society as he felt such a society would also affect individuals in different ways. Some

---

[42] Straw Dogs by John Grey, Granta Books; New edition edition (1 Sep 2003) ISBN-10: 1862075964

would show more resilience than others. In following his interests Bettlheim came to the conclusion that the good life meant,

"living a subtle balance between individual aspiration, society's rightful demands and man's nature ; and that an absolute submission to any one of them will never do[43]."

For Bettleheim modern industrial society had produced a situation where people often perceived themselves as cogs in a machine and that this created an imbalance between aspiration, society and nature leading often to mental illness. In these circumstances, personal autonomy is undermined and the resilience to coping with change adversely affected. He argues that rapid social change does not allow people enough time to develop attitudes needed for dealing with that change in the outside environment. As he says,

"What we now fear is a mass society in which people no longer react spontaneously and autonomously to the vagaries of life, but are ready to accept uncritically the solutions that others offer....[44]"

But we know from others as in the work of Carol Ryff, that people can cope given the right circumstances. In her work she has found that when people have goals and projects that they enjoy (eudaimonic well being) then resilience is stronger. Preliminary findings on a sample of ageing women showed that those with higher levels of eudaimonic well-being had lower levels of daily salivary cortisol, pro-inflammatory cytokines, cardiovascular risk, and longer duration REM sleep compared with those showing lower levels of eudaimonic well-being. Hedonic well-being, however, showed minimal linkage to biomarker assessments[45].

---

[43] The Informed Heart (The Human Condition In modern Mass Society) Bruno Bettleheim, published by HarperCollins; n.e. edition (6 Aug 1970) ISBN-10: 0586080171
[44] Ibid
[45] Ryff, Carol D.;Keyes, Corey L.; Hughes, Diane L. Status inequalities, perceived discrimination, and eudaimonic well-being: do the challenges of minority life hone purpose and growth? J Health Soc Behav. 2003 Sep;44(3):275–291

So the maintenance or recovery of health and well-being in the face of cumulative adversity is possible but it needs both outer directed goals and inner personality self knowledge to be successful.

Our Survival

Bettleheim's concept of the "extreme situation" is interesting today. He lived through the 1930's and saw economic depression, war and concentration camps. Today we are living in a dangerously changing world where genocide is again possible, where the collapse of advanced and developed societies is an ever real probability as resources run out, climate change takes place and weapons of mass destruction become more available. The 21st Century has produced a chain of possible "extreme situations" How to avoid the Bettlheim scenario where people are not allowed enough time to develop resilience in the face of such challenges is now a major concern for us all. Our survival may in the end depend on how resilient we are.

Part 2 – The Knowledge Crisis

There is a crisis in the knowledge we have about both our selves and the world. It is not that there is too much or too little knowledge but a question of how we perceive the knowledge that does exist and how we organise it to give us some sort of coherence. In chapter 5 we say,

There are two dilemmas facing us. The first is that the reality we see is not the reality out there – the real world. It is a construct in our mind. The second dilemma is that the way we act to change or cope with the world around us is not always rational. Often it is not based upon a conscious decision at all. This leads us to face up to four problems of survival in the 21st century.

First we have to acquire some knowledge of ourselves so that we know what is and what is not possible – what our limitations are and what are our strengths. Secondly we need to have some idea of what the external environment around us is and what the dynamics of change are in this present age. Thirdly we need to develop constructs within our mind that reflect the gravity of the environment around us and those constructs have to be based upon worldviews that are not antiquated but relevant. Finally we have to contemplate more on our actions and what the right actions are in this world of 21st century turbulence.

In this part of the book we try to address some of these issues. What are the delusions that face us that colour our worldview? We have looked at some of the problems of our status driven society but the problem goes deeper than that. The personalities we create for ourselves are part of our existing acquisitive society; but through time we have always created our own realities from the information we receive from our environment as it interacts with our psyche. What are the barriers that prevent us from seeing more clearly?

And if we do begin to see then what is it that we see in ourselves and in the world around us. How can we acquire self-knowledge that will empower us rather than delude? And what is the world we see as it changes in the 21st century? We have found ways and devices to understand our world over time but when the changes have been so fast and so traumatic as they are today then how is it possible to understand that world?

These are some of the issues that we discuss in the chapters of this section of the book by confronting the crisis of knowledge that faces us all.

CHAPTER 5 - Living With Illusion

The Noble Lie

In the United States there has always been many myths but none so strong and enduring as the "American Dream." This is the idea that any person can be successful as long as he or she is prepared to work and use his or her natural gifts. It has often been expressed in the phrase "from log cabin to white house" – the belief that however lowly your origins you can still become President.

Of course it was not true, and took as long as 2008 before a woman or an African American could run for the Presidency. Most Presidents came from well connected and well to do families and wealth became a key factor to getting elected. However until well into the 20th Century the "American Dream" was widely believed because it gave Americans a good feeling about themselves, their country and their hopes for the future.

It was Scott Fitzgerald's book "The Great Gatsby" that in many ways symbolised to many Americans that the dream was over and that the reality was very different from the illusion that their countrymen and women had been weaned on. Indeed Scott Fitzgerald wrote in 1924, while working on The Great Gatsby,

"That's the whole burden of this novel -- the loss of those illusions that give such colour to the world so that you don't care whether things are true or false as long as they partake of the magical glory"

In the book, Gatsby tries to chase the American Dream, yet his idea is tarnished. He throws parties to fit in with the socialites around him. Gatsby's idea of the American Dream fails because he tries to buy his way into a society that will never accept him. The American Dream excludes him and brings the United States face to face with a reality that it would rather not have known.

For decades the "American Dream" had been a noble lie that many if not most believed. For Plato the idea of a noble lie was the essential myth on which most states were formed. In Plato's Republic inhabitants were organized into categories: The Rulers,

Auxiliaries, Farmers, etc. They were the men of gold, silver and bronze. The noble lie was that the categories defined by Plato were laid down by God and were not a social convention. It was God who had put gold, silver, and iron into each person's soul, and those metals determined a person's station in life. The dream of Plato's Republic was opposite to the American one but both were false yet both served a purpose.

Appearance & Being

Illusion is part of our lives both collectively as in the examples above and individually in the images we have of ourselves. It was Jean-Jacques Rousseau who denounced the chasm separating "appearance and being" among his contemporaries when he said,

"We no longer dare seem what we really are, but lie under a perpetual restraint. In the meantime the herd of men, which we call society, all act under the same circumstances exactly alike, unless very particular and powerful motives prevent them. Thus we never know with whom we have to deal... What a train of vices must attend this uncertainty! Sincere friendship, real esteem, and perfect confidence are banished from among men. Jealousy, suspicion, fear, coldness, reserve, hate, and fraud lie constantly concealed under that uniform and deceitful veil of politeness..[46]"

To what extent these illusions are deceptions that we are consciously aware of or whether they are also deceptions that we inflict upon ourselves is an important question. Certainly some commentators like Erich Fromm believe that we delude ourselves because we live in societies where journeying beyond the chains of illusion becomes difficult. He says,

"To see himself without illusions would not be so difficult for the individual, were he not constantly exposed to being brainwashed and deprived of the faculty of critical thinking. He is made to think and feel things that he would not feel or think, were it not for uninterrupted suggestions and elaborate methods of conditioning. Unless he can see the real meaning behind the double-talk, the

---

[46] Rousseau - Discours Sur Les Sciences / Discours Sur L'Origine De L'Inegalite, Editions Flammarion ISBN-10: 2080702432

reality behind the illusions, he is unable to be aware of himself as he is, and is aware only of himself as he is supposed to be.[47]"

What is interesting in this is the view that the image we have ourselves is the image that we think we are supposed to be – the one that others often think we are. And it is this "magical glory" that Scott Fitzgerald believes we partake of in our daily lives. What we are is less important than what we think we are. It reminds us of the words of Edgar Allen Poe

All that we see or seem
is but a dream within a dream[48].

Philosophers have always been intrigued by the physical world and how we perceive it. John Locke for example had argued that external objects acting on our senses caused all knowledge. Perception was simply passive and the mind merely reflects the images received by our senses. Kant on the other hand saw the mind as an active participant continually shaping our experience of the world. Kant discussed forms that appear in our mind and that he calls *phenomenon* and the external world that gives rise to this perception he calls *noumenon.* He argues that we will never know the latter and the phenomenon is all that we will ever know. Reality, he saw, as something we each construct for ourselves.

Constructed Reality

Construction theory is a modern area of study that argues that we construct our own personal, family and social worlds in order to adapt and cope. These constructions then help us view the world in a certain way and can shape our behaviour. It has been a useful device not just for analysis but also for therapy as well where new

---

[47] Erich Fromm, The Art Of Being, Continuum International Publishing Group Ltd.; Reprint edition (31 Dec 1997) ISBN-10: 0826406734
[48] Edgar Allan Poe: A Dream Within A Dream: The Life of Edgar Allan Poe, Publisher: Peter Owen Publishers; First edition (1 Dec 2008) ISBN-10: 0720613221

constructs in people's lives help to provide a healthier perceptual environment.

Gestalt psychology founded at the end of the 19th century emphasised that when we perceive an object then the whole is more than the sum of the parts. It was a reaction to the atomistic or reductionist school that argued that we could understand our environment by breaking it down into its separate and component parts. This school was being made popular at that time through the behaviourist approach of Pavlov and Watson. Watson drew heavily on the work of Pavlov, whose investigation of the conditioned reflex had shown that you could condition dogs to salivate not just at the sight of food, but also at the sound of a bell that preceded food.

Watson argued that such conditioning is the basis of human behaviour - if you stand up every time a lady enters the room, you're acting not out of 'politeness', but because behaviour is a chain of well-set reflexes. He claimed that *recency* and *frequency* were particularly important in determining what behaviour an individual 'emitted' next: if you usually get up when a lady enters the room, you're likely to get up when one enters now. There is little construction here. You merely reacted to stimuli and understanding the world is merely the comprehension of people's behaviour through cause and effect.

Gestalt theory rejected this because it advocated a holistic approach to both personal and social interaction. For Gestalt psychologists *form* is the primitive unit of perception. When we perceive, we will always pick out form.

The Rubin vase as shown above illustrates this. It is just black and white shapes and that is the same stimuli that are received by anyone who observes it. Yet if we look at it closely then what do we see? Some people see a white vase in the centre whilst others see two black silhouettes staring at each other. As we stare then the impression can change in our minds. From those basic shapes, our minds make a whole that is more than the separate parts.

Begging Many Questions

This may show us that we do construct reality from the real world but it does little to tell us how we construct it or why. Nor does it tell us how we can reconstruct a world in our mind that reflects more accurately what is happening in the external environment. How do we see more than the shadows on the wall of the Platonic cave and grasp more closely what is actually there? Of course it may be a forlorn quest. We may always be dancing with shadows and never see the pure image by light of day. For some that may be a constant concern. The fact that we always live an illusion may cause despair for many. But if we understand the finite nature of what it is to be human then it allows us to accept that their maybe alternative truths and not just a single holy grail that as our ultimate quest.

I once had a friend now sadly deceased and who had the distinguished honour of being the only person to have, in my knowledge, ever been expelled from a book group. His problem was that he was an unrepentant 1945 Socialist who believed in nation state socialism, which involved the nationalisation of the "commanding heights of the economy" carried out through the parliamentary method. Nothing could shake him from this model throughout his life.

Everything in life centred on this belief and it governed most of what he did and discussed. So when he joined a book group then discussing a book that examined the state of the British economy (do book groups actually discuss this) was perfect as he could bring in his old and well-tried ideas. However when the book was about passionate love and sex then it was a different matter. If the love affair went desperately wrong then my old friend could not resist letting those know there that this would never have happened if all the industries had been nationalised in 1945. After a while this one-dimensional approach to all of life became tedious for the book group and they asked him to leave.

This rather affable but dinosaur of a man had views so fixed that he saw the entire world through his nationalised tinted glasses. Nothing seemed to shake him. The Vase in the centre of the Rubin image had become a nationalised mindset and everything around that had no form or shape without that vase being just as he saw it.

Well we are all like that to a certain extent. The example of my friend probably offered up an extreme example. Yet the extreme example does show how difficult it is to shift mindsets and to get people to perceive new forms in the tapestry of life. It is even probably more difficult for those of us who believe we are not fixed in our attitudes because that view is an illusion upon illusion. We all have mindsets and we perceive the Rubin vase in our own way. We all sometimes resist the idea of alternative truths.

The Quest For Alternatives

In this world where muddling through has become the process that all of us follow to a greater or lesser extent and in an environment where our past maps and blueprints have been torn up, then the need for alternative constructs of the world and our place are needed more than ever. The danger is that in the vacuum of meaning we may seek a one-dimensional approach to truth like my friend in the book group. Fundamentalism of all kinds has been on the rise as the millennium has come and gone. Some in search of meaning have sought new forms of certainty. Like my friend they have sought to see reality through tinted glasses so that everything seems put in its place. His was a kind of nostalgia – a looking back to a past truth or for him the golden age of parliamentary socialism. For others it is the certainty of some future utopia hidden in the text of religious scriptures or the uttering of some latter day messiahs.

For those lost in a changing world confusion is painful. When we move from one age to another then as Toffler[49] pointed out our attitudes can be confused as they reflect both the old and the new. That is not enough for some who want clarity so they again know their place in the universe. But certainty is dangerous in an uncertain world. If around is the turmoil of a new world with all the certainties of the past torn up and with a planet increasingly unsustainable then to fall into new instant certainties is like hiding your head in the sand. What is important in the ever changing 21st century is to have a head clear enough to question our assumptions and to live with the flow of change. One of the often referred to quotes of Spanish-American philosopher George Santayana is,

"To be interested in the changing seasons is a happier state of mind than to be hopelessly in love with spring.[50]*"*

Santayana was a life long agnostic who spent his last years in a convent in Rome. Over the years he had maintained a rather decorous love affair with the Catholicism of his youth. He said that he felt a deep attachment to Catholicism because of its historical and aesthetic qualities, although he described himself as being entirely "divorced" from religious faith. It was this that made him look upon agnosticism as a state of constant being rather than an end state. He felt that whatever belief you held then you should always question its basic assumptions. A Catholic should be an agnostic one as a communist should be agnostic too. His thoughts found expression in the poet Philip Larkins's famous quote

---

[49] The Third Wave, Alvin Toffler Pan Books; New edition edition (15 May 1981) ISBN-10: 0330263374
[50] http://thinkexist.com/quotes/george_santayana/

"I'm an agnostic, I suppose, but an Anglican agnostic, of course[51]."

Having this open agnostic view to life is one that allows people to be open to alternative views, to experiment with themselves in their environment and to become affective agents of positive change. And it is this attitude to life that is needed more than ever as the growing challenges of the 21st century descend upon us. People from different backgrounds and cultures faced with the social and environment challenges of the next few decades have to somehow build bridges that will hold back the danger of the world falling into a new nightmare of tribalism and intolerance.

But how can we construct a worldview that allows us to adapt to the changes around us. Our illusions are ones created over many decades and will be hard to shift; and there are many barriers in the way.

Barriers To Deconstruction

What is it that within us creates barriers to deconstructing the world as we see it and helping us to see life in different ways?

In previous chapters we have looked at some of the work of the early Post Freudians who have argued that there is an unconscious side to our being that acts on us in ways that prevent us from being free and spontaneous. Reich sought to free up our life instinct by releasing us from sexual repression. Fromm saw that a competitive and acquisitive society created a social character that made it difficult for us to adapt to a changing world. And Jung saw shadows deep within us that influenced how we behaved even if we were unaware of them. All of this came from the work of Sigmund Freud who felt that the subconscious was often a dark force in our lives and had negative effects on our adult behaviour.

Much of this work is still relevant today even if the therapy derived from these theories have been surpassed by modern cognitive and positive psychology. Its relevance lies in the understanding that in

---

[51] Phillip Larkin "The Less Deceived" The Marvell Press (1988) ASIN: B00110A2SS

what we do we do not always act as reasonably as we think and that irrational forces lie deep within us. These forces act as barriers to reconstructing our world in a positive way. They are the illusions that we need to be aware of.

Often these illusions are the result of emotions taking over our reason and being turned into consuming passions. It was Jung who told us that reason could only work well if emotionality was at a relatively low level. It is Daniel Goleman who has written a great deal about the emotional side to our lives and describes what happens when passions overwhelms reason.

In his book "Emotional Intelligence[52]", Goleman quotes the case of Mr. Crabtree. He entered his home one night and heard noises. Thinking his daughter was at a friend's house he proceeded to find his handgun later killing his daughter when she surprised him by jumping out of a closet. This then became the springboard for discussing what happens when emotions take over our lives.

Emotions can often become destructive and these shape our perception of other people and our worldview. Goleman has argued that the emotional brain responds to an event more quickly than the thinking brain. If the brain senses an emotional emergency then it can take over before the rational side clicks in. Although this may have helped in our evolution where we have had to respond instantly to daily emergencies, it does not help us have a calm worldview. What we then often rationalise is the after effects of our emotions and try to convince ourselves it is reason.

But it is not just emotions individual or collective that shapes our illusions of the external environment. Goleman also argues that we

---

[52] Daniel Goleman Emotional Intelligence: Why it Can Matter More Than IQ Bloomsbury Publishing PLC; New edition edition (12 Sep 1996) ISBN-10: 0747528306

often use self-deception when we form a view. As he says in his book, Vital Lies, Simple Truths[53],

"Self-deception operates both at the level of the individual mind, and in the collective awareness of the group. To belong to a group of any sort, the tacit price of membership is to agree not to notice one's own feelings of uneasiness and misgiving, and certainly not to question anything that challenges the group's way of doing things."

Goleman talks about "the intelligent filter", which gives us a clear concept on how we often screen out ideas and information that do not fit our assumptions. It is this that leads us to reject innovative ideas as we filter out new pieces of information even before we are aware of them. We do this according to Goleman because

- The mind can protect itself against anxiety by dimming awareness.
- This mechanism creates a blind spot: a zone of blocked attention and self-deception.
- Such blind spots occur at each major level of behaviour from the psychological to the social[54].

Goleman like many others points to the process that goes on in our brain that makes us on an individual basis not the rational creatures of the Enlightenment that many think we are. We view life often not through reason alone but through a whole series of filters that create an illusion of the external world and that helps us to cope both individually and collectively.

What About Science?

But all around is the proof of the pre eminence of reason in our life. Our modern world would not be as it is unless the reasoned enquiry of scientific method had not grown out of the Enlightenment and created what we have today. All around us are great cities with huge

---

[53] Daniel Goleman, Vital Lies, Simple Truths: The Psychology of Self-deception Bloomsbury Publishing PLC; New edition edition (8 Jan 1998) ISBN-10: 0747534993
[54] Ibid

transport systems, we can fly from city to city at a moment's notice, our energy is extracted from land and the deepest seas and transformed into fuel for our homes and cars and our hospitals are full of new drugs and technology. All this has been delivered to us by the reason of the human mind focussed on continuous improvement.

The scientific method at one level is an attempt to minimize the influence of bias or prejudice in the experimenter when testing a hypothesis or a theory. It has four steps.

- Observation and description of a phenomenon or group of phenomena.
- Formulation of an hypothesis to explain the phenomena. In physics, the hypothesis often takes the form of a causal mechanism or a mathematical relation.
- Use of the hypothesis to predict the existence of other phenomena, or to predict quantitatively the results of new observations.
- Performance of experimental tests of the predictions by several independent experimenters and properly performed experiments.

If the experiments bear out the hypothesis it may come to be regarded as a theory or law of nature. If the experiments do not bear out the hypothesis, it must be rejected or modified. It is often said in science that theories can never be proved, only disproved. There is always the possibility that a new observation or a new experiment will conflict with a long-standing theory.

Although science may have progressed by inter subjectivity – the subjective mind of one scientist after another testing theories that have been created within a viewpoint or paradigm, it has given us both progress in our understanding of the world and increasing income and health. Yet science progresses inductively. It focuses on specific areas of investigation. However it is not holistic and does not take account of unintended consequences. If science and technology helped to develop the coal age in the 19th century it was not holistic enough to see the impact of that age on the atmosphere and the impact of greenhouse gases. This was because most science was reductionist and more concerned with breaking things down to their component parts. James Lovelock in his book "The Revenge Of Gaia[55]" argues that the failure of scientists to understand the significance of global warming for many years was because of its division into different disciplines and each of these was limited to seeing only a tiny part of the planet. There was no coherent or holistic viewpoint. As he says,

"Science is a cosy, friendly club of specialists who follow their numerous different stars; it is proud and wonderfully productive but never certain and always hampered by the persistence of incomplete world views."

Consequently the idea of the earth as a self-regulating system did not really become apparent until the 1970's and this took decades to be even partially accepted. Science because of its reductionist approach was unable to perceive the impact outside of the component parts under study. It was concerned with cause and effect in a huge variety of different areas but there was no overall view. There was no system science that looked at this problem early enough.

Many scientists today are attempting to create Grand theories that embrace all or system theories that look at the impact of all on all including the consequences of actions both intended and unintended. But that is some way off yet and we still live in the scientific age of singular cause and effect science.

Science had changed since the early 20th century of course. For example with the advent of quantum physics in the early part of the 20th century the certainty of objective observation in scientific method came to be questioned and particularly by Werner Heisenberg[56] who argued first that an object being observed can

---

[55] ."The Revenge Of Gaia, "James Lovelock, The Revenge of Gaia: Why the Earth is Fighting Back - and How We Can Still Save Humanity Penguin (22 Feb 2007) ISBN-10: 0141025972

.
[56] Werner Heisenberg Physics and Philosophy: The Revolution in Modern Science Publisher: Penguin Classics; New edition edition ISBN-10: 0141182156

alter merely by the presence of the person observing it. Secondly he suggested that science was not about seeking objectivity but that the outcome was really intersubjectivity. This raised important question about the nature of science itself and of the scientific method. Yet it was not until late into the 20th century that system science began to have an impact.

Despite that some humanists sometimes elevate this method of inductive reasoning to a religion and argue that it is the standard by which all human endeavours should be judged. The problem is that although this method of reasoning is good when focussed at individual experiments it is not always adequate for grand theories that cover the whole of life. Developing the "grand theory" has become the holy grail of many a scientist but we are still far away from that prospect yet.

What we have rather than grand theories that cover everything are paradigms that represent a cluster of values at any one time. And these can often be changing illusions over centuries but illusions that have fired many a generation of effort. A paradigm is a thought pattern that determines our worldview. Thomas Kuhn wrote in 1962 in "The Structure of Scientific Revolutions[57]" that - *"a paradigm is what members of a scientific community, and they alone, share."* A paradigm then is not simply a theory but a worldview. This changes only when science encounters anomalies, which cannot be explained by the existing paradigm of the time.

When a paradigm is generally accepted then Kuhn calls this a period of "normal science" The work of scientists usually proceeds normally until anomalies arise that result in a new theory being proposed that results in a different understanding of concepts and this can lead to a rejection of some or part of the old. A paradigm of a scientific revolution in Kuhn's sense would be the *Copernican revolution.* Here the idea that the earth was the focal point of God's creation was replaced with the idea that the earth was but one planet of several orbiting around the sun. This changed the view of the world and the context in which scientific exploration proceeded.

---

[57] Thomas Kuhn, "The Structure of Scientific Revolutions," University of Chicago Press; 2nd Revised edition edition (1 April 1970) ISBN-10: 0226458040

So although the process of scientific method can be very powerful, it takes place in the context of worldviews that change over time because of shifts in understanding some of which are initially intuitive. These shifts present new perceptions of the world that remain in tact until anomalies take us from one overarching viewpoint to the next. This does not mean that scientific progress does not take place but it also means that it does so within a view of the world that is a construct in the mind.

The Two Realities

But there is also another reason for this dilemma and that is that the implementation of scientific achievement is usually not in the hands of scientists but of others and usually decision makers like politicians or consumers who wish to benefit from cheaply produced commodities. Politicians and consumers are often fed by power or status, recognition and instant gratification. Their reality is different from the scientist,

In a way there are two realities. There is the physical reality of what is out there – the reality that stimulates our senses. But there is also the personal reality that we construct in our minds to understand the physical reality that is out there. Both are very real but the one in our mind is a construction and maybe at times even an illusion. The illusion comes when we confuse the reality we experience with the physical reality, the thing-in-itself.

The ancient philosophers of India called this illusion maya and by this they meant a false perception of the world. In a sense it is a delusion rather than an illusion because it is the way we learn to deceive ourselves. If we believe that what we see is actually what is there that is the deception. What appears in our mind or what we think we see is often very different from the actual physical world and two people may see or hear things differently.

As human beings we filter the physical world as it affects both our senses and our consciousness. We are constrained by our own frailty as a human being. When we think we see something then we only see what our eyes and brain allows. For example we only see light in the narrow frequency range and light that is outside that range like ultraviolet or infrared light we just do not experience. So what we actually see and what registers as an object to us is only part reality. The same is true of our other senses.

It is also true of our consciousness. We often believe that what distinguishes the human from other animals is that we are conscious of what we do and that this consciousness allows us to apply reason to the world. Well we have already discussed how we bring irrational forces to our reason turning it into rationalisations. Passion can cloud our thoughts only too easily. Yet it goes further than this. Our behaviour is often the result of acts that we do almost automatically and without thought – as John Gray puts it is Straw Dogs,

"Our acts are end points in long sequences of unconscious responses[58]."

Gray points out in his book to the work of Benjamin Libet on "the half-second delay" where he has shown that the electrical impulses to our brains that initiates action occur a half second before we take the conscious decision to act. Our delusion is that we think we have taken a conscious decision to act whilst in actuality our brain has taken the decision to act in a certain way even before we give it conscious consideration. As Libet points out, *"cerebral initiation even of a spontaneous voluntary act .... Can and usually begin unconsciously."* In this sense there is the possibility that we are not the authors of our own acts. And yet we think we are and most post Enlightenment philosophy has been based on the fact that we as humans make conscious decisions. Yet if Libet is right then it does raise the question of how conscious our decisions are and to what extent we delude ourselves into believing that our decisions are rational.

Again as Gray argues our actions generally do not reflect our decisions. Conscious awareness only plays a small part. Most of our lives just go on even without us thinking and it is the consequences of this that we spend much of our time coping with. Perhaps the

[58] John Gray, Straw Dogs: Thoughts on Humans and Other Animals Granta Books; New edition edition (1 Sep 2003) ISBN-10: 1862075964

ancient Chinese understood this more than most. Much of philosophy, and not just Western but to some extent Indian and Buddhist as well, have been about metaphysics - which is concerned with the structure of reality. Much of what is written here is about that – the discussion around reality and appearance. The question asked is what is ultimate reality and how can we possibly get to know that. This obsession has led to Platonic philosophy as well as monotheistic religions and to modern science. Chinese philosophy, on the other hand, is more about how we should act rather than how we perceive what is out there in the external world – the ultimate or the reality. If we are not masters of how we act through conscious decision-making, then ancient Chinese philosophy questioned what is the right way to act in these circumstances. What is "right action" or "wu wei" that allows us to behave in a way that is appropriate to the flow of nature and indeed our own nature. This is a debate that we have lost in the post Platonic world but one we may need to come back to if we are to have a sustainable planet.

Coping With The Dilemma

So there are two dilemmas facing us. The first is that the reality we see is not the reality out there – the real world. It is a construct in our mind. The second dilemma is that the way we act to change or cope with the world around us is not always rational. Often it is not based upon a conscious decision at all. This leads us to face up to four problems of survival in the 21st century.

First we have to acquire some knowledge of ourselves so that we know what is and what is not possible – what our limitations are and what are our strengths. Secondly we need to have some idea of what the external environment around us is and what the dynamics of change are in this present age. Thirdly we need to develop constructs within our mind that reflect the gravity of the environment around us and those constructs have to be based upon worldviews that are not antiquated but relevant. Finally we have to contemplate more on our actions and what the right actions are in this world of 21st century turbulence.

This is not easy task because for most of our past we have held worldviews that were comfortable for most of us in that they provided ready answers. They were either the worldview of the pre industrial era where everyone knew their place in the world and that place determined who we are and how we acted out our lives. Or they were the worldview of the industrial age or early post industrial one where the dynamics of the world was seen through one of several blueprints that were like scripts for us to act out. We played our roles as part of a class or nation and that gave us some meaning to life however deluded that might have been.

Today those blueprints are gone and the danger is that we will create delusions that are worse than any of those experienced in the industrial age. Because the world is increasingly incomprehensible to many and increasingly becoming unsustainable then the risk is that we will retreat into tribal or parochial perceptions of reality. To break free from this then we will need to do something that is unique in our modern age. We will need to become truly autonomous individuals confident in our self-knowledge and able on the basis of that to engage in "right actions" to not only cope and survive but effect sustainable change.

It was Bettleheim in "The Informed Heart" who understood how closely our external and internal lives are interwoven. His argument is that unless we are able to solve inner conflicts – those between our desires and what our environment demands – *the more we come to rely on society for the answer to any new challenge that it may offer.*" Relying on a society that is in chaos as the world rapidly changes provides no compass for us to act. In such a world there is a greater need for self-reliance based upon our inner strengths. However Bettleheim had observed behaviour in extreme situations and knew that at a time of such rapid change then there is often not enough time to develop new attitudes. People then become confused and uncertain and in those circumstances the more people emulate others or dissolve themselves in groups who claim certainty. This then make individuals accept uncritically what others offer. Fast change in the world challenges personal autonomy. However Bettleheim believed that a person who has even a little autonomy can accept a fast rate of change. So to cope in the world of the 21st century we may well have to develop personal autonomy at the same time as we try to change our environment. One cannot happen without the other.

So in the next chapter we look at self-knowledge and autonomy, then go on to examine our fast changing external environment. From there we discuss how we can construct a worldview in which our autonomy is important. Finally we look at the concept of "right action" that is sustainable and how that may be effective in a world where we muddle through.

CHAPTER 6 - Knowing Ourselves

Shaking The Foundations

In my early life as a child and teenager I accepted my religion almost as a given. What I had learnt through the church and through the scriptural texts seemed to me to be the map for my understanding of the world. At 17 when I began to doubt all of this I found myself first doubting and questioning the institution of the church itself and then doubting the message that the Christian church was broadcasting to the world. Although my Protestant based religion had not got behind it the authority of the Catholic Church and the hierarchy of legitimacy that that entailed and although it did give me free range to interpret the scriptures as I saw fit, I was still faced with the assurance that these scriptures were the word of God.

As I began to question all of this and read around the subject I found myself struggling with constant doubt. As I did, I came across a book that had just been published by the then Bishop of Woolwich John Robinson called "Honest To God" and also a book by one of the great theologians of the 20th century Paul Tillich, "The Shaking Of The Foundations." The message of those books was striking and although I never quite understood it at the time I came back to it in later years especially when I began to study the development of the early church in the years after Christ's death. What both those books were saying was that religion did not come from the sounding brass of august institutions or the revealed word written in gospels or creeds but that it came from deep within us. The true path to religious experience was self-knowledge rather than belief and the acceptance of external authority.

John Robinson had argued that the notion of God as being "out there" external to us and a universal supremo was a view that we should abandon in favour of the idea that God should be within us – the very depth of our being and existence. Paul Tillich had been saying the same – that God was not some sort of fantasy in the sky but the very ground of all our being. To understand this Tillich went further and argued that to make the jump from God "out there" to God as the ultimate depth of all our being, one should forget everything traditional that we have learnt about God in the past and perhaps even the word itself.

Paul Tillich had to some extent followed the line of both Søren Kierkegaard and Sigmund Freud in believing that in our most private moments of introspection and contemplation we come face to face with the terror of our own nothingness. In doing that we realise our own mortality and that in essence we are finite beings. What was so important about Tillich's argument was that he believed that finite beings could never be sustained by another finite being or by some imaginary comfort zone out there. What can sustain finite beings is being itself, or the "ground of being". Although Tillich identifies this as God others have referred to it as self-knowledge.

Alternative Visions.

When I was a teenager struggling with these ideas it was only some 20 years since some major discoveries had been made in the Middle East that shook the very foundations of the Christian faith itself as proclaimed through the orthodox Catholic and Protestant churches. These discoveries were first the Dead Sea Scrolls that placed the development of Christianity into its Jewish context with all the turmoil of that time and the many movements of dissent, rebellion and retreat - particularly that of the Essenes. The second major discovery was the Gnostic Gospels found at Nag Hammadi and revealing a different tradition of Christianity from that proclaimed by the church and cemented into dogma in 325 at the First Council of Nicaea.

It was two farmers who discovered the Nag Hammadi Library accidentally in December of 1945. This was a substantial and important find as there were 52 texts altogether. They contained, secret gospels, such as the Gospel of Thomas, the Gospel of Philip. The Gospel of Mary Magdalene had been found earlier and was also a Gnostic Gospel. Many contained conversations between Jesus and his disciples and contained within them a different view of Christianity than that expressed through the Biblical gospels and the modern churches. As Elaine Pagels[59] has shown early Christianity was far more diverse and varied than it is today. Contemporary Christianity, as varied as it is, shows more unanimity than the Christian churches of the first and second centuries. She explains that,

"For nearly all Christians since that time, Catholics, Protestants, or Orthodox, have shared three basic premises. First, they accept the canon of the New Testament; second, they confess the apostolic creed; and third, they affirm specific forms of church institution."

But this unanimity of view only emerged towards the end of the second century and became the "state creed" after the fourth century when Constantine converted himself and the Roman Empire to this orthodox view. Before that time many different gospels existed, as did a huge variety of Christian groups. Those who called themselves Christian during that time organised themselves in ways that differed widely from one group to another. Gnosticism was a varied but substantial part of early Christianity.

Like Buddhism, Gnosticism begins with the fundamental recognition that earthly life is filled with suffering. Gnostics hold that the potential for self-knowledge (Gnosis), and thus, of salvation from pain is present in every man and woman, and that salvation is individual and not the product of accepting an external saviour. However the early Christian Gnostics did accept that Jesus was the "Messenger of Light" and came to assist humans in their search for Gnosis. Gnostics do not look to salvation from sin (original or other), but rather from the ignorance of which sin is a consequence. The "Messenger of Light" is an enabler to help each human individual achieve this knowledge that will help him or her in a world of constant struggle.

Gnostics were a substantial part of early Christianity and had no central organisation like the growing Orthodox Church. Theses new insights into early Christianity began to make clear that the early church was a very fragmented one but it was Orthodoxy which eventually won the power struggle for ascendancy and quickly

---

[59] The Gnostic Gospels by Elaine Pagels. Phoenix; New edition edition (6 April 2006) ISBN-10: 0753821141

moved to rid the world of the evidence of these early traditions and proclaimed many of them as heresies so that they were forbidden fruit. This went on right down to the 13th century when one of the most dramatic examples of suppression and persecution was that of the Gnostic Cathars in Languedoc by Pope Innocent III when a rampant Catholic church burnt hundreds of Cathar Christians at the stake.

The Gnostic tradition proclaimed Christianity through self knowledge rather than acceptance of a creed ordained by external authority. Self-knowledge is a very dangerous concept because it places the individual and their discoveries of themselves centre stage. For those wanting conformity and acquiescence then it is often a challenge too far. Most movements from early orthodox Christianity to modern day Marxism have been based on a "gospel" that is central to belief and enforced often with great cruelty by the guardians of the given word or proclaimed method of understanding history. Often self-knowledge has been discouraged as dangerously anarchic and the expression of individual self indulgence.

In one sense it was self-indulgence as early Christian Gnosticism maintains that the spark of knowledge resides in an elite, not in all humanity. In that sense it is not anarchic but elitist rather like Plato's Philosopher Kings. But not all Gnosticism was like that.

The Tyranny of Creeds

In 1926 Katherine Tingley published her book "The Gods Await[60]," which expressed her philosophy that our salvation is found within ourselves. She said,

Too long have we been thrall to the "blinding and crippling tyranny of creeds and dogmas." It's time to step out of the shadow of fear and self-doubt and claim "the freedom to breathe the broad sweet air of life and find infinity within ourselves; . . . we are immortal, inheritors of all the good in the universe"

---

[60] The Gods Await, Katherine Tingley, Kessinger Publishing, LLC (January 20, 2003) ISBN-10: 0766132633

Her view was that no matter how degraded anyone may have become; everyone has within them a divine spark and the god-given power to learn from mistakes and change. We need no intercessor to save our soul: we are our own destroyer, our own saviour.

Katherine Tingley was an altruist who in the early 1890's set up soup kitchens in New York City's East Side as well as emergency relief missions. She worked with orphaned children, unwed mothers and destitute families. As well, she worked with prisoners, was against the death penalty and was a champion of peace and against the "vileness of war." Her causes were numerous and broad based. William Q. Judge, the cofounder of the Theosophical society, influenced her with his belief that the divine rests in us all no matter what our state in life.

Theosophy is essentially a modern version of Gnosticism. It seeks the knowledge that is deep within each human being and considers this important for autonomy in a complex society. It does not emphasise outward religious observance at the expense of the search that is within us. What matters is one's inner awareness and commitment to understanding self, not outward acceptance of belief or social forms.

Katherine Tingley was influenced by this philosophy because it gave her the inner strength to stand out against the pressure and injustice of society around her. It gave her the potency to make a difference in her own world. She like her fellow theosophists and Gnostics down the ages was deeply suspicious of belief systems and creeds.

The 20th Century has seen a renewed interest in Gnosticism. It is seen not just as an early Christian sect but also as an idea that predated Christianity and had an influence on it in its early days. There were Jewish and pagan Gnostics. Many now see the Gnostic tradition as one in its own right and is now often taken as an ancient religion that strongly influenced other traditions. Voegelin in his book, *Science, Politics and Gnosticism*[61] argues that there is a "Gnostic attitude" that shares the following values:-

- dissatisfaction with the world;
- confidence that the ills of the world stem from the way it is organized;
- certainty that amelioration is possible;
- the assumption that improvement must "evolve historically";
- the belief that human beings can change the world;
- and the conviction that knowledge-gnosis-is the key to change

Since the early Christian era the Western world had been the subject of one belief system or another and most had subscribed to the creed of their belief. But creeds and beliefs were about political power rather than conviction. When the Orthodox Church won the battle of Christianity in the early centuries after Christ's death then they won the battle of political power. They dismissed from sight the view that Christianity was about inner knowledge and thus a personal path to salvation. Instead they instituted a Church hierarchy with members who had signed up to the creed at baptism and were thus ever under the control of the Church establishment. Battles between beliefs when they did happen were thus battles about political power. When people died in the 30 Years War after the Reformation they died not for a belief as much as the right of one establishment to control at the expense of another.

When the Enlightenment heralded in the age of reason then belief systems and creeds took on a secular form with the growth of liberalism and socialism, nationalism and conservatism. People soon signed up to these new secular creeds as easily as they had the religious creeds of the Middle Ages. The French Revolution and the Napoleonic Wars as well as the Russian Revolution were all a battle of control. None of these secular beliefs allowed individual paths to salvation through self-knowledge, as that was a challenge to the new status quo. Creeds or manifestos were a way of recruiting foot

[61] Science, Politics, and Gnosticism: Two Essays, Intercollegiate Studies Institute (January 30, 2005) ISBN-10: 1932236481

soldiers to one belief system or another. The bankruptcy of all this began to become apparent in the second decade of the 20th century.

Filling The Vacuum

It was not surprising that after World War 1 that many people developed this scepticism over belief systems and creeds. The First World War was the "war to end all wars" and although it failed at that it did succeed in becoming a catalytic fatal blow to the creeds of the 19th century that left the world in a vacuum. The 19th century had seen with the repeal of the Corn Laws in a laissez faire form of international liberalism in the UK that had suddenly faced the challenge of tariff reform at the beginning of the 20th century. Those who argued then for tarrifs and imperial preference gave warning that the age of liberalism were at an end. The 19th century had also seen the growth of international socialism and social democracy. There was a growing belief that the international proletariat would come together in a global crisis and that the loyalty they had to each other would surpass that of the nation state. However when the War broke out in 1914 the working class of all belligerent countries flocked in their masses to the flag of their nation to fight against fellow workers in other countries. The whole concept of internationalism, whether liberal or socialist, had broken down in the trenches of northern Europe; and it never really recovered.

It was in this vacuum that the scourge of Fascism entered centre stage. When all the old belief systems had failed or seem to and religion was on the decline then National Socialism became the appeal to young men and women in a hurry. Oswald Mosley in the United Kingdom was the graphic story of one man in a hurry. His life reflects what lengths that individuals will go to when all else has failed and the world is still in turmoil. He like so many others was deeply influenced by the First World War and never wanted that repeated again. He felt that such a tragedy not happening again depended on creating a fair society and once in the then growing British Labour Party he set out to advocate a new economic policy based on the principles of John Maynard Keynes, the great early 20th century economist. When economic crisis struck the world he was exasperated with the response of a Labour Party that took up an almost classical economic position and did very little. He saw the world slide into crisis and eventually started up his own political

Party, the New Party, and then the British Union Of Fascists as his answer to that crisis. Fascism was action in the absence of either the individuality of self-knowledge or the existence of the collective maps and blueprints of the past century. It was the cry of people in panic as the world fell in to despair.

Finding An Anchor

It was during this period between the wars that people looked for an anchor that would moor them somehow to the world in a meaningful way. Well some sought the drug of action to find meaning in a world without – a path that led to the battles between communism and fascism seen dramatically in the Spanish Civil War, others sought inner meaning as the main way forward. This battle of uncertainty was brought to an end in World War II and in the post war world reconstruction through Keynesian economics saw people have hope again as economic growth took hold on the developed world.

Somehow economic growth acted like a drug and gave people a false sense of security. There was the hope that growth would be continuous and that every generation would enjoy a better life than the previous one. The two major ideologies of the age American led capitalism and Soviet communism both competed with each other over who could provide the fastest economic growth. Such growth was not only tied up with personal aspiration but also national prestige.

But the period that saw the close of the 20th Century and the beginning of the 21st brought that optimism to an abrupt end. The fall of Soviet Communism, the triumph and then increasing demise of growth orientated Western capitalism, the fragility of the planet on which we live and the growth of religious fundamentalism and terror created a new world. That new world needed more than just blue prints and maps based upon external creeds or ideology. Fundamental religion and the proliferation of belief systems and cults, both religious and secular, no longer have the overarching understanding that was provided by the old beliefs and creeds. They added a new landscape of chaos to our world. It will probably take some time before we have any new blueprints to direct us in the new world in which we find ourselves. What is certain is that we do need to understand ourselves if we are to work in the world in which we live today. And then we have to transfer that understanding to also comprehending the world, which is our only home.

We saw earlier that Bettelheim in his book "The Informed Heart" believed that for people to survive in extreme circumstances then they not only have to understand the world they are in the they also have to fill empowered in order to cope with that world and maybe change it. Of course Bettelheim was talking about life in concentration camps during the war; but he was also talking about the industrial society in which we were living and that was creating change around us at an increasingly fast rate. In that growing industrial society people's lives were being uprooted and their values challenged. It was difficult enough for people in those circumstances to be able to cope with themselves let alone tackle a world that seemed in chaos.

Today changes are faster than ever before and the fragility of our planet makes our future uncertain. We are most certainly in this situation of extreme circumstance. In these conditions, it is important to try both to understand the world and our self simultaneously. Like the early Gnostics at the very beginning of organised Christianity, we need to find our roots in some knowledge about ourselves rather than following prescribed creeds or beliefs imposed upon us from outside. Common action and collective organisation is equally important but if that action is based upon false creeds that we accept without question, any changes we make are likely to be counter-productive. Indeed our actions are most likely to be determined by the chaos of society around us rather than what is required. We have discussed earlier how our behaviour in an acquisitive society is often based upon the desire for recognition and status. Erich Fromm introduced the term social character in order to describe the mechanism that we created within us so as to behave in a way that reflected the society we lived in. That social character often prevented us from seeing outside the boundaries of that mechanism. The importance of self-knowledge is that it gives us the tools to step outside of those boundaries and to perceive the world differently. Today, it is that skill that we need more than ever.

Our Alienation

Self-knowledge is important to counter our own alienation. For Karl Jung, modernity is marked by our alienation from our self. Human beings project their alienation onto the world, but the world is only the manifestation, not the source, of alienation. In a way this produces a double whammy effect. Not only is the world in crisis but also we project our own dysfunction onto it in our efforts to cope. But these coping mechanisms are false; and an endangered world is misunderstood by our own delusion. The Jungian goal is the reconciliation of ego consciousness with the unconscious.

Marx had a different theory of alienation. His view is that in the emerging industrial world - under capitalism - workers inevitably lose control of their lives and selves in not having any control of their work. Because their labour is not of their ownership, they are not autonomous or self-realized individuals. What is needed to correct this is self-actualisation – the process whereby individuals realise their inherent potential by whatever avenues are open to them. Yet Marx considered self-actualisation of secondary importance because capitalism increases the impoverishment of workers (the proletariat) so rapidly that they will be forced into revolution just to stay alive – and self actualisation would be a by product of a more favourable environment.

For Marx, alienation was rooted not in the mind or in religion, as it was for his predecessors Hegel and Feuerbach. Instead Marx understood alienation as something rooted in the material world. Alienation was loss of control and specifically the loss of control over labour. Once a worker has that control then alienation ceases. The secret to self-actualisation was a revolution whereby the proletariat controlled their labour. Marx thus developed a materialist theory of how human beings determined the society they lived in, but also how they could act to change that society. In his theory, people are both 'world determined' and 'world producing'.

The problem for Marxists is that the revolution did not happen and generations of people still suffered alienation. As the second half of the 20th century moved on, it also became more complicated. The industrial Society that Marx had analysed and written about had begun to change rapidly into a service economy and later in many societies into a post-industrial one. This made the whole idea of labour a complex one. For example, many people began to work from home whilst others began a programme of flexible working or part-time occupation. Others combined voluntary work with paid work and the whole process of labour became more diversified. At the same time many people became unemployed and lacked the skills to work in the new economy. This meant that alienation was less to do with the traditional patterns of labour and more to do with the separation of self from a total lifestyle that had been forged by the new post-industrial and service economy. In these circumstances, the view of Karl Jung became more relevant and alienation became separation from our self. The problem of modern society is that we project that alienation of our self onto the wider world. Perhaps rather than pursue a revolution that either will not happen or will likely be betrayed, it becomes more important to understand ourselves and our own alienation so that what we project upon the outside world is a self actualised and empowered individual who can make a difference in a positive way. Self-actualisation is about the revolution in our selves rather than in our environment. But what is self-actualisation?

Self-Actualisation

If self-actualisation is "the process whereby individuals realise their inherent potential by whatever avenues are open to them" then what does that mean?

Carl Ransom Rogers (January 8, 1902 – February 4, 1987) was an influential American psychologist and among the founders of the humanistic approach to psychology. Much of his work was based around self-actualisation whish he defined as an essential condition of our being. As he said,

"*The organism has one basic tendency and striving - to actualize, maintain, and enhance the experiencing organism*" (Rogers, 1951, p.487).

Rogers rejected the deterministic nature of both psychoanalysis and behaviourism. He argued that we behave as we do because of the way we perceive our situation. "As no one else can know how we perceive, we are the best experts on ourselves." For him self-actualisation was to "fulfil one's potential and achieve the highest level of 'human-beingness' we can."

To achieve self-actualisation Rogers believes that a person must be in a state of congruence and by this he meant a person's "ideal self" (i.e. who they would like to be) is consistent with their actual behaviour (self-image). Self-image is how we see ourselves, which is important to good psychological health. For example, we might perceive ourselves as a good or bad person, beautiful or ugly. Self-image has an affect on how a person thinks feels and behaves in the world. When congruence happens and our self-image reflects what we believe we are – our ideal self – then we are autonomous and empowered.

But for that congruence to take place then there has to be a sense of self worth as well – the third important concept in Roger's ideas. Self worth (or self-esteem) – is what we think about ourselves. If we think well about ourselves, become the person we want to be and behave to reflect that then there is integration. Of course a person's ideal self may not be consistent with what actually happens in life or of a person's experiences. When there is a difference between a person's ideal self and that person's actual experience then there is what Rogers calls incongruence.

Much of what Rogers describes has been used in therapy. Rogers argues that if one person can offer another unconditional positive regard, empathy, and genuineness then there is a therapeutic relationship and by that he meant a healing or growing relationship. This view of therapy has influenced a generation of counsellors and therapists from those dealing with partnership relationships to those dealing with conflict resolution and negotiations where a win-win situation is the key to success.

However Rogers's work has not been used so much when it comes to analysing the mechanisms of social change. But it is the relationship between his idea of congruence and the way that impacts on a person's potency to change the environment that is crucial to the 21st century.

Recreating A New Balance

Mental illness can arise when an individual has a different view of him or herself than they actually are. Perhaps this is a simpler way of describing what the earlier psychoanalysts believed. Jung's view of alienation from our self, Reich's view that we develop a "character armour" to protect our inner self from the real world and Fromm's view that "social character" was the medium that connected our inner psyche with the outside world all have a resonance with the concept of congruence. Almost all of the humanist tradition argues that mental health and personal empowerment comes when we have a self-image of ourselves that reflects what we truly are. To have an image of our selves that does not reflect our "ideal self" is to create a dysfunctional society and neurotic individuals. We referred in an earlier chapter to Oliver James' book "Affluenza[62]" where he argued that the constant goal of affluence in the Western world and especially the English-speaking world has led to a contagion of mental illness because an acquisitive society creates unrealistic aspirations and the expectation that they can be fulfilled. This is an example of incongruence in the modern world where expectations creates within us a self image that is itself acquisitive and does not reflect the real world where achievement is constantly frustrated.

Living in an environment of constant frustration results in a blinkered view of the world. The imperative of our age is to make it an age of congruence whereby our idea self is the same as what we believe we are. The problem is having the means to discover our ideal self – to gain that self-knowledge which is the basis for authenticity.

Yet it is hard to get the right balance in the 21st Century between image and reality and often the transformation movements of our time do not help. One can understand the religious ones seeking salvation through a messiah or nirvana or ones like Alcoholics Anonymous mentioned in the previous chapter. That is about transformation as therapy to change behaviour. It is not about changing the world. However there are some transformation movements that believe that if we meditate and get inner calm or if we reflect on ourselves to transform negatives into positives then that is all that is needed. The world will then look after itself.

Self-knowledge cannot be so introspective that it excludes everything outside of us as that makes it isolated and self-defeating. Nor can self-knowledge be about reflection on our beliefs and ideas alone. That is inadequate. In an earlier chapter we mentioned that the Chinese approach to philosophy was more concerned with

---

[62] Affluenza by Oliver James and published in 2007 by Vermillion.

behaviour rather than belief. This approach to life is also seen in there view of self-reflection.

Inner Digging And Drilling.

The humanist tradition of China dates back twenty-five centuries. We often think of humanism as emerging with the ancient Greeks and Socrates but there is another tradition of humanism that predates that and is more embracing. When humanism developed in China then it was often characterised as "inner digging and drilling" that is needed to discover a self-awareness of our selves. In the Chinese tradition the self was not a mental construct but rather an experience of reality. Western humanism has been characterised by emphasising the mental constructs that humans create and their capacity to think and develop ideas. Learning was about the development of ideas.

However for Confucius, learning could not occur without silent reflection and to be an authentic person then we have to be truthful to both our self and our sociality. Being true to our self was more than developing ideas; it also understood our place in the cosmos as instinctive beings. Reflection was about not just our ideas but also our relation to the world around us. Reflection took us deeper than our thoughts and made us aware of our instinctive nature too. There needs to be an internal integration between self and nature. It is this integration that is missing in our Western tradition and it is this that has made Western humanism at times so arrogant with its emphasis alone on reason. There are some now who are beginning to question this like James Lovelock and John Grey. They believe that the perilous state of our planet is that we have failed to integrate self with nature and instead tried to elevate self over nature. Their view, as that of the ancient Chinese, is that we need reflection that reveals our total self and its place in the natural world.

And of course, from this came behaviour and an understanding of the right way to behave with others. Confucius focuses on the cultivation of the inner experience, both as a way of self-knowledge and as a method of true communion with the others. Self-reflection should rid us of four things that stand as barriers to true communication and they are arbitrariness of opinion, dogmatism, obstinacy, and egotism. Reflection to gain self-knowledge was never just an exercise in self-discovery or enlightenment for the ancient Chinese – whether of Confucian or Taoist tradition – but as a way of opening ourselves up to communicate with others and behave to others through "right action." This meant that reflection was not about our self but about our relationship with others and the planet on which we live. It is relearning this old tradition that is important for us now as we move into the 21st Century. A new form of humanism has to emerge that is not just about the ascendancy of human reason but one that reflects the needs of our planet and our place on it as one species. Once we see ourselves in this manner then it has an impact on how we behave.

Transformative Learning

Despite the many cults of enlightenment and self-discovery there has been a move in the latter part of the 20th century that could form the basis for a new form of humanism and that development centres on what has been called reflectivity or transformative learning. This is a recognition that learning has to be meaningful and not just the assimilation of factual knowledge. Both John Dewey[63] and Paulo Freire[64] argued against learning as a "bank of knowledge" and valued meaningful learning that gave facts substantive and contextual sense. This meant questioning beliefs, values and assumptions and challenging our reasoning consistently.

As the 20th century progressed then the debate emerged as whether transformation is merely intellectual or whether it also embraced emotional, spiritual and environmental intelligence. Much of Daniel Goleman's[65] work is based upon stressing the importance of emotional intelligence and trying to identify the EQ or emotional quotient. And for Paulo Freire then transformation included political and social awareness as our intellect continually reacts with the

---

[63] John Dewey and the Art of Teaching: Toward Reflective and Imaginative Practice, Sage Publications, Inc (8 Feb 2005) ISBN-10: 1412909031

[64] Pedagogy of the Oppressed (Penguin education) by Paulo Freire Penguin; 2nd Revised edition edition (25 Jan 1996) ISBN-10: 014025403X

[65] Emotional Intelligence by Daniel P. Goleman Bloomsbury Publishing PLC; New edition edition (12 Sep 1996) ISBN-10: 0747528306

environment around us. For him transformation inspires action that should change the world and the unfair distribution of resources and power that exists. He describes the concept of conscientization, a process that achieves a deepening awareness of both the sociocultural reality which shapes our lives and the capacity to transform that reality through action upon it.

It was probably Jack Mezirow who was the main force behind the transformation learning movement, in recent decades, as he believed that individuals could be transformed through a process of critical reflection. According to Mezirow learning occurs in one of four ways:

- By elaborating existing frames of reference,
- By learning new frames of reference,
- By transforming points of view, or
- By transforming habits of mind.

He argues that,

"Transformation theory's focus is on how we learn to negotiate and act on our own purposes, values, feelings, and meanings rather than those we have uncritically assimilated from others -- to gain greater control over our lives as socially responsible, clear thinking decision makers."

For learners to change their beliefs, attitudes, and emotional reactions then they must critically reflect on their experiences in order to achieve perspective transformation and question why their existing assumptions have constrained the way they perceive. Transformative learning occurs when individuals change their frames of reference through critical reflection of their assumptions and beliefs and then making conscious choices to bring about new ways of the defining their world.

This theory is a start but is probably incomplete. Some, for example, have criticised Mezirow because his theory emphasises rationality and is a process that is rationally driven. Intuitive learning and emotional intelligence is not included.

Transformation Plus

The development of self-knowledge has to be about the world we live in and not just our inner self and there has to be some process of connection between the two. The early Gnostics sought self-knowledge as a way of knowing the divine but the later Gnostics like Katherine Tingley and the theosophists sought inner knowledge and used reflection to empower themselves in this world and change it. That is the view of thinkers like Paulo Freiere and although the ancient Chinese may have not considered changing the world, they did consider inner knowledge as a way of influencing our behaviour in our relationship with others.

However they also added the point that inner knowledge is not just about mental constructs but is also about integrating our self with our instincts so that we live within a world that exists rather than one in our imagination.

The problem is that many of us see the world as how we want it to be rather than how it is. We create a self image of ourselves that reflects our perceived view of the world and when that conflicts with our "Ideal self," who we really are, then that impacts on our self esteem and causes mental illness. To understand ourselves we also have to understand the world out there so it is no longer a wish fulfillment but rather an understanding of what is. Only then can we create new frames of reference for ourselves that shift our perception of how we interact with that world and only then can we begin to make a difference. Self and environment exist together and we have to integrate that as well.

Part 3 – The Global Crisis

There is not only a crisis in the knowledge we have about ourselves but there is also a crisis in the knowledge we have about our environment and the planet in which we live. Generations have been shaped by a worldview that science and technology have brought in their wake a world of abundance and all that matters is how we distribute that abundance. The great maps that saw us through the last two centuries increasingly focussed on that distribution and the political debates flared up around that issue. As the 21st Century dawned so did the realisation that it is not the distribution of resources that is the main issue but the abundance of those resources themselves.

The section of the book is concerned with the recent realisation that we do not live in a world of abundance but one of increasing scarcity and that this one fact changes everything. Old structures now have to be challenged and new structures created if we are to live in a world where the guarantee of plenty is not just there. The fact that our planet is finite will change our view of the world and how we can tackle the problems of sustainability and social justice.

However there is still within the ruling economic and political elites the view that we benefit from an infinite global economy and that through free trade this should be allowed to flourish. This dichotomy between the finite planet and the infinite global economy is one of the major tensions of our age and will define the nature of politics for years to come.

But politics itself is also in a sorry state and is ill equipped to tackle the tensions of our new age. There are glowing deficits in the way we structure and deliberate our political life that creates disillusionment and stalemate. In order to renew the structures of our finite world then we have to recreate politics in a way that people relate to it with confidence. So this section looks at the finite world and the tensions that this causes to the global infinite economy and also at the poor state of our democracy in tackling this tension of our global age.

CHAPTER 7 - New Social Structures

Virtual Teddy Bears

When a local councillor gets a present of a virtual teddy bear, joins up to booze mail and a friend tells the world she is painting her nails pink then you know that suddenly you are in the world of social networking. Suddenly a whole host of people are licking whipped cream from a virtual belly button and having pillow fights online. They are forming strange and nonsensical groups to engage new friends and prove to the world that they are cool! Their life becomes a virtual playground, as a reversion to childhood is no longer the music of sweet innocence but the play of adults being artificially childish.

Social networking has exploded across the globe and virtual teddy bears are flying everywhere. People of all ages from the very young to grand parents in cardigan and slippers are now making virtual friends by the dozen. People they would not have dreamed of meeting let alone talk to are now proudly on their friends list for all to see. From Myspace to Facebook and from Netlog to Second Life sites are springing up to find people, friends and create virtual communities. Second Life even boasts its own currency through which people can play and do business that can be converted into hard cash. No one can fail to believe anymore that large slices of life are illusions and that those illusions are becoming many people's enduring realities. People connect to words and images as once they connected to human flesh and an illusion is created that has the force of reality. I found this out when I joined Facebook myself.

I joined to use it to develop the idea of 21st Century Network referred to in the Introduction. I began writing to people in groups that expressed social concern telling them about the concept of 21st century Network and inviting them to join. In next to no time I was banned from Facebook. Apparently I had been spamming! This led me to research the web to see if I could find out what to do if sent to purgatory as I was.. The advice was to write an abject and grovelling letter of apology in hope that they would take me back. I did just that and they reinstated me. I felt myself thinking that there were so few people of my age on Facebook that they wanted to keep as many as they could as tokens and so here I was back and in action but this time with caution.

What was interesting and revealing was that there had been huge numbers of people who had been summarily banned from Facebook and the web was full of young people complaining that their life had been destroyed. Their whole life had revolved around the contacts and silly games of that social networking site. Without it they were left complaining, that life suddenly had no purpose. Without a sexy poke or two whole lives became suicidal!

An Age In Transition

Of course with the web there is much cooperation and collaboration and emerging virtual structures and such virtual communities and teams are increasingly important in business and social activities. Also virtual communities of all kinds have galvinized change and been responsible for the creation of specific subcultures, and the emergence of network organisations to extend or replace existing organisations.

With the advent of social action networks and means of building social networks through the web, there is a great opportunity to create a new form of activist democracy that will liberate people from a sense of hopelessness that at the moment pervades the traditional political environment. All of that is fast developing in the near future and there is hope that the web generation will create a new way of transcending the limitations of virtual teddy bears and mindless play. However there is also danger.

The Internet age has also produced a new sort of person that some researchers have dubbed as Internet Addiction Disorder sufferers. Those who have researched this believe this disorder has created a new kind of dependency in users which can often result in withdrawal affects when deprived.. This is similar to many other addicts like gambling addiction for example and the addict becomes just as isolated as them. Such people often use the Internet as a route to escape the real world and this becomes a mood altering experience.[66]

And for vast sections of social network users if there is not a dependency there is enough interaction around trivial pursuits that mood and attitudes change. When Michael Houellebecq wrote his book "The Elementary Particles:" he was trying to illustrate how the post 1960's generation had been through a mood-changing decade that had produced an illusion of freedom rather than a reality. Often considered the first novelist since Balzac to capture contemporary "social realities,"*The Elementary Particles"* refers both to Houellebecq 's scientific worldview and sense of an atomized society. Houellebecq attempts to show that modern society's emphasis on the individual, on individual rights and freedoms is actually what has made modern man feel dispossessed and lonely. He writes from a Christian perspective but strangely uses the techniques of pornography to expose its shallowness. He believes that the solidarity of communal societies is being weakened by the focus on the individual that became pronounced in the 1960's and took on another form in the 1980's. His book looks at the search for self-gratification and shows it as producing the guilt and dysfunction of modern western society. For him the antidote to this is to find new ways of connecting people.

Without mentioning some of the great writers before him like Marx, Freud, Fromm or Jung, Houellebecq was, as a novelist, trying to illustrate what many of them had said before and that is that our world view and social character is an interaction between our inner selves and the artificial world that surrounds us. Many of us would not totally agree with his analysis of the 1960's but we can see looking back how that decade often produced the illusion of freedom rather than autonomous freedom itself. Just as the 1950's had seen the growth of suburbia and the status seeking society so the 1960's onwards gave a sense that the individual was the centre of what should be empowered rather than the community. As a result social character, in the Fromm sense, took on an unreal flavour because when the individual became increasingly powerless in the

---

[66] Ferris, Jennifer R. Internet Addiction Disorder: Cause, Symptoms, and Consequences. http://www.files.chem.vt.edu/chem-dept/dessy/honors/papers/ferris.html

face of a complex and globalised world then that individual sought their own reality in personal development, self gratification and the pleasure of the moment. Personal experience was what counted rather than community and social change and the world became atomised – a collection of individuals playing as Rome burned.

Wave After Wave

The Internet age was born in this time of individualism and it became the playground increasingly for those seeking the pleasure of the moment as social networking took off with a vengeance. The generations following the 1960's were well equipped to embrace this and take it one step further. Research is now growing on the impact that the Internet and particularly social networking is having on our lives and it will be interesting to see if there is growing evidence of the internet generation being affected in terms of their social character as earlier generations were by the environment around them. We have already looked at the work of those who have examined the relationship between inner self and outer environment in the past; but finding out how this will manifest itself in the post industrial age is often seen in the works and thoughts of futurists.

One such futurist is Alvin Toffler who has looked at how different economic substructures (or "waves" as he calls them) impacts on both social structure and our own selves. In his book *The Third Wave* Toffler describes three types of societies, based on the concept of 'waves' - each wave pushes the older societies and cultures aside although there is a transition period between each wave as the dynamics of change takes place.

A soon as people discovered they could raise crops and no longer had to hunt and gather to survive then the first wave began in Toffler's typology. This was an agricultural society where people stayed in their place within extended families that cared for one another. Generations of families lived in the same place and on the same land and there was a sense of the world being cyclical as seasons changed yet people, stayed the same. The farm was the central production unit in an economic system of self-sufficiency and there was little waste.

The second wave was the industrial one where we learnt to harness technology to create factory production. Wind, water, coal, steam and oil fuelled the second wave creating our industrial world. In this new world self sufficiency was replaced with the "law of comparative advantage" whereby people concentrated on manufacturing products that gave them a comparative advantage in a competitive world. This led to a division of labour to enhance the wealth of nations. Investment, factories, managers and legal corporations became the essence of the industrial order. The concept of the factory as the place of work extended far beyond the manufacturing sector as schools became factories for learning, hospitals factories for treatment, and asylums factories for the sick. Instead of the farm being the basic unit of production, people moved to the cities and the nuclear family became increasingly prominent. Men worked and most women stayed at home creating a gender gap of inequality.

Since late 1950s many countries began moving away from a Second Wave Society into what Toffler called a Third Wave Society or the post industrial one. This new age is an information one started through telephony and now dominated by the computer. Today, Radar systems warn us of incoming missiles, robot callipers detect tiny variations in ball bearings, and CD-Roms store our accumulated knowledge. The factory is no longer the sole production unit and many have downsized, outsourced, relocated around the world or shut down.

The postindustrial society is the digital age. Digital information, once in a computer, can be whisked anywhere in the world with one click. It can be rapidly moved without delay and without degradation. Customers now interact directly with manufacturers. You call their phone centre or order online and your sweater with your initials is delivered the next day. That sweater wasn't lying around, ready to be delivered; increasingly, the product isn't finished until just before it goes into the package. In the post industrial age,

- Work is done everywhere: at home, on the road, even in the office!
- Continual education is the necessity of the age and for success.
- Size doesn't matter: Small companies can compete with large and bureaucratic, companies.
- Location, Space, and Mass do longer matters.

- Time matters dearly, and we call the new timeframe Internet time.
- Often people consume and are also producers. There is not the rigid distinction of the indusial age. The post-industrial age is the age of both – called by Toffler The Prosumer.

Diversity & Subcultures

In this post-industrial society, there is a lot of diversity in lifestyles or subcultures. Toffler gives an example of the family where once we had either the extended or nuclear family in the post-industrial age we have "57 varieties!" In addition to these more traditional models of the family there are also single parent families, same sex relationships and families, communal living and increasing numbers of people choosing to live alone. Culture also becomes diversified, as creative innovators no longer depend on mass communication to be successful. Blogging, video blogging and sites like YouTube can reach huge audiences and a huge variety of subcultures can find their own audience.

This growing fragmented society where individual preference dominates the social and political agenda will effect how people view the world. However the world actually is, the growing diversified society of the post-industrial age will create new ways through which a person's inner self makes sense of the chaos all around. In this world of individual endeavour where knowledge transfer is important then different impulses emerge within society. The knowledge society is often driven not so much by labour as in the industrial age but more by creativity and sometimes play as people experiment across the globe crossing national boundaries and cultures. This often creates a countervailing response from nation states and organisations that seek to set agendas and insert control. So social character is often developed in the dichotomy between individual creativity and control and this can impact on both individual and social character.

It was Erich Fromm who developed the idea or concept of social character as we have seen earlier. For him social character is made up of " *the essential nucleus of the character structure of most members of a group, which has developed as the result of the basic experiences and mode of life common to that group*."

In the very individualised and diversified post industrial world then there are many groups that help define social character and this creates problems for social cohesion. This has always been the case in the United States that developed in the 19th Century through waves of immigration. Now this is also happening in the more established European countries as social cohesion is being challenged by greater and greater diversity.

The Digital Divide
Not everyone is in the postindustrial age and some countries have hardly started. There is a gap that needs bridging as the global digital divide poses a serious challenge in today's world. While millions in the developed world have access to the vast information, communication and economic resources available through the Internet, much of the world's population continues to exist without the benefit of Internet access and information resources. Although this gap is closing access and the ability to use the new technology is still and will remain for some time a very real problem.

The Information revolution is the dynamic energy behind the postindustrial world and the *global digital divide* may hinder the ability of non-industrialized economies to catch up with the living standards and productivity of the industrialized world.[67] It is true that the growth of personal computers has been striking. In 1990 there were only 2.5 personal computers per 100 people in the world but by 2001 this had changed to 8.1% of the world being able to access computers. But this growth hides the fact that access is not even around the globe. In 2001, there were 61 computers per hundred people in North America, and only 1 per 100 people in sub-Saharan Africa and 0.5 per 100 in South Asia but over the years since access has grown considerably in much of Asia, and Latin America.

---

[67] Chinn, Menzie D., Robert W. Fairlie. 2004. "The Determinants of the Global Digital Divide: A Cross-Country Analysis of Computer and Internet Penetration." *California Digital Library.* Retrieved 13 July 2004. http://repositories.cdlib.org/cgirs/CGIRS-2004-3/

Over recent years growth has been dramatic, but this can hide the fact that a substantial disparity still exists and time will be needed for developing nations to catch up.

But it is not the disparity between nations that is all-important. It is also the disparity within them. The United Nations Report on the Millennium Goals 2007 stated that the proportion of people living in extreme poverty fell between 1990 and 2004 and that the number of extremely poor people in sub-Saharan Africa has leveled off, with the poverty rate declining by almost six percent. However they also say,

The benefits of economic growth in the developing world have been unequally shared, both within and among countries. Between 1990 and 2004, the share of national consumption by the poorest fifth of the population in developing regions decreased from 4.6 to 3.9 per cent (in countries where consumption figures were unavailable, data on income were used). Widening income inequality is of particular concern in Eastern Asia, where the share of consumption among the poorest people declined dramatically during this period.[68]

Widening income inequality both within nation states and between them creates a divide and this is seen in the digital revolution – a revolution that has been the engine of most modern economies. So on one hand there is a new social structure emerging in the developing world around social networks, mobility and increasing diversity whilst because of widening inequalities there is also huge sections of the world's population who do not share this and face the reality of being dispossessed and that can lead to the culture of humiliation.

---

[68] The Millennium Development Goals Report 2007, UNI T ED NAT IONS
NEW YORK, 2007, Website
http://mdgs.un.org/unsd/mdg/default.aspx

The Culture of Humiliation

But of course as Toffler argues in his book "Third Wave" countries do not transform from one wave to the next immediately and as change takes place then agricultural, industrial and postindustrial economies and attitudes live side-by-side adding to the tension and lack of cohesion. At a time of traumatic change such as our present time when past blueprints are no longer adequate then this can lead to a sense of humiliation by the dispossessed.

We know that September 11th 2001 saw the United States attacked on its own soil for the first time since the Second World War and the attack on Pearl Harbour. But this was not the only act of terrorism on American soil since that War.

On April 17, 1995 Timothy McVeigh reportedly picked up a 20-foot Ryder truck from Elliott's Body Shop in Junction City. The truck was filled with roughly 5,000 pounds (2,300 kg) of ammonium nitrate, an agricultural fertilizer, and nitromethane, a highly volatile motor-racing fuel-a mixture also known as Kinepak or ANFO. At 9:02 a.m. on April 19, 1995, the truck exploded in the street in front of the Alfred P. Murrah federal building. The attack claimed 168 lives and left over 800 injured. The Oklahoma City bombing was the worst terrorist attack on U.S. soil until the September 11, 2001 World Trade Centre attack.

Timothy McVeigh said he was doing this as revenge for the standoff between the FBI and the Branch Davidian cult (led by David Koresh) at the Davidian compound in Waco, Texas which ended in tragedy in April 1993. When the FBI tried to end the standoff by gassing the complex, the entire compound went up in fire, claiming the lives of 75 followers, including many young children. The death toll was high and many people blamed the U.S. government for the tragedy. Timothy McVeigh, angered by the Waco tragedy, decided to enact retribution to those he felt responsible -- the federal government, especially the FBI and the Bureau of Alcohol, Tobacco, and Firearms (ATF).

The Federal Government tried to paint McVeigh as a lonely man and the sole perpetrator of this act. In no way did they seem to want to link what he did to a feeling of rage that was sweeping across much of mid America. The author Gore Vidal, a libetarian and opponent of the mid west and bible belt politics of America wrote a long article trying to get Americans to understand the mind set of McVeigh and those who felt frustrated by the march of Federal Government. He made it clear in a famous article that the Federal Government wanted to portray this act of terrorism as that of a depraved individual. He said,

There was to be only one story; one man of incredible innate evil wanted to destroy innocent lives for no reason other than a spontaneous joy in evildoing.[69]

But Gore Vidal after a long interview with Timorthy McVeigh saw it rather differently and argued that McVeigh saw himself as the *"John Brown of Kansas", the anti-slavery campaigner who was executed after leading a raid into the south which sparked the American civil war."* And he also argued that McVeigh was not alone either in the act he perpetrated or in his hatred of the government. McVeigh felt he was acting on behalf of all those who had been humiliated by Washington.

In Joel Dyer's book "The Harvest of Rage" he explores the deep rural routes of the growing anti government feeling amongst much of middle America.Dyer states and starkly states that between 1991 and 1995 there were 4,046 pipe-bomb incidents in the United States and 75% of those bombs exploded.

Pipe bombs are easy to make and Ron Cole, Branch Davidian and leader of one of the many American militias (this one in Colorado) is recorded as saying that is the only reason they are used and if bigger bombs were easier to make they would be. Biological and chemical weapons are becoming easier to procure and manufacture and terror in America may come from within just as well as outside its borders.

Dyer quotes Howard Zinn the author of "A People's History of the United States" when he argued,

---

[69] Gore Vidal, *Vanity Fair*, September 2001

"What we're seeing now is recognised as the growing polarization of wealth in the country, with just 1 percent owning 40 percent of the wealth, with the middle class shrinking as people lose their jobs and become part of the homeless poor."

The "rage" often experienced by people in the Mid West of America towards the Washington Establishment is often the rage engendered by social change as more traditional Mid Western cultures clash with East and West Coast America and the finance Establishment – a rage that spread across the country in the financial collapse in 2008/09.

World Views Asunder

Of course September 11th 2001 was also an act of revenge for humiliation too. For decades the West had divided the Arab world in pursuit of oil resources, supported a growing Israel that became armed with nuclear weapons and failed to tackle the Palestinian question that had resulted in the longest refugee problem on record. Young people humiliated, highly educated in some cases, but without jobs or prospects felt alienated and angry and this grew as the 21st century dawned upon us. The collapse of the twin towers saw a collapse of a world that made sense. For half a century the bi polar battle between the Western and Communist worlds had given some semblance of meaning to our understanding of events around us. When the Berlin Wall fell then the hegemony of the United States and the triumph of its liberal philosophy led some to believe that this was the "end of history" and that there was now but one world view.

Of course it was not true then and never was true but it was the prevailing establishment philosophy. And yet the growth of rage in the United States made manifest in the Oklahoma bombing challenged the one worldview at the very moment that it was being proclaimed. And when the twin towers collapsed then what went down as well was the belief that a new world order had been achieved. There was no longer a one-world view. As the Western world embraced the digital age and a post industrial future much of that same world as well as much of the rest of the globe felt left out and humiliated. Side by side with the diversity of the new world of social networks and individual gratification were the worlds of the dispossessed espousing fundamental creeds and living the culture of despair. It was a world in fragments cast asunder without framework or apparent meaning. Making sense of this new chaos that had suddenly hit our imaginations in the first decade of the 21st century was now the imperative of our age.

CHAPTER 8 - Knowing Our Environment

Our Place In The World

When I was a young arrogant and very priggish seventeen year old, as I mentioned earlier, I approached my Methodist Minister in my hometown. I had just given up my religious beliefs and thought politics was the answer to all. I remember telling him that once the welfare state was perfected then no one would need religion and it would be a thing of the past. Everyone would have security and that environment of well being would change people's hearts and minds relegating superstition to some unwanted nether region of the mind. How wrong I was! Whatever our state of welfare, the world out there created unmet needs that shaped us and formed insecurities and these insecurities were often formed by what went on around us and how we coped with that within our inner selves.

Our environment may change us, and help to create new possibilities so that new worlds of opportunity appear in our mind; but what appears is an interaction between our mind and the world out there. Understanding who we are and how we can cope in that world means understanding both that external world and ourselves. Here we want to look a little at that external world and then ask what we can do to change ourselves so that we can not only cope more effectively but also make a difference that matters. It seems a futile goal to spend time trying to make a better world without understanding how we fit into the changing mosaic about us. Equally it seems almost self indulgent to concentrate on ourselves alone and exclude what is going on around us. We are part of a greater whole and understanding that in the 21st century is about understanding how that can change our behaviour. It is about liberating our inner self from the chains of illusion and creating new constructs that place us in the world in which we live as empowered individuals.

When Bettleheim discovered that people in extreme circumstances acted in ways that were not predictable he began to also understand that it is how we relate our inner selves to the circumstances that we face daily that determines our potency to act. Giving attention to both is important not just for survival as a human being but in the

21ST century for the survival of the planet as well. It the next five chapters we want to look at our changing external environment and how the knowledge of that impacts on the knowledge of ourselves. We will look at these five areas.

Our Social Character

In understanding the world we have to also understand our place within it and how that world affects our social character. It is not enough to describe the 21st century world as an academic exercise. We also need to understand how that affects ourselves and influences our behaviour and then find ways to see beyond the surface.

Those of us brought up since the Second World War in the Western world has seen a landscape of devastation transformed by reconstruction. What was an existence of bare necessity with rationing, community self help and a return to the normalcy of family life suddenly became transformed through economic aid and growth to one of consumerism and ever-higher expectations. Suddenly markets grew up amongst the middle classes, the young and then working people everywhere. Suburbia became part of modern life, new public housing was built and young people found a liberating independence in music and fashion.

In that consumer society character was formed (as discussed in previous chapters) through the quest for recognition and status. Small things suddenly became important as symbols of our place in the world and this determined the image we had of ourselves and how we saw the world.

In the new millennium we are developing new social structures that affect our social character and these create new illusions that can blind us from alternative visions of a world in turbulence. One of these is the Internet and particularly the growth of social networks. In one sense the Internet has created opportunities for a coming together of people on our globe and it offers a positive form of globalisation. At the same time it has produced a new virtual suburbia online that masks the world out there through the constant trivia and play of people in search of contact.

As many engage in these new interactive structures, there are many that are deprived of contact through the Internet and are part of the "digital divide" – the new division between those who have access and those who do not. That divide is even greater when the web and social networks are dominated by the influence of West and their life styles are projected to the under developed world where such life styles seem out of reach.

So the new structures of the new century can offer opportunities, illusions and growing inequalities of access. It is these structures that we need to examine as Fromm, Jung , Bettleheim and many others did for structures of the 20th Century.

A Divided Planet

But it is not just the division caused by the digital age that is important to understand. There is the basic division between those who have power and resources in the world and those who do not and we need to consider how this is changing in the 21st Century. The advent of "globalisation" in the latter part of the 20th Century has created new power structures, greater dependency and a mountain of debt not only in the poorer nations but within the richer ones too and this has created a world built on a foundation of sand.

As we create our lives particularly in the developed world around the new social structures that shape our behaviour, it is important to place that behaviour in the context of the unequal world we live in and the fragility of it all. Unless we do that then we will be creating an illusion of what life is like whilst underneath the reality cries out a more uncertain future for us all.

Somehow we have to develop a worldview that encompasses the powerful as well as the dispossessed. Often our focus on our own immediate needs and gratification blinds us from this. One has only to spend a little time on social network sites to see how many if not most people there are in a virtual world of isolation rather than engagement from a truly global view. A global view in the 21st Century is important for individual behaviour.

Population & Resources

We are also in a world that has come to the end of the bonanza of the previous two or three centuries of growth. Many of the resources that fuelled that growth are running out. Oil is reaching its peak and will no longer provide the fuel base of the 21st Century. This will produce an energy gap between the depletion of oil and the advent of new and alternative technologies. That gap could be one of tension and crisis.

But it is not only oil that is becoming scarce. So are many of the other resources that not only feed our growth economies like copper but also those that are essential for life like water and food. And as technologies such as bio fuel are being exploited then that will take land away from essential food production.

When such shortages are linked to a growing world population then the crisis looms ever more serious. A population of 6 billion today has risen from half of that in less than 40 years and will increase to over 9 billion by the middle of this century. This will put enormous pressure on resources especially as the new giants of our century, China and India, try to emulate the life styles of the West.

Almost all the people born in the next 50 years are expected to end up in urban areas, and some of these can barely provide minimal services for people now.

The UN is predicting widespread future food shortages as well as sanitation and health problems in cities and others have linked population increases with social tension, and breakdown in law and order.

An Unsustainable Future

All of this is creating an unsustainable future; but it is not just an unsustainable one of shortage and population growth. We are also reaping the harvest of our past growth as that growth slowly damages our planet through pollution and even more important the emission of greenhouse gases.

The growing emissions of methane and most importantly carbon dioxide over the years have slowly warmed our planet and of this there is an overwhelming scientific consensus. The debate now is not whether this will create global warming but what is the extent. Predictions of 2% to over 10% by the end of the century hide within them different scenarios about our existence as a species on this planet.

Lower rates of growth will see melting ice and rising sea levels and produce migrations of population on an unprecedented scale. The higher rates could see much of human life become extinct as life itself struggles to survive and the resources needed to support it are not just there.

Global warming is probably the greatest single threat to human life on this planet and not understanding the seriousness of it as we play within our new found social structures is a little like fiddling while Rome burns. This new and apocalyptic scenario of the planet's future has to and must become a part of our consciousness.

Democracy In Crisis
But then there is another problem. Even if we are aware of the vast changing world out there then what can we do about it. Even if the external world is part of our inner self and our worldview then to what good is that if we can change nothing?

For over two centuries we have seen the growth of democracy in nation states. It has not been achieved without considerable struggle in almost all countries. Now having achieved democracy in many parts of the world, we are now seeing it being eroded as decisions are taken across national borders by bodies that are often unaccountable to local electorates. This has created a sense of hopelessness amongst electorates in the developed world let alone the underdeveloped where national assemblies, democratically elected are constrained by the globalisation and the concentration of decision making.

How we reinvent democracy and make it relevant to the 21st Century is now one of the great issues facing us. How do we create a democracy that is both local and cosmopolitan? It is hardly being discussed in political circles although it is a great debate amongst academics.

To make any change in consciousness in ourselves because of a changing world also must have with it a feeling of empowerment so that we believe we can make a difference. Only then can our behaviour be meaningful.

Right Action

As we have already discussed the post Enlightenment world saw the creation of a number of blueprints that gave us some sort of navigation to understand the world. Those blueprints now seem faded as the world rapidly changes. In time new blueprints may emerge but the debate over those will probably take decades. The crisis of the 21st century does not have decades to spare and so we have to find ways around mobilising ourselves not only to understand ourselves in the world but to change both the world and ourselves.

In previous chapters we have looked at the impact that our environment has on our worldview that we develop within ourselves. In the next chapters we will look at how we need to change in order to reflect the dramatically changing environment but looking at the imperatives that this environment presents to us.

In the final chapters we look at 21st forms of social action that we can take to make a difference and also at how behaviour should become our focus rather than belief. It is our collective behaviour that may get us through the next few decades rather than creeds or dogma, as that is more likely to divide us at a time when such division may prove fatal.

CHAPTER 9 - The Major Issues – The Finite Planet

Moments Of Revelation.

There are times in life when events happen that can change your whole approach to life and the ideas that underline it. Such times are uncomfortable as they put in doubt so many of the truths that until then you thought self-evident. Then you either hide your head under the duvet hoping for the world to go away or you find excitement and challenge in the new revelations and struggle to adapt.

Such a time for me was when I discovered the world we live in is actually finite. Until I was about 30 I had always lived in an illusory world of continuous improvement or so I thought. The debates of my teenage years and twenties had always been about not whether but how that continuous improvement would take place. And for almost all of us that improvement would be through economic growth.

However it was in the 1970's that I began to understand the precarious state of our planet. First I realised that our fossil based economy was not sustainable, secondly I came to understand that the same profligacy that we applied to our economy we also used in organising our education and care systems making them unsustainable too. Finally I became aware that it was not our economy and social system that was under threat but that our planet itself was as an ecosystem that sustained life. We were threatening our own survival as our population increased unchecked.

The post Second World War years had been deeply influenced by the ideas of the economist John Maynard Keynes. The post War Labour Government in the UK and Roosevelt's New Deal in the USA had set about putting his ideas into practice through a managed economy. It was through such an economy and full employment that wealth would be created and most political parties in the Western world were united in accepting this. The main divisions at that time were about whether that wealth should be redistributed in favour of the less well off or not.

But as wealth increased the new middle class did not want to see their new found riches redistributed and this caused a crisis on the political left as the growing middle class could only be ignored at the expense of political oblivion. So in the 1950's the reformists (or revisionists as they were often derisorily called) in the left in Britain took Tony Crosland as their new guru. He was a passionate man who once lost his temper at me when I suggested he was being too political at a Labour Party meeting in his constituency in Grimsby. Silly question really but at least I got to know that Crosland was no cold calculating machine but a man who felt passionately about politics. His book "The Future Of Socialism[70]" became the new bible for those modernisers on the left of British politics who wanted to see redistribution whilst at the same time paradoxically try to woo the emerging middle class. He wanted the nation as a whole and not just a privileged class to enjoy the benefits of a libertarian society where you could find,

"… more open-air cafes, brighter and gayer streets at night, later closing hours for public houses, more local repertory theatres, better and more hospitable hoteliers and restaurateurs, brighter and cleaner eating houses, more riverside cafes, more pleasure gardens on the Battersea model, more murals and pictures in public places, better designs for furniture and pottery and women's clothes, statues in the centre of new housing estates, better-designed new street lamps and telephone kiosks and so on ad infinitum."

Crosland was a major influence on the left and did get minds focussed on the difference between means and ends. Public ownership was to him but one means to managing an economy and achieving economic growth but it was not to be the only means.. In arguing this, Crosland endorsed the principle of economic growth and sought to identify measures that would enhance the dynamism of the private sector.

For him equality was to be achieved through making the education system one where all could benefit equally. But central to his argument was the importance of economic growth and the redistribution of that growth if not of basic wealth itself.

---

[70] The Future Of Socialism, Anthony Crosland, Robinson Publishing; 50th anniversary ed edition (14 Sep 2006) ISBN-10: 1845294858

All of this became the conventional wisdom of my early years. I remember campaigning in mock elections at school on the basis that sound economic management and growth would create a fairer society, repeating this five-year's later as a student campaigning in London & the West Country and then repeating it myself ten years later as a Parliamentary candidate in my own right. I had passed on what had become the illusion of our age – that economic growth was the panacea to wealth and happiness for all. It was like a mantra and all political parties chanted it. I too joined the chorus

A year after my minor clash with Tony Crosland, I joined the BBC to work as a Production Assistant making programmes for Open University Courses. This was 1969 and the last year of the 1960's. I had been one of the post war spoilt generation brought up in the absence of War or unemployment, bred on the "never had it so good" outlook on life and alive with the rock music of the new age and the thought of oblivious pleasure if not the reality of it all. Two particular decades in the second half of the 20th century stand out as creating the greatest of illusions. The 1980's created the illusion that wealth was possible for all by the pursuit of self-interest. It saw the yuppie generation come of age and the bright young things who thought happiness was found through having as much as possible and consuming it as ostentatiously as one could. This was the generation that formed the base for the later neo cons in the US and the Blair lads and babes of the late 1990's. The other and perhaps more significant decade was the 1960's. Having gone through the post war period where our parent generation wanted to return to "normalcy" after years of depression and war and after the sounds of rebellion broke through in the 1950's with the beatnik generation, rock and roll and teen age spending power, the 1960's was explosive. A generation suddenly sprung up who wanted to experiment with life and enjoy it to the sounds of music more thrilling and optimistic than any previously. This was the age when anything was possible and turned the Enlightenment of the 18th century into popular culture. Some called it a counter culture but it was very much in the tradition of the past – as in our excitement with life we thought we could remake the world and everyone was invited to get on board.

And so in 1969 I joined the BBC – a working class kid from the West country now a producer in the most respected broadcasting organisation in the Western world making programmes for the most innovate educational organisation for decades. And of course, it was an exciting job and I was surrounded by a wealth of very talented people. I started by making Psychology, Sociology and mainly Politics programmes for the Foundation Course in Social Science and I admit to having the statutory long hair, flowered shirt and flairs! Three years in and I found myself involved with a course called Statistical Sources. We decided that we would make programmes that highlighted some of the sources from which statistics were collected. We wanted to show that statistics was not a cold and dull subject of painstaking calculation but was based upon assumptions and actual sources. It turned out not to be the most exciting course I had worked on and was remarkable for only one or two programmes and one of these was on energy. And it was here that I was confronted with the views of Marion King Hubbert.

Peak Oil

In 1956, a Shell Oil geologist named M. King Hubbert stood up before a meeting of the American Petroleum Institute and predicted that oil production in the United States would peak and begin to decline starting in the early 1970s. He had noticed that oil discoveries graphed over time and tended to follow a bell shape curve. Shell tried to stop Hubbert from making his projections public, but he went ahead and did so.

Hubbert was right; US continental oil production did peak in 1970 even though in 1970 US oil producers had never produced as much oil. The peak was only recognised several years later after much denial from politicians and vested interests as well as those who wanted life to go on as usual. Yet America never again produced as much as it did in 1970, despite drilling four times more oil wells each year. Since then, oil production has been in steady, rapid decline.

Hubbert went on to predict a global oil peak between 1995 and 2000. Although the oil shocks of the 1970s slowed our use of oil globally, since the mid-1980s, oil companies have been finding less oil than we have been consuming. The Association for the Study of Peak Oil and Gas (ASPO) latest model suggests that 'regular' oil peaked in 2004. If heavy oil, deepwater, polar and natural gas liquids are considered, the oil peak is projected for around 2010[71].

For me brought up on the belief of unending progress that would guarantee well-being for all, this came as a sudden shock. As an undergraduate I had read Thomas Malthus and his pessimistic projections about population explosion and the impact this would have on society. It was Malthus who first drew our attention to demand pressing on ever dwindling resources. However like most others I accepted that he was not mainstream and his view of economics gave it the aura of the "dismal science." So like others it was Ricardo, Marx, Marshall and others that reflected the true nature of economic activity and the intellectual conflicts were not because of progress but were within the paradigm of progress itself.

Now along comes King Hubbert raising the spectrum of Malthus all over again. We now have to face the real possibility that oil had peaked and "Peak Oil" means not 'running out of oil', but 'running out of cheap oil'. For societies based on ever increasing amounts of cheap oil, the consequences could be dramatic. Our industrial societies and economic systems were built on the assumption of economic growth – continuous growth based on ever more readily available cheap fossil fuels.

Oil currently accounts for about 43% of the world's total fuel consumption, and 95% of global energy used for transportation. For decades oil has dominated Western economies as the bloodstream of its life. If that begins to slow then its impact will be felt across geopolitics, security, lifestyles, agriculture and economic stability. It will have global impact. Oil-based economies do not need to deplete their reserves of oil in its entirety before it begins to collapse. A shortfall between demand and supply of as little as 10 to 15 percent is enough to cause major disruption.

The issue is not the end of energy but the end of cheap energy as it is this that has sustained the growth mania of our mass consumption societies. Moving to alternative energy systems such as nuclear, hydrogen or biodiesel and ethanol fuels will not produce cheap

---

[71]From the ASPO Web site at
http://www.peakoil.net/uhdsg/Default.htm

energy. What is critical is the concept of Net Energy, or the Energy Returned on Energy Invested ratio (ERoEI). This measures the ratio between the amount of energy input to produce a given energy output. In the early days of oil, one barrel of oil of energy input was capable of producing 100 barrels oil equivalent in energy output and was thus cost effective and efficient. More recently, as oil recovery becomes more difficult, the ratio has become significantly lower. Exploration in the sea or on tar sands has made this input/output ratio less attractive and such alternative sources of energy normally have ratios that will not produce cheap energy.

It is not just that energy is getting more expensive to exploit and produce but also that demand is growing and set to grow further. There are over six billion people on the planet and five billion of those barely use energy at all. But that is now changing as China and India are catching up at a fast rate.

And this is happening when new oil fields are difficult to find. In 2000, there were 16 discoveries of oil "mega-fields," eight in 2001, and in 2002 only three discoveries were made. Today, we consume about six barrels of oil for every one new barrel discovered.

The U.S. Dept. of Energy estimates that the world will require 120 million barrels a day by 2025. To meet that demand we need to find the equivalent of 10 new North Sea oil fields within a decade. Today, we are hard-pressed to discover one new mega-field, let alone 10.

So it looks as if Malthus is having the last word and the impact will be severe. If population growth and demand push against a dwindling resource that is the lifeblood of our economic well being then it almost certainly will result in serious political and cultural turmoil ahead. Industry and the agricultural, manufacturing and retail trade will change considerably and not without much disruption on a global scale.

So by making one programme for an Open University course, my world had been turned upside down. I realised that the dream of continuous improvement founded on cheap energy based economic growth was an illusion. King Hubbert was saying to me that the "emperor has no clothes." How to find new apparel was difficult.

Future Wars

Once a new revelation hits you like the world we live in is finite then everything can change. Slowly one has to reconstruct ideas and thoughts around an entirely new paradigm or reject it all together. It seemed that to reject it was an act of arrogant self-indulgence and so coming to terms with a finite world was the only intellectual choice possible.

In early 2008 there were riots in Egypt, Tibet, Haiti, The Ivory Coast, Cameroon demonstrations or strikes in Jordan, Mauritania, Mozambique and Senegal and protests in Uzbekistan, Yemen, Bolivia and Indonesia – and all because of rising food prices. In March of that year Josette Sheeran,, director of the UN World Food Programme, said: *"We are seeing a new face of hunger. We are seeing more urban hunger than ever before. We are seeing food on the shelves but people being unable to afford it*[72]*."* And Robert Zoellick, president of the World Bank, also said *"many more people will suffer and starve" unless the US, Europe, Japan and other rich countries provide funds. He said prices of all staple food had risen 80% in three years, and that 33 countries faced unrest because of the price rises*[73]*."*

The shortage of basic resources is a major cause of conflict and unrest but is also almost certainly the spark that will ignite future wars. Resource scarcity has implications for almost everything and one thing that became increasingly obvious was that it began to change our perceptions of war. Being born at the end of World War II I lived in an era where warfare was dominated by the theories of Carl von Clausewitz – the champion of total war! To Clausewitz war must never be seen as a purpose to itself, but as a means of physically forcing one's will on an opponent. For him, "war is the continuation of politics through other means." The Oxford English Dictionary[74] defines total war as "a war to which all resources and

---

[72] David Adam report in The Guardian on Wednesday 9 April 2008

[73] Reported in Spiegel Online on October 4th 2008 at http://www.spiegel.de/international/world/0,1518,546551,00.html

[74] Oxford Dictionary of English (Hardcover) by Catherine Soanes (Editor), Angus Stevenson (Editor,) Publisher: OUP Oxford; New Ed edition (11 Aug 2005) ISBN-10: 0198610572

the whole population are committed; loosely, a war conducted without any scruples or limitations."

Clausewitz wrote his book "On War" because as a Prussian officer in the 19th century he was curious at how the French Revolution and Napoleon had changed the very nature of war by unleashing it on a grander scale than ever using all resources that were possible. It was total.

Not only was the backdrop to my early life the theory of total war as illustrated in two world wars of the twentieth century but also the belief that war was about misunderstandings that could be sorted out by rational discussion. I remember chairing a meeting recently when a leading Opposition front bench spokesperson took part as a leading participant. She represented a constituency with a strong Jewish lobby and was herself a strong supporter of Israel but she clearly thought that if called upon she could act as an honest broker in discussions between Palestinians and Israelis. I kind of understood that even though I found it hard to agree with her because she had this naïve view that I held in my teens that discussion could solve all whatever your views.

1962 was the year of the Cuban Missile crisis when total war meant annihilation. It was a year that made it clear that such war between East & West was no longer possible and that survival meant discussion and negotiation. However when American placed missiles in Turkey and The Soviet Union responded by shipping missiles to Cuba then an American blockade placed the world on the very edge of nuclear war. In my teenage naivety I still felt rational discussion could stop it so in my small West Country town I was travelling from Youth Club to Youth Club to get support to put pressure on our local MP who would then pressure the then Prime Minister to influence President Kennedy. I really felt that we could influence our MP and that he could influence the Prime Minister and that in turn the Prime Minister could change the mind of the American President. Everything could be settled by reason. And in a way during the Cuban Missile crisis reason did prevail.

But today in the era of resource depletion war will never be total nor will it be resolved by reasonable discussion alone. There is now the fear that future wars will not be about a "balance of power" as in the

19th century or a battle of ideologies as in the 20th century but it will be a battle for ever scarce resources.

Many people argue that because of the decline or oil resources that the United States is heading for an economic crash and the collapse of the dollar will affect every nation on earth. Richard Heinberg of the New College of California in his book "Power Down: Options and Actions for a Post-Carbon World[75]" argues that

"It's too late to maintain a 'business as usual' attitude. What is required is to manage the change that peak oil will bring in a way that causes the fewest casualties. This must be done at an economic and geopolitical level, to fend off resource wars. The US invasion of Iraq is clearly a resource war,"

The US response to the crisis of Peak Oil is rather than cut oil consumption by scaling back on economic activity and making major lifestyle changes, it is to use the military to maintain control over oil in the Middle East.

"The long-range plan is for the West to control the Middle East by the military so it can control the price of oil."

Michael Klare, an expert on warfare and international security looks at the impact of resource scarcity his book on resource wars and sees the effect in the Persian Gulf and in the Caspian and South China Seas, And it is not just oil scarcity that he considers crucial but other basic resources too and particularly water in the Nile Basin and other multinational river systems and also scarcity over timber, and minerals from Borneo to Sierra Leone.[76] China for example has 7% of the world's water resources and roughly 20% of the world's population and it has a regional imbalance with about four fifths of the water supply in the south. Today the North China plain, once a

---

[75] Powerdown: Options and Actions for a Post-carbon Society (Paperback) by Richard Heinberg Publisher: Clairview Books; 2nd Revised edition edition (23 Jul 2007) ISBN-10: 1905570104
[76] Resource Wars by Michael T. Klare, Holt Paperbacks (March 13, 2002) Publisher: Palgrave Macmillan; First edition (5 Jul 2002) ISBN-10: 0805055762

healthy ecosystem, is parched. Most of the wetlands have dried up and natural streams have vanished. When there is scarcity then the danger of war or internal strife is high. Egypt is concerned about the water developmental activities of the upstream users of the Nile. It has warned Ethiopia and Sudan it will bomb any dam they build on the Nile.

According to Michael Renner of the World Watch Institute about a quarter of the wars in 2001 had a strong "resource dimension[77]". It is predicted that the world's population will increase from 6.1 billion to perhaps 9 billion by 2050. This will increase the demand for resources and increase conflict.

Wars will no longer be the total wars of the 20th century – the total Wars fought on the Clausewitz model of the nation state. Over 90% of violent armed conflicts classified as wars in 2001 were wars within a state, between groups fighting for political control, over natural resources or other causes. These wars are low intensity ones between groups within states often warlords, clans or gangs. But also the major industrial countries have also been involved in such wars as in the case of Iraq's oil and the fight over oil transportation in the Caucasus. When they become involved then organised gangs will fight back not in total confrontation but through asymmetric warfare – through terrorism and insurgency.

Unless the issue of resources is addressed at an international level, my teenage wish of disputes being resolved through rational discussion will be another illusion. The underlying dark shadow of resource scarcity will have to be tackled first and a sustainable planet the main international objective. But sustainability is not just about resources.

---

[77] Michael Klare, Resource Wars: the new landscape of global conflict, Carnegie Council: Books for Breakfast, as facilitated by Joanne Myers, 22 May 2001

Silent Spring

Once you are confronted with a new perspective on life – that is the frailty of it all and the finite nature of our planet then your views develop in areas that you once thought unlikely.

For example when I was a young champion of economic growth and progress then I found environmentalists difficult to accept. They struck me as middle class conservationists who wanted to protect their England from ordinary working people. I think many of us felt that on the left in those days. We saw environmentalists as those who wanted their old England whilst we were fighting for a new and modern one. We wanted "Jerusalem in England's dark Satanic mills" rather than heritage sites and greenery where only those with cars could visit.

But once resource scarcity hits you as a concept then suddenly the rational model of progress breaks down and the optimism in technological advancement takes a knock. So you begin to question your old assumptions and begin to think afresh.

In 1962 when I was busy saving the world from nuclear annihilation and seven years before the concept of peak oil hit me like a strike of lightening a lady from a small farm in Pennsylvania who had spent much of her working life in the Bureau of Fisheries (later the U.S. Fish and Wildlife Service) in Washington, D.C wrote a book that changed the balance of power in the world. Her name was Rachel Carson and the book was "Silent Spring."

Before "Silent Spring" environmentalists were all about protecting an image of the past and wanting to conserve this view they had of their environment. Inner city estates were not a major item on their agenda. After "Silent Spring" environmentalists were about saving the health of our environment for everyone. It became mainstream and radical.

The book claimed that pesticides had a detrimental affect on the environment and wild life especially birds. The main culprit that Carson highlighted was DDT one of the most powerful pesticides the world had known. It had been developed at the beginning of

World War II and had been used in the South Pacific islands to destroy malaria-causing insects. In Europe it had been used alarmingly as a delousing powder.

DDT was not a narrow targeted pesticide. Once sprayed it was capable of killing hundreds of different kinds of insects all at once. Rachel Carson was the first to show that the unintended consequences of such an approach were far-reaching and serious. *Silent Spring* described how DDT entered the food chain and accumulated in the fatty tissues of animals, including human beings. The effect of this was to cause cancer and genetic damage resulting in reproductive problems and death.

Of course the chemical industry did not like it and launched a counter attack. She was accused of spreading disinformation and they questioned her competence to write such a book. There were threats of lawsuits. American Cyanamid, Monsanto and Velsicol together with much of the chemical industry led their attack supported by the Federal Agriculture Department. But she had done her research well and eminent scientists rose to her defence. As a result the President's Science Advisory Committee under president Kennedy examined the issues and supported Rachel Carson's assertions. She had been vindicated. As a result, DDT came under much closer government supervision and was eventually banned.

No longer could chemical companies assume that what they did would not be scrutinized. The balance of proof suddenly rested on them. "Silent Spring" showed that science and technology was not automatically a force for good and that how they were used was as important as their use itself. But it went further than that. Her book raised questions in people's minds about progress. The wanton destruction of nature in the name of modernity now became questioned as never before. And not just with DDT. Other chemicals and indeed pollutants were poisoning our lakes, rivers, oceans, and ourselves. Environmentalism was no longer about saving a nostalgic dream. It was about saving our planet and ourselves from the unintended consequences of progress and self interested corporate gain.

From then on the environmental movement became radicalised and technological progress faced much stiffer scrutiny. This laid the foundation for the deep ecology movement to develop and the environmental grassroots movements of the 1960's that sprung up almost as a new and refreshing injection onto the political landscape.

Environment & The Poor

And it could not have come at a more important time. Bringing environmental issues into the mainstream of politics rather than allowing it to be the preserve of the conservationist middle class changed the debate fundamentally. The more one investigated it then it was the poor and less powerful who suffered most from corporate inflicted environment disaster. But as the 20th century turned into the 21st more and more people were affected – privileged or not – and this created a new and powerful alliance.

On December 3rd 1984 the news of a major pollution incident spread around the world. This took place just after midnight in Bhopal, India. The Campaign For Justice In Bhopal described what happened.

Shortly after midnight poison gas leaked from a factory in Bhopal, India, owned by Union Carbide Corporation. There was no warning; none of the plant's safety systems were working. In the city people were sleeping. They woke in darkness to the sound of screams with the gases burning their eyes, noses and mouths. They began retching and coughing up froth streaked with blood. Whole neighbourhoods fled in panic, some were trampled, others convulsed and fell dead. People lost control of their bowels and bladders as they ran. Within hours thousands of dead bodies lay in the street.[78]

Bhopal is home to more than 900,000 people - many of whom live in slums. Nearly 3,000 people died immediately from the disaster and ultimately 15,000 to 22,000 total deaths resulted. There are still toxic chemicals in the area because of groundwater and soil contamination and 20,000 people live in that vicinity. Many people

---

[78] http://www.bhopal.net/

there continue to suffer cancer and birth defects as well as general lethargy, aches and pains and constant exhaustion.

One of the major problems is that developing countries often lack the resources such as communication and training to maintain advanced technologies but because of the state of development, they are eager for hi tech industries. This attracts multinational companies who can often ignore the safety and health standards required in developed countries. It almost becomes a catch 22 situation.

And even in developed countries industries that pollute are often located in working class areas and away from the sensitivity of middle class pressure groups. In the Borough in which I live in London there is a notorious incinerator that according to Greenpeace is expected to result in fifteen deaths every year.

In 1999 when Michael Meacher was Minister of State for the Environment he stated,

"The emissions from incinerator processes are extremely toxic. Some of the emissions are carcinogenic. We know scientifically that there is no safe threshold below which we can allow such emissions. We must use every reasonable instrument to eliminate them altogether."

Pollution and congestion hit the urban poor hardest. For example the poorest parts of towns often suffer the health impact of urban car use even though it is people from suburban areas that use the cars most. And as far as industrial pollution is concerned it is those with average incomes of less than £15,000 who often find themselves twice as likely to be located close to industrial complexes and polluting factories.

So environmental issues have now become ones that impact on low income areas and environmental concerns are no longer the preserve of the rich; but of course, pollution knows no boundaries.

Acid rain was one of the world's worst pollution problems of the 1970s and 1980s, affecting large areas of upland Britain, as well as

Europe and North America. The pollutants come from cars, factories and power stations as they all burn fuels and as a result produce polluting gases. When gases like sulphur dioxide, nitrogen oxide and hydrogen chloride combine with water droplets in the atmosphere then the chemical reaction that occurs results in weak sulphuric and nitric acids and this is the basis of acid rain.

Its effect on soil, trees, buildings and water can be deadly and the rain can fall many miles away from the source of the pollution, so it neither has respect for national or even continental boundaries. Forests are affected as well as lakes. In some areas of the world like Scandinavia some lakes are dead with no plant life or fish. In the UK freshwater fish is under threat and fish eating animals and birds can be affected too.

Although action has been taken in much of Europe in the last 20 years or so to clean up acid pollutants from power stations, and industry in general, research has shown that the improvements are nowhere near as great as expected. In parts of the UK many streams are still highly polluted with acid.[79]

So environmental issues once the preserve of the conservationist middle classes now impact on everyone and no one is exempt from detrimental effects. Once the concept of peak oil had struck me in the 1970's then looking at the world, as a fragile ecosystem with valuable finite resources became an almost automatic response.

The Emperor Has No Clothes

The belief that growth is all-important to well being is not one just applied to the economy. After World Way II it was a belief that began to pervade the whole of the social fabric of the Western World. Buildings got bigger and taller, homes increasingly high-rise, hospitals and schools ever larger and years in school longer. Increasingly we were given the message that progress depended on providing the most up to date technology available and that this could only be done if large economies of scale were met. As accountability to users became less and less tangible then in its

---

[79] This includes research from the School of Biosciences

place came the notion of users as customers with a new industry in customer service appearing, targets being set and policy being formulated through focus groups and opinion polls.

It was in the 1970's and early 80's that this philosophy began to take hold. Until then there had been a debate emerging about how to make our services and industry more accountable. These were the decades following the 1960's and the watershed year of 1968 when students took to the streets in many countries, and in Paris for a moment it looked as if a participatory form of democracy might win the day. The next two decades saw debates on workers councils, campaigns for a democratic health service, patients committees, and education as empowerment. It was the age that saw the development of consciousness movements amongst women, children ethnic minorities, the disabled and the gay communities.

But behind this counter culture of participation and involvement the doctrine of continual growth carried on unabated. It was in the 1960's that we saw the growing institutionalisation of society with professionally dominated institutions ever present in organisations of increasing size. But as this was happening there were some observers who were saying as Marion King Hubbert had of our oil based economy – the emperor had no clothes! One of these was Ivan Illich in the 1970s with a series of brilliant, short, polemical, books on the major institutions of the industrialized world.

Illich believed that the growing institutionalised world was unsustainable, as King had argued over the oil based economy. Illich once famously said that if every child in the United States had spent on them the same about of money for their education as the best and most talented then it would make the expenditure on the Vietnam War look like a drop in the ocean. Just throwing money at a problem was in Illich's view wasteful because it did not work and often added to the problem; and it just was not possible. As Illich said himself,

Universal education through schooling is not feasible. It would be no more feasible if it were attempted by means of alternative institutions built on the style of present schools. Neither new attitudes of teachers toward their pupils nor the proliferation of educational hardware or software (in classroom or bedroom), nor finally the attempt to expand the pedagogue's responsibility until it engulfs his pupils' lifetimes will deliver universal education.[80]

Illich believed this has resulted in a disaster, which has the following outcomes:

- the poor have even less chance at a fully developed and realized world.
- in the process of "protecting" us society has taken over much too much of our lives and freedom.
- society itself has suffered since we have substituted "process" for "substance" in our quest for objective and fair standards of measurement and in wishing to make up for genuine differences in achievement.

For Illich, modern societies were more and more dependent on expensive institutions that undermined people and diminished their confidence in themselves, and in their capacity to solve problems. It killed convivial relationships. The case against expert systems like schooling is that they can produce damage, and this outweighs any potential benefits. Learning becomes a commodity,' and like any commodity that is marketed, it becomes scarce. Illich argued,

Schooling - the production of knowledge, the marketing of knowledge, which is what the school amounts to, draws society into the trap of thinking that knowledge is hygienic, pure, respectable, deodorized, produced by human heads and amassed in stock..... [B]y making school compulsory, [people] are schooled to believe that the self-taught individual is to be discriminated against; that learning and the growth of cognitive capacity, require a process of consumption of services presented in an industrial, a planned, a professional form;... that learning is a thing rather than an activity. A thing that can be amassed and measured, the possession of which

---

[80] Ivan Illich, *Deschooling Society* Publisher: Marion Boyars Publishers Ltd; New edition edition (1 Jan 1995) ISBN-10: 0714508799

is a measure of the productivity of the individual within the society.
[81]

Social value is thus based on the consumption of education as a product rather than learning as a value in itself. In questioning the 'messianic principle' that schools as institutions can educate, Illich was also questioning the post war obsession with quantitative growth at the expense of qualitative human conviviality. He questioned the 'messianic principle' that schools as institutions can educate in a meaningful way that was also sustainable.

The advent of the 1980's, with politicians like Ronald Reagan and Margaret Thatcher, saw an attack on professional institutionalisation but it never got to the root of the malaise of the post war world. Schools got bigger and hospitals too as smaller unites were closed and A&E departments such down in many areas. Industry also saw increasing rationalisation as mergers took place and small business was curtailed. The areas of entrepreneurship were in the Internet industries that expanded and sometimes burst but there were still fortunes to be made. Citizens and clients suddenly became customers of health, education and social services rather than partners in social processes that affected them. Managements became more and more divorced from the grassroots, shareholder and citizen opinion as polling and focus groups took over from meaningful participation. Civil society was under threat as people were considered objects to be manipulated by marketing techniques rather than consulted as citizens. So the criticism of those like Illich still largely held true though the format was changing and rather than the deschooling of society the post 1980's saw the schooling of society extend and reach far beyond the classroom.

And as this expansion took place so did the inefficiencies that Illich noticed and of course he was not the only one. E. F. Schumacher in the 1970's wrote a series of essays called "Small Is beautiful[82]"

---

[81] Ivan Illich, *Deschooling Society* (1971) ISBN 0060121394
[82] Small is Beautiful: A Study of Economics as if People Mattered by E. F. Schumacher Publisher: Vintage; New edition edition (16 Sep 1993) ISBN-10: 0099225611

extolling the virtue of appropriate technology rather than wasteful huge scale development. As he said,

"The most striking about modern industry is that it requires so much and accomplishes so little. Modern industry seems to be inefficient to a degree that surpasses one's ordinary powers of imagination. Its inefficiency therefore remains unnoticed."

The Emperor had no clothes but all the dignitaries of the Court – the Government and Establishment and the captains of the growing globalised economies did not notice. For them consumption was the path to profit and success but it was also the path to waste as well. Again Schumacher commented

"[A modern economist] is used to measuring the 'standard of living' by the amount of annual consumption, assuming all the time that a man who consumes more is 'better off' than a man who consumes less. A Buddhist economist would consider this approach excessively irrational: since consumption is merely a means to human well-being, the aim should be to obtain the maximum of well-being with the minimum of consumption. . . . The less toil there is, the more time and strength is left for artistic creativity. Modern economics, on the other hand, considers consumption to be the sole end and purpose of all economic activity."

For Schumacher the pursuit of consumption as the path to well being was a false one as it often did the opposite. Yet the belief in more and more that became the battle cry of the globalised economy was one that hid the underlying emptiness of it all and gave those who pursued it an empty idea. Again Schumacher,

"The way in which we experience and interpret the world obviously depends very much indeed on the kind of ideas that fill our minds. If they are mainly small, weak, superficial, and incoherent, life will appear insipid, uninteresting, petty, and chaotic. It is difficult to bear the resultant feeling of emptiness, and the vacuum of our minds may only too easily be filled by some big, fantastic notion – political or otherwise – which suddenly seems to illumine everything and to give meaning and purpose to our existence. It needs no emphasis that herein lies one of the great dangers of our time."

And as it turned out it was the great danger of our time – the 21st century. The inefficiency of our social and economic systems was producing not only waste but also a whole series of unintended consequences and this was shifting our planet into another gear.

Revenge of Gaia

The new gear was one that could accelerate our planet into a crisis greater than any known since humans inhabited the earth and one that threatens their dominance of it. It is not just that environmental changes will deplete us of resources making future conflict almost inevitable but those changes could also threaten the support systems of life itself.

Planet Earth has seemed to have two stable conditions in the last two million years and that is glacial and interglacial. The latter is much shorter in duration and we are living in an interglacial period right now. How the planet moves and transforms from one state to another is now a question of great importance especially at this time of climate change.

The Intergovernmental Panel on Climate Change (IPCC) was founded by the World Meteorological Organisation and the United Nations Environment Program in 1988 and is acknowledged around the world as the authoritative source of advice on climate change science. Its role is to assess the scientific, technical and socio-economic information relevant for the understanding of the risks of human-induced climate change.

In its Fourth Assessment Report[83] published in 2007 it warned that global warming would have a far more destructive and earlier impact than previously estimated and predicts that the frequency of devastating storms will increase dramatically. It also reports that sea levels will rise over the century by around half a metre; snow will

---

[83] Climate Change 2007 - The Physical Science Basis: Working Group I Contribution to the Fourth Assessment Report of the IPCC (Climate Change 2007) (Paperback) by Intergovernmental Panel on Climate Change (Author) Publisher: Cambridge University Press; 1 edition (30 Sep 2007) ISBN-10: 0521705967

disappear from all but the highest mountains; deserts will spread; oceans become acidic, leading to the destruction of coral reefs and atolls; and deadly heatwaves will become more prevalent; and this if change is only moderate.

But as we have seen there are growing voices that the change facing us could be far more dramatic and that anthropocentric or man-made climate change is beginning to rapidly change our world.

Some evidence from the Arctic and Greenland ice-cores going back thousands of years - suggest an increasing likelihood that we will see abrupt and possibly catastrophic changes in the Earth's climate within our lifetimes. Fred Pearce in his book "The Last Generation[84]" looks at some of this evidence that the feedback caused by moderate change could unlock a far more dramatic change than we thought possible. He shows that in the past Europe's climate has switched from Artic to tropical in three to five years and that could happen again. He says,

"We have been lured into a false sense of security by the relatively quiet climatic era during which our modern complex civilisations have grown and flourished. This security has left us unexpectedly vulnerable as we stumble into a new era of abrupt change."

Recent analyses of ice core samples from Greenland and Antarctica have shown that in the past, roughly half the warming between the ice-ages and the post-glacial world took place in a single decade.

And Elizabeth Kolbert in "Field Notes from a Catastrophe[85]" argues

---

[84] Last Generation - How Nature Will Take Her Revenge for Climate Change (Paperback) by Fred Pearce Publisher: Eden Project Books (1 Jan 2007) ISBN-10: 1903919886
[85] Field Notes from a Catastrophe: A Frontline Report on Climate Change (Paperback) by Elizabeth Kolbert Publisher: Bloomsbury Publishing PLC; New edition edition (20 Aug 2007) ISBN-10: 0747585504

"Ice core records ... show that we are steadily drawing closer to the temperature peaks of the last interglacial, when sea levels were some fifteen feet higher than they are today. Just a few degrees more and the earth will be hotter than it has been at any time since our species evolved."

In February 2007 the International Panel on Climate Change judged that world temperatures would rise by up to 6.4C over the next century but there are now some who predict it will be much higher because of feedback mechanisms releasing carbon sinks in both the oceans and on land. Fred Pearce in his book tells us of a workshop at the Hadley Centre in 2004 where reputable scientists illustrated graphs showing temperature rises of up to 10% and even 12% because of the feedback into the atmosphere. As he says this would be cataclysmic. Elizabeth Kolbert states,

"It may seem impossible to imagine that a technologically advanced society could choose, in essence, to destroy itself, but that is what we are now in the process of doing[86]".

In 2008, James Hansen, head of the Nasa Goddard Institute for Space Studies in New York warned that the EU and its international partners must urgently rethink targets for cutting carbon dioxide in the atmosphere because of fears they had grossly underestimated the scale of the problem. He argued that carbon dioxide must be slashed to 350 parts per million not the 550ppm targeted by the EU as even a 450ppm concentration held long enough would probably melt all the ice - that's a sea rise of 75 metres. He argued our present target is a disaster[87].

The basic reason for his reassessment was the "slow feedback" mechanisms that are now only becoming apparent. Positive feedback amplifies the rise in temperature thus increasing greenhouse gases in the atmosphere. Ice and snow reflect sunlight but when they melt, they leave exposed ground, which absorbs more heat.

---

[86] Ibid
[87] Climate target is not radical enough – study The Guardian, Monday 7 April 2008

The most important and influential scientist who changed the consciousness of both the general public ands scientists themselves was James Lovelock. It was he who described our planet as a self-regulating mechanism that would respond with revenge on human behaviour. He called this the principle of Gaia[88].

The principle is simple. Life has modified and been modified by the biosphere over hundreds of thousands of years. The organisms that survive and thrive on the planet are those that help maintain the biosphere in a way that is favourable for their own life.

Lovelock illustrates this through the analogy that he calls "Daisy World". Here black and white daisies colonize an imaginary planet. The black daisies absorb light as heat and warm the planet, while the white daisies reflect light and keep the planet cool. Too many black daisies cause the planet to overheat, making the world uncomfortable for them, but better for the white daisies. Too many white daisies cause the world to become too cold, thus favouring the black daisies that can absorb heat. This is self-regulation. Of course, the real biosphere is much more complex, with countless independent life forms acting as a check-and-balance system to maintain the biosphere in a way that is conducive to life as a whole. Lovelock believes that through human action we are destroying that bio diversity and the complex mechanisms and processes that our planet has developed over millions of years to regulate itself making it today a life supporting planet. Our society based upon waste, consumption and growth is

"As if we had lit a fire to keep warm and failed to notice, as we piled on fuel, that the fire was out of control and the furniture had ignited. When that happens there is little time left to put out the fire

---

[88] Gaia: A New Look at Life on Earth by James Lovelock Publisher: Oxford Paperbacks; New edition edition (Aug 1982) ISBN-10: 0192860305

before it consumes the house itself. Global heating, like a fire is accelerating and there is almost no time left to act.[89] "

So a world running short of vital resources, bent upon growth and ever increasing consumption is one that is leading us to the point of extinction if the more dramatic predictions of climate change are right. However if they are not then we still face a very rocky ride that will change our lives fundamentally.

Not Quite Revenge but Chaos

In early 2008 senior EU Foreign officials warned that in the decade ahead millions of environmental migrants would flood Europe as a result of climate change. They argue that the devastating effects of global warming will be felt far away from Europe, with the poor suffering disproportionately in south Asia, the Middle East, central Asia, Africa and Latin America, but that Europe will ultimately bear the consequences. The Intergovernmental Panel on Climate Change predicted that

"the effects of climate change are expected to be greatest in developing countries in terms of loss of life, and relative effects on investment and economy".

Livelihoods built for generations on particular patterns of farming may quickly become impossible. Climate change is likely to place an additional 80-120 million people at risk of hunger and over 70 million of these will be in Africa. [90] The Tearfund study, has already estimated that there are 25 million environmental refugees

---

[89] The Revenge of Gaia: Why the Earth is Fighting Back - and How We Can Still Save Humanity by James Lovelock Publisher: Penguin (22 Feb 2007) ISBN-10: 0141025972
[90] Climate Change 2007 - The Physical Science Basis: Working Group I Contribution to the Fourth Assessment Report of the IPCC (Climate Change 2007) (Paperback) by Intergovernmental Panel on Climate Change (Author) Publisher: Cambridge University Press; 1 edition (30 Sep 2007) ISBN-10: 0521705967

resulting from changing rain patterns, floods, storms and rising tides and they predict this figure is likely to rise significantly.[91]

Javier Solana and Benita Ferrero-Waldner, the EU's chief foreign policy coordinator warn,

"The multilateral system is at risk if the international community fails to address the threats. Climate change impacts will fuel the politics of resentment between those most responsible for climate change and those most affected by it ... and drive political tension nationally and internationally[92]."

With a global population of 6.6 billion and growing, the self regulating mechanism that supports life will be stretched to the very limit because of record levels of consumption.

- In 2006, the world used 3.9 billion tons of oil. **Fossil fuel** usage in 2005 produced 7.6 billion tons of carbon emissions, and atmospheric concentrations of carbon dioxide reached 380 parts per million.
- More **wood** was removed from forests in 2005 than ever before.
- **Steel** production grew 10 percent to a record 1.24 billion tons in 2006, while primary **aluminum** output increased to a record 33 million tons. Aluminum production accounted for roughly 3 percent of global electricity use.
- **Meat production** hit a record 276 million tons (43 kg per person) in 2006.
- Meat consumption is one of several factors driving **soybean** demand. Rapid South American expansion of soybean plantations could displace 22 million hectares of tropical forest and savanna in the next 20 years.

---

[91] Feeling The Heart, Report from Tearfund 2006 - http://www.tearfund.org/webdocs/Website/News/Feeling%20the%20Heat%20Tearfund%20report.pdf
[92] EU told to prepare for flood of climate change migrants The Guardian, Monday 10 March 2008

- The rise in global **seafood consumption** comes even as many fish species become scarcer: in 2004, 156 million tons of seafood was eaten, an average of three times as much seafood per person than in 1950.[93]

The rapid growth of population in the world, the desire of massive countries like China and India to industrialise and grow at a fast rate and the record levels of consumption that go with this will cause huge dislocations in our societies and add intense pressures on scarce resources. The future will be one of uncertainty and conflict.

As many of us still live in the mindset of the late 20th century where all seemed possible we have not adjusted out perceptions to the world, as it will be – either individually or collectively. We live on a foundation of sand because we are obsessed with the false belief that the future will be the same as our immediate past. As James Lovelock says,

"Economic growth is as addictive to the body politic as is heroin to one of us, perhaps we have to keep the craving in check by using a safer substitute, an economist's methadone.[94]"

To change ourselves we have to understand the imperatives of the real world we now live in and not the fantasy of the pleasure boat of continuous consumption. We are beginning to but it is not yet deep enough in our consciousness to take effect but as Lovelock says there is little time left.

---

[93] Share The World's Resources website at
http://www.stwr.net/content/view/2199/36/
[94] The Revenge of Gaia: Why the Earth is Fighting Back - and How We Can Still Save Humanity by James Lovelock Publisher: Penguin (22 Feb 2007) ISBN-10: 0141025972

CHAPTER 10 - The Infinite Global Economy Global

Capitalism In Crisis

The world is getter more finite as each year goes by as resources are depleted and the planet's support system is being threatened by our own behaviour. That very behaviour is based on an economic system that does not understand the term "finite." We still live in a global economic system that believes in the infinite and it is that that drives the engine of growth and consumption.

In 2008 the EU was being urged to take action on a trading scam that involved the bio fuel industry. The scam has been called "splash and dash" and involved shipping bio fuel from Europe to the US and there a dash of fuel was added that allowed traders to claim 11p a litre subsidy to the entire cargo thus undercutting EU prices. Although the trade was not illegal it did involve shipping fuel across the Atlantic needlessly and adding to carbon emissions. There was thus cheaper fuel, more sales, higher consumption but the impact on global warming was to increase it. The infinite quest for higher consumption conflicted with the finite needs of the planet.

The drive to use resources so that consumption can increase and profits materialise clearly drives the economic system and the needs of the finite planet comes second when the market is left unfettered. It is the engines of a growth society – the consumption of the consumer, the accumulation of the investor and the profit of the company - a combination of individual behaviour and company gain. The constant danger in this is that the consumption or investment drive of individuals can take on a surreal nature as in the 18th Century South Sea Bubble when people invested in a company that had a monopoly of Southern American trade in return for underwriting the then war against France. It seemed a safe bet and share prices soared until the bubble burst. Stocks crashed and people all over the country lost all of their money. The Clergy, Bishops and the Gentry lost their life savings; the whole country suffered a catastrophic loss of money and property. Porters and ladies maids who had bought their own carriages became destitute almost overnight.

Of course the South Sea Bubble burst in the mercantile 18th century and from the 19th century we seem to believe that our economic system is now based upon "forces" that are neutral or above human invention. Politicians of the right often extol the free market because they argue only it can offer choice to all. No regulator has that infinite wisdom to provide optimum satisfaction whilst the free market can provide infinite choice. The market has a magic quality about it – the "invisible hand" of Adam Smith that makes all things possible. That feeling of confidence in the objective role of the 19th century laissez faire market has in the late 20th century been transferred to the global financial markets of the world. As the famous international speculator and commentator on globalisation George Soros has said, financial markets,

".. continues to maintain the approach established by classical economics. This means that financial markets are envisaged as playing an essentially passive role; they discount the future and they do so with remarkable accuracy. There is some kind of magic involved and that is, of course, the magic of the marketplace where all the participants, taken together, are endowed with an intelligence far superior to that which could be attained by any particular individual[95]."

And yet there are three weaknesses in the argument that markets are neutral and stand like a god created system above human endeavour. One is that they discount the future. Markets are about a moment in time – the present moment. They adjust to meet current situations and the future consequences of that adjustment is discounted. In the long run, as Keynes pointed out, we are all dead – so markets eat, drink and become very merry! Carbon emissions are an example of markets discounting the future. We produce for the moment using the cheapest possible fuels and carbon fuels provide that energy source. That they had "externalities" that impacted on our environment was of no consequence. Markets are supposed to adjust to take account of all challenges. But with global warming they were unable to discount enough.

---

[95] The Crisis of Global Capitalism: Open Society Endangered by George Soros Publisher: Little, Brown (7 Dec 1998) ISBN-10: 0316849162

The second weakness is that markets are based upon what is effective rather than what is right. Again George Soros has said.

"No longer is there any need to profess moral principles other than self interest. Success is admired above all considerations. Politicians gain recognition for getting elected, not for the principles they represent. Businesspeople are esteemed for their wealth, not for their probity or the contribution of their business to social and economic well-being. What is right has been subordinated to what is effective and this has made it easier to succeed without paying any heed to what is right. Needless to say, I see a grave danger here to the stability of our society."

If politicians and businesspeople are judged by targets as well as accumulated power and wealth rather than by achievement and meaningful outcomes, then the drive behind our political economy will be solely self interest and that interest will always be measured in the present moment of time. Markets and human behaviour reinforce one another in a vicious circle of never ending profligacy. Again as Soros says,

" the participants' views and the actual state of affairs enter into a process of dynamic disequilibrium which may be mutually self-reinforcing at first, moving both thinking and reality in a certain direction, but is bound to become unsustainable in the long run and engender a move in the opposite direction."

What George Soros is saying is that the behaviour of individuals can impact on the "invisible hand" and reinforce it in one-way or the other. And this is the third weakness to the argument that markets are somehow independent of human intervention and thus superior to it. Identity and reality reflect one another rather than exist as two separate forces. This is often referred to as reflexivity and one that Soros pays great attention to but it is similar to what others have argued in the past – Fromm and social character is but a more psychoanalytic version of it. To have an identity for our self we need to compare ourselves to a perceived exterior reality. What we think is real in the exterior world, we then use to define what is real in our own interior world. If the market is about power and wealth then we reflect this in our inner self. To change ourselves we have to find a new external world to compare ourselves with – and that world must be one that does not discount the future.

In a sense the separation of identity from reality, the division between observation and the observer is one that has dominated classical science for many years. Since the 18th Century philosophy and natural science has laid great emphasis on the separation of events from the observations, which relate to those events. Events are facts and observations are true or false, depending on whether or not they correspond to the facts. As George Soros has indicated,

"Classical economics was modelled on Newtonian physics. It sought to establish the equilibrium position and it used differential equations to do so. To make this intellectual feat possible, economic theory assumed perfect knowledge on the part of the participants. Perfect knowledge meant that the participants' thinking corresponded to the facts and therefore it could be ignored. Unfortunately, reality never quite conformed to the theory.[96]"

However with the advent of sub particle and quantum physics the classical view of Newton has been challenged and Heisenberg introduced the concept of the "uncertainty principle" whereby there is an "observer effect" on reality – on what is being observed. This effect states that the act of observing will make a difference on the phenomenon being observed. Hence for us to see an electron a photon we must first interact with it, and this interaction will change the path of that electron. So we become an interacting part of the reality we observe and change it. Although modern science now takes account of the "observer effect" economics based upon classical Newtonian science does not. Again as Soros states,

"There is an active relationship between thinking and reality, as well as the passive one which is the only one recognized by natural science and, by way of a false analogy, also by economic theory."

---

[96] The Theory of Reflexivity by George Soros at
http://www.geocities.com/ecocorner/intelarea/gs1.html

The fact that there is this relationship provides both dangers and opportunities. The danger is that both economists and politicians will ignore this "observer effect" and continue to believe that economics is a value free science independent of human observation and intervention and the future will continue to be discounted at our cost. The opportunity is presented by the knowledge that by changing the behaviour of humans and linking them to a different reality then the future will be preserved from the harm created by the constant moments of mass consumption.

The End of History

And yet not long ago, the age of endless consumption was seen by some as the "end of history." When the Berlin Wall came down it seemed as if the West had won the Cold War with the total collapse of viable alternatives to Western liberalism evidenced in the increasing spread of consumerist Western culture. This was seen in such diverse contexts as peasants' markets and colour television sets spread throughout China, the cooperative restaurants and clothing stores opened in Moscow, and the rock music enjoyed alike in Prague, Rangoon, and Tehran.

Commentators like Francis Fukuyama argued this was different and in a way turned Marx upside down. Karl Marx had seen the end of history in the dialectic march towards an end state – a communist society. Fukuyama saw not just the end of the Cold War but the end of history as such in the triumph of the West. For him, the end point of mankind's ideological evolution and the universal acceptance of Western liberal democracy was the final form of human government.

But of course history did not come to an end. Nations remained strong and the cold war is now being replaced by new struggles between nation states as India and China emerge as potential economic superpowers of the future. The world is still dominated by the United States but that is not a permanent feature that will go on forever. Robert Kagan another American commentator on the changing world pattern argues,

"Struggles for honour and status and influence in the world have once again become key features of the international scene.

Ideologically, it is a time not of convergence but of divergence. The competition between liberalism and absolutism has re-emerged, with the nations of the world increasingly lining up, as in the past, along ideological lines. Finally, there is the fault line between modernity and tradition, the violent struggle of Islamic fundamentalists against the modern powers and the secular cultures that, in their view, have penetrated and polluted their Islamic world.[97]"

Others like Sam Huntington[98] have written that we are in a period where there is a growing "clash of civilisations" He argues that world politics is entering a new phase, in which the great divisions among and the dominating source of international conflict in the 21st Century will be cultural rather than ideological or economic. He argues that the "fault lines between civilisations will be the battle lines of the future." Although this theory has come under immense criticism it is still a view that suggests the idea that history is at an end and that we have come at last to the final state of equilibrium is not one that reflects the world as it is.

In his book "Black Mass," John Gray puts the view of secular utopianism into perspective when he argues that the great secular movements of the Enlightenment are no more than secular faith movements. He argues,

"The very idea of revolution as a transforming event in history is owed to religion. Modern revolutionary movements are a continuation of religion by other means.[99]"

The decline of the ideologies and blueprints of the 19th and 20th centuries has seen religion begin to assert itself again often in new

---

[97] End of Dreams, Return of History by Robert Kagan at http://www.hoover.org/publications/policyreview/8552512.html
[98] The Clash of Civilizations: And the Remaking of World Order by Samuel P. Huntington Publisher: Free Press; New Ed edition (5 Jun 2002) ISBN-10: 074323149X
99 Black Mass: Apocalyptic Religion and the Death of Utopia by John Gray Publisher: Penguin (24 April 2008) ISBN-10: 0141025980

and fundamental forms. For Gray this is business as usual. The secular belief that we can have heaven on earth has reverted to the older belief that those on earth should be prepared for heaven in the life here after.

So instead of the 21st century being one where history has come to an end, it is more than likely the age where history repeats itself in a new cycle of conflict. The nature of that conflict is still uncertain, as are its roots. It maybe economic, cultural, religious or power based but it is there. What is so amazing is that when it is clear that conflict is still a driving force of human affairs the dominant economic forces of the Western world operated on the "end of history" thesis believing that their view of globalisation was one that extended the western liberal ideology to the entire world in an act of messianic fervour ignoring all alternatives as relics of the past. Globalisation became the watchword of this new utopia and it meant the globalisation of the Western and particularly the American "neocons" view of the world – one where trade was liberalised in a way that favoured the corporate giants of the Western world often at the expense of the developed world and of the dispossessed in the Western world itself. It was a view of the world that took off with a vengeance in the decade before the millennium – the roaring nineties!

The Roaring Nineties!

In 2001 there was a recession that followed years of growth and seeming prosperity in the 1990's – often now referred top as "the roaring nineties." When the recession did come, it also exposed the fault lines that had been hidden in the 1990's and that were sown a decade before. And those fault lines also showed that the market was not the neutral mechanism that stood above us as the invisible hand – but that it was influenced and directed by corporate greed that had a detrimental effect on society that when left unchecked led to deception, distortion and economic disaster.

One person who helped to expose this and analyse the malaise of the post 1980 world was Joseph Stiglitz, Professor of Economics at Columbia University. As the chairman of Bill Clinton's Council of Economic Advisers, and subsequently as the chief economist of the

World Bank during the East Asian financial crisis, Joseph Sitglitz was well placed to observe what was happening around him.

Stiglitz noted that the recovery after the 1980's slump that began in the early 1990's was facilitated by reducing the US federal budget deficit, which in turn allowed interest rates to decline resulting in sharp increase in investment and growth. For the traditional economist this provided a problem as it went against the then conventional wisdom of modern economics – a view that accepted that you should institute counter- cyclical policies of increasing both spending and budget deficits to get out of a recession. Certainly under the Clinton administration, the budget deficit was reduced but instead of leading to an economic downturn, it led to a period of growth and recovery. At the height of that economic boom American capitalism seemed triumphant with unprecedented growth. Globalisation became the buzzword and was taken on as the new gospel across the globe. As Stiglitz said,

"Asians were told to abandon the model that had seemingly served them so well for two decades but was now seen to be faltering. Sweden and other adherents of the welfare state appeared to be abandoning their models as well. The U.S. model reigned supreme."

In doing all of this the global economy was being set up for the problems of years if not decades to come. During that period accounting standards were allowed to slip, deregulation was taken to extremes by the ideologues of the globalisation mission and corporate greed was often encouraged. Stiglitz argues that the scene was set for all this in the 1980's when President Reagan cut taxes when there was poorly designed financial-sector deregulation. This led to savings-and-loans debacle where the Government had to support banks that were devastated by non-performing real estate loans and this adversely impacted on the economy particularly as interest rates were not reduced quickly enough to counteract the possible recession.

This was added to by the issuing of long term bonds whose value was likely to fall if interest rates rose and thus creating uncertainty. He explained that the economic downturn of the early 1990s was partially due to banks shifting from lending to buying long-term government bonds. He noted that much of the move towards bonds was based on bad information. As a result, long-term bonds were considered safe investments although their prices were quite volatile. When banks shifted away from lending, it was more difficult for businesses to expand and this hurt the economy.

In this environment there arose a high degree of what Stiglitz refers to as "Creative Accounting and Crony Capitalism" whereby the U.S. government became involved in options accounting, to the detriment of financial markets. They took deregulation too far and allowed companies the freedom to engage in practices that put strain on the economy. This allowed companies to use stock options as a way of remuneration for their top executives and this in turn diluted the stock prices for other shareholders. Consequently CEOs began to look for accounting measures that boosted stock prices artificially. This was the art of creative accounting and did not reflect the real world.

Enron was one company that used creative accounting practices to dress up profits and conceal losses. When the managers saw disaster looming, they sold off their shares at a profit. Those footing the bill were the employees, their pension fund and all investors without insider connections.

Chief executive officers' compensation provided incentives to take advantage of the limitations in our accounting systems. Such bad accounting led to bad information and this led to hyped up activity around the world's markets creating bubbles ready to burst. There were conflicts of interest and this led to false or inaccurate information being available to shareholders and investors. Short term interests prevailed over longer term interests and often Government legislation made matters worse.

The market was no longer an abstract concept but something that was being manipulated by self-interest. The balance between government and the market had been destroyed by corporate greed and bad information. By following private gain, individuals could not contribute to the whole society, because of the asymmetry of information. Some market participants had information that others did not and this was used against the general interest. Governments were often too influenced by the forces of "crony capitalism" and refused to intervene or regulate sufficiently. As Stiglitz[100] commented,

"In the past three decades, the world has seen close to a hundred crises and many of them were brought on by some form of too-rapid deregulation. Though the economic downturn in 2001 is only a milder form of these more virulent diseases, there is no question that major parts of the downturn resulted from the deregulation of the Nineties."

The Globalisation of Debt

But from the 1980's onwards regulation became a dirty word as major corporations attempted to create an environment where they could expand unhindered especially in those parts of the world favourable to that expansion. This was the driving force behind globalisation. It is true that policies created since the end of the Second World War have shaped how decision makers have viewed the global economy. The door seemed to be left open especially since the *Uruguay* Round of trade talks which created an unfair international trade arena as wealthy countries sought to open up the markets of poor countries, but not their own. As well as this, developing countries were often encouraged strongly to liberalise their capital markets and this added instability. At a time of development there is often a stage of growth where protectionism is important. The developed world had largely gone through this stage before they even thought of liberalising. The underdeveloped world was not given that chance. It is this that makes many commentators believe that the liberalisation of trade is not about efficiency or spreading wealth worldwide but is more about control by those who already have power. Noam Chomsky for one has argued,

What is called "globalization" is a specific form of international integration, designed and instituted for particular purposes. There are many possible alternatives. This particular form happens to be geared to the interests of private power, manufacturing corporations and financial institutions, closely linked to powerful

---

[100] The Roaring Nineties: Why We're Paying the Price for the Greediest Decade in History by Joseph Stiglitz Publisher: Penguin; New Ed edition (3 Jun 2004) ISBN-10: 0141014318

states. Effects on others are incidental. Sometimes they happen to be beneficial, often not.[101]

The liberalisation of trade so beloved by the modern advocates of globalisation often means opening the markets of the underdeveloped world to the goods of the developed whilst at the same time closing the developed world's borders to the agricultural goods of the developing world. This is all about national and corporate power and not free trade. This makes it almost impossible for those in the developed world to compete and also adds to their debt. Interest payments are devouring a big chunk of the debtors' national income, leaving very little for growth and development. In Mexico, for example, interest payments consumed 46.23% of the government's entire expenditure in 1986 and 56.20% in 1987.

Also many loans taken out by developing countries come with conditions that include such constraints as preferential exports. Something like 80% of America's foreign aid is returned through its exports. In effect then, more money comes out of the developing countries than goes into them.. This depresses wages even further and makes development more difficult. According to a working paper prepared by the UN Sub Committee on Human Rights,

"The history of third world debt is the history of a massive siphoning-off by international finance of the resources of the most deprived peoples. This process is designed to perpetuate itself thanks to a diabolical mechanism whereby debt replicates itself on an ever greater scale, a cycle that can be broken only by cancelling the debt[102]."

Since the burden of colonisation, developing countries have faced grave economic, political and social problems that pose a danger to their existence and their population. This has prevented individual

---

[101] Globalization and its Discontents, Noam Chomsky debates with Washington Post readers Washington Post, May 16, 2000,

[102] New 'Working Paper' on 'Effects of debt on human rights' prepared by **Mr. El Hadji Guissé** for current UN Sub Commision on Human Rights (E/CN.4/Sub.2/2004/27

human rights from being protected in such countries as a result of the debt owed and poverty resulting. Debt creates poverty but also dependency too and countries in such a conditions are open to exploitation and domination and Western corporation are often willing to exploit that.

The International Monetary Fund (IMF) and the World Bank administer third-world debt, and the G8 governments largely control these two institutions. Although they began with a Keynesian approach to economics during the latter part of the 20th century they changed to become neoliberal organisations and instead of pump priming local economies they imposed stringent conditions as they began to micro manage the markets of developing economies. Since the early 1980s, the IMF and the World Bank have offered loans if nations complied with "structural-adjustment programs" which were basically economic-reform policies with a free market bias. Developing countries have to prove that they are implementing economic reforms at a satisfactory pace in order to have a portion of the loan requested. Rather than provide protection for local economies to grow they opened them up to competition when they were least able to withstand that. The role of the state was curtailed as the private international investment complex took over economic development.

The debt of the developing world is only part of the problem. What has made the situation more precarious is that debt is now a part of everyday life in the developed world as well. The developed world has a growing debt burden, as it has been a major tool for many to increase their daily spending power. This has led to the world financial system becoming hostage to the developing countries growing debt. The World Bank has warned of a "serious risk" or "sustained setback" to the development of many debtor countries that could lead to a breakdown of debtor-creditor relations resulting in a crisis to the world economy itself.

Debt At The Edge

In March 2008 when it was reported by Halifax that housing prices had taken their biggest fall since the 1990's Malcolm Knight, general manager at the Bank of International Settlements - the central bankers' central bank - described the current economic turmoil as "probably the most serious in the advanced countries since the second world war." These comments followed those of the former chief of the International Monetary Fund, Dominique Strauss-Kahn. He called for co-ordinated government intervention at a global level to tackle the credit crisis. *"I really think that the need for public intervention is becoming more evident, the crisis is global,"* he told the Financial Times.[103]"

Clearly this was an appeal for politics to catch up with the global crisis and intervene on a global scale. The years of crony capitalism had been catching up on us, and fast. Author, Italian economist and journalist Loretta Napoleoni has defined crony capitalism as rogue economics and by this she means,

"A sort of umbrella under which we find the criminal economy, the illegal economy, but also those grey areas, grey areas where there is not a proper regulation, where there is not legislation for the economy. Now, these grey areas in this particular crisis are being created by globalisation. Now, this happens generally when there are great transformations. We have seen it during the Industrial Revolution, but we also have seen it during the crisis in 1929. The economy suddenly starts moving faster than politics, and politics can't manage to keep pace with it, so it can't manage to regulate the economy. So, the current crisis is the product of the 1990s, of the easy money, cheap credit of the 1990s[104]"

By the close of the first decade Governments were in panic mode as the credit crisis emanating from the US hit the western world. After years of passing responsibility to central banks and away from

---

[103] As reported in The Guardian, April 8th 2008
[104] Interview with **Amy Goodman on** World Prout Assembly at http://www.worldproutassembly.org/archives/2008/04/loretta_napol eo.html

government, the US and the UK particularly found themselves intervening. In the UK the Government was willing to take over the mortgage commitments of banks in return for new government bonds. The aim was to give banks back the confidence to lend again and prevent economies falling into recession. However whether governments were acting fast enough to keep up with an economy that had been shaped in the roaring nineties remained to be seen. And certainly as 2008 turned into 2009 the crisis became global as banks began to collapse under a burden of debt. Governments had to step in to support or partly nationalise many banks to increase the flow of loans to householders and small businesses. However that flow was slow arriving and by the beginning of 2009 a deep recession hit the world economy and the future looked unsure.

The growing problem was that of debt. The US and UK boom of the 1990's onwards was a credit led boom that freed up new sources of money for consumers to spend. But by the end of the first decade of the 21st century both these countries had moved from being the world's largest creditors to that of the world's major debtors. This posed a threat not just to the countries themselves but also to the global economy. Despite a declining dollar the US external deficit had risen to 6% of GNP by the middle of the decade and this in a country that held the leading world reserve currency. Ann Pettifor in her book "The Coming First World Debt Crisis," states,

"In contrasts to the 'golden era of tranquillity' between 1945 and 1970, since 1980 these debts and imbalances have led in turn to political crises within and between nations that have wreaked civil war, pain, unemployment, loss and havoc on the lives of millions of innocent people affected."

The crisis of the latter years of the first decade of the new millennium was not just one of external debt but also of internal debt as well. In the same book Ann Pettifor points out that in the US and the UK in particular debt has become a way of life that has allowed citizens of both countries to live beyond their means. She points out in early 2006 UK individuals and households owed £1,174 billion, which is almost exactly equivalent to total UK income or GDP of £1,210 billion. Every UK adult owed on average £25,200 more than the median annual earnings (which according to the Office of National Statistics was in 2004/05, only £22,900.

The same was true in America. US household debt including mortgages in 2005 was £11,497 billion and this compares with US income or GDP of around £12,410 billion. By 2007 the ratio of debt to income for US households was nearing 122%.

In 2008 the debt-based economies faced a growing crisis because of what was called the "credit crunch" originating from the sub-prime mortgage situation in the United States. This lead to plunging property prices resulting in a slowdown in the US economy, with billions in losses by banks. This crisis had its origins in the way mortgages are funded and this in itself reflects the debt base of the American economy.

The traditional way that banks financed their mortgage lending was through deposits that they received from customers and this put a limit on what they could lend. However the practice had grown where banks sold their mortgages to bond markets in order to secure additional liquidity. This lend to slackness where banks were not as careful in checking the mortgages that they issued. And with the growth of the private sector in the lending market this new situation led to some specialising in the sub-prime market where those with poor credit histories who had traditionally been shunned were now accepted despite the risk. At first this was profitable for banks and more and more of these mortgages were sold making the mortgage bond market the single largest part of the US bond market – one that was even bigger than Treasury bonds.

It was this situation that led to a financial crisis in 2007 and 2008 and it started with unsustainable debt. About six million people in the USA have borrowed money to the full extent of the price of their house – in other words 100% mortgages. Many of these are people with bad credit histories and these are the sub prime borrowers. They are at risk whilst the companies lending did not originally have to worry because they financed the lending through bonds rather than just customer deposits. Because bonds are bought and sold it meant that the risk was often passed on with the bonds. Yet as they were sold on Mortgage backed securities were checked for credit risk and whether borrowers were likely to go into default. And of course those with bad credit histories might indeed and this led to an increasing number of foreclosures. It was this that triggered the financial crisis. Once housing prices started to drop in

2006-2007, refinancing of mortgages became increasingly difficult in the USA and foreclosure activity increased. In 2007 nearly 1.3 million US housing properties were subject to foreclosure activity and increase of 79% on the previous year.

Speaking after Hurricane Katrina in 2005, President George W Bush told the nation that poverty among black people needed to be addressed and that home ownership was the answer. "We have a duty to challenge this poverty with bold action," he said. "So let us restore all that we have cherished from yesterday and let us rise above the legacy of inequality.

"When the streets are rebuilt, when the houses are rebuilt, more families should own, not rent, those houses."

But black Americans often have bad credit ratings or are the victims of discrimination, so they tend to be given sub-prime loans. And now, with a nationwide housing slump, they are facing disaster. [105]

Debt has now become a major problem in both the developed world and the developing one too and the dreams that had given people their place in the world and their hopes for the future were being shattered. The underlying reality of the myth of progress was being made obvious to all.

Fair Trade For The Few?

The infinite global economy has been based on the belief that the world is infinite in its resources and opportunities and that if trade were unhampered and free then wealth would become the gift of all as growth continued unimpeded. But we have learnt to our cost that the world is not finite and that resources are becoming scarcer and in such a world free trade turns from being a fair and level playing field to being one where the powerful seek to hold onto their position in the world market whilst the poor suffer because they cannot get a foot in the door. And this is not only true for the poor and dispossessed of the developing world: it is also true for those in the developed world who are trying to compete with the giant

---

[105] Guardian 5 April 2007 00:05 UK

corporations. They also find it difficult to break through and are faced with a power structure that seems impenetrable.

At an international level the fair trade movement has grown up because of the belief that producers in developing countries do not get a return on their labour that is "fair" and often they cannot earn a living. The Trade Justice movement has grown up in the belief that,

"Everyone has the right to feed their families, make a decent living and protect their environment. But the rich and powerful are pursuing trade policies that put profits before the needs of people and the planet. To end poverty and protect the environment we need Trade Justice not free trade[106]."

When Governments, business and Regional structures such as the European Commission or the North Atlantic Free Trade Association work with the developed world then they do so on terms that protect the powerful. The Trade Justice movement has long argued for example that the Economic Partnership Agreements (EPAs) negotiated between Europe and Third World countries favours trade liberalisation over the needs of development. Such agreements are supposed to help the developing world by opening European markets to the goods of the developed nations. However as the Trade Justice Movement has pointed out agreements like for example those drawn up with African, Caribbean and Pacific countries in 2007 require far reaching trade liberalisation by those countries in return for continued entry of their goods into European markets. This means that growing local and national industries in third world countries have to face the competition of large European businesses and stand no chance of development. They do not get the advantages that Europe itself enjoyed in the 19th century when protectionism was used to help national development. Instead many countries are put into the position of having to choose between supporting existing livelihoods and industries or succumbing to EU pressure and leaving the door open for future industry controlled by global corporations at the expense of local development.

It has also been argued that the North Atlantic Trade Association (NAFTA) adopts the same practises and has

---

[106] Trade Justice Website at http://www.tjm.org.uk/about.shtml

resulted in negative impacts on Mexican farmers who find themselves faced with cheap food produced by US agribusinesses. The North American Free Trade Agreement (NAFTA) is a trade agreement among the United States, Canada, and Mexico that liberalizes restrictions on trade among the three countries. Yet the agreement has done little to encourage Mexican wage levels to rise and it is possible that along the border living standards have not risen at all. The agreement is about opening up free trade so there is nothing there to prevent American corporations from exploiting Mexican workers.

During the Primaries for the 2008 US Presidential election both the then Democratic presidential hopefuls Hillary Clinton and Barack Obama threatened to pull the United States out of the free trade agreement with Canada and Mexico unless it was renegotiated. Though this was not because of the impact on Mexican workers: it was about the effect that agreement was having on their own workers in the United States. It is unlikely that either candidate, if they win, would pull out but their utterances were made to win votes from working class Americans who were suffering through job loss as a result of NAFTA.

For many free trade is not fair trade as it causes poverty and unemployment not just in the developed world but also in the developed nations as well as corporations seek the cheapest labour and resources for their business. Many like those in the Adam Smith Institute in the United Kingdom believe this the right policy as they see free trade as being fair and any attempt to impose regulations on the market they think will cause an inefficient distribution of world resources that in the long term will make more farmers poor in the developing world rather than help them. In a Paper written for the Institute by Marc Sidwell, he argues

"Fairtrade is not an answer to poverty. For those who promote it, Fairtrade is not even necessarily intended to aid economic development. Instead, Fairtrade operates to keep the poor in their place, sustaining uncompetitive farmers on their land and holding

back the changes that could give their children a richer future by encouraging mechanization and diversification[107]."

In some ways it is strange that an organization with the name Adam Smith in its title should argue this as it assumes that fair trade practices and initiatives encouraged by the Fair Trade Foundation and the Rainforest Alliance are the main reasons for interrupting free trade. Clearly it is not as the main reason is the structure of the world economy organised around oligopolistic corporations. Adam Smith argued in the "Wealth of Nations" that perfect competition could take place only when no organization could affect price by its own operations such as increases in production. It is only in a world where such conditions prevail that perfect competition exists and there is an optimum distribution of resources because of it. That world was as idealistic as the utopian communist dream of the later 19th century. As economic organizations and companies increased in size they became more powerful and do impact on price. Today we have large multinational producers and companies that can easily affect the market by merely altering their level of production. These organizations are political rather than economic and are the main obstruction to Adam Smith's idea of perfect competition and today's concept of free trade. They intervene in the market on a daily basis to further their own interest. In such circumstances countervailing intervention by government and fair trade organizations becomes necessary.

The Diseconomies of Scale.

Classical economists have argued the case that scale can create savings and result in efficiency – the famous economies of scale. In a finite world the opposite is increasingly becoming true. Large organisations are causing diseconomies of scale and the wasteful use of resources. This was the essence of the "limits to growth" debate that began in the 1960's and 70's. The early 1970s saw the oil crisis due to the Arab oil embargo and this led many to question the value of growth and scale in a world of scarce resources. The "Club Of Rome[108]" report that was written following that period

---

107 Unfair Trade by Marc Sidwell, Adam Smith Institute, London

108 The Limits to growth: A report for the Club of Rome's Project on the Predicament of Mankind by Donella H. Meadows (Author),

questioned the importance of growth at a time of resource depletion. This was also a time when Schumacher published his book "Small Is Beautiful[109]," advocating the philosophy of appropriate technology rather than large-scale solutions to every problem. And Leopold Kohr[110] argued that it was over development rather than underdevelopment of nations that posed the greatest challenge for the coming decades. Large-scale development had favoured the powerful and allowed the domination of some American companies on the global market. However the argument subsided when oil began to flow again and globalisation made large-scale development yet again acceptable.

But in a time of climate change and the need for developing a sustainable future, questions of size and sustainability has again raised its head. It is the large corporations that have been the most profligate in the use of energy and thus the least efficient in terms of sustainability. The growth of large multinational corporations may have produced some undeniable benefits such as the ability of large corporations to seek out low-cost production opportunities that provides a benefit to consumers in the form of lower prices.

But of course economic activities often impact on those who are not involved in the activities themselves and are external to it. So a corporation manufacturing automobiles can pollute the surrounding area and this pollution is borne by local residents. External costs (or benefits) arising from economic activities are referred to as externalities. Almost any firm is responsible for some externalities, but multinational corporations can use their political influence to avoid bearing responsibility for significant external costs.

Jorgen Randers (Author), Dennis L. Meadows (Author), William W. Behrens (Author) Publisher: Universe Books; Second edition (18 Feb 1974) ISBN-10: 0876631650

[109] Small is Beautiful: A Study of Economics as if People Mattered by E.F. Schumacher Publisher: Vintage; New edition edition (16 Sep 1993) ISBN-10: 0099225611

[110] The Breakdown of Nations by Leopold Kohr Publisher: Green Books; New Ed edition (26 April 2001) ISBN-10: 1870098986

They can be big enough to ignore "externalities" - the costs that their activity has on the environment and that are not costed into a company's accounts. The benefits firms obtain from being able to impose externalities and shift costs to others are difficult to measure in economic terms but at a time of climate change then it is vital to do so and ensure that companies act responsibly regarding the impact that their economic activity has on global warming. One way to do this is to make companies internalise many of these costs through the pressure of public opinion and the acts of government. Another way is to shift economic focus towards those smaller sized companies that are following a sustainable path to growth from the outset. However there is a problem there.

Small businesses represent an overwhelming majority of companies in our economies. In many developing countries, the self-employed comprise more than 50 percent of the labour force. They create more new jobs, train more employees and produce more innovations than larger companies. Despite this they are the losers when it comes to competition for capital. The world global market is geared up to rewarding larger companies and the deregulation of the world financial services industry has helped to strengthen this trend. Small businesses and local communities tend to be ignored in favour of larger well-entrenched companies when it comes to loans and capital.

World markets are not geared up to help smaller companies and so those with the larger external cost that impact on the environment often win out. There has to be some way of shifting capital to those smaller industries that are sustainable and minimise the adverse effects of externalities to the environment. Some of this is beginning to happen and we look at this in the final two chapters but there is a long way to go and not much time left if we are to restructure our society towards a sustainable future.

A Sustainable Future

A report in the UK in mid 2008 showed that very few top executives of major corporations got fired for bad performance. The system is entrenched and so is the inefficiency and power that goes with it. Eventually this creates a fragile economy. Major Western economies are building their success on internal and external debt and free trade is protecting the powerful rather than opening up markets fairly

Much of what has happened in the world is the result of corporations seeking ways of expanding their sphere of influence and increasing their profits. This is often reinforced by the bonus and stock issuing culture whereby managers are given huge bonuses for success measured in terms of company gain. This gives them an incentive to follow greed rather than the common good. Responsibility has to be personal as well as corporate and government has a role in setting the framework through which responsible behaviour is made possible.

For companies it is important that they readjust their culture and way of thinking to be able to sustain their existence in a fast changing world. It is little use just aiming for short-term gain when it damages the long term irreparably. Government and companies need to consider their approach in a number of areas. The corporate responsibility movement goes some way to encouraging this but government needs to set the framework so that this is real rather than window dressing.

One of the most important innovations that government can begin to impose on companies is that they internalise costs. Normally companies externalise their costs onto the environment rather than bear it themselves. So pollution costs are often offset or externalised by a company so that others have to bear the cost of cleaning up. Roads that are built come from taxes rather than profits even though companies demand their use more than most. Stress caused by working practices is taken up by the health services with the company happy to allow this to happen. There are countless examples whereby costs are never measured in any total accounting way and this gives companies free range not to think about them. Somehow we have to move towards an accounting system that measures the unintended consequences of company behaviour as well as the intended outcomes.

Secondly our bonus culture should be changed so that remuneration is neither based on bonuses or share issues to managers. Both encourage the drive to increased dividends at the expense of sustainable growth. Executives will always look towards the quick fix to higher income rather than planning the realistic growth of their companies in a complex environment. This leads to waste and conspicuous consumption more than almost anything else. Advertising is based on convincing consumers that they need what they do not and want is constantly confused with need. And as we have seen, current levels of consumer spending are sending personal debts rocketing placing families at great risk. A company acting in the social interest would have to only sell goods that were needed and could be afforded, rather than encourage consumer spending beyond the means of individuals or the future sustainability of the planet. The current rate of degradation of the natural systems that are vital for our survival, forests, oceans, soil, fresh water and the earth's capacity to absorb pollution, can only be stemmed by an urgent reduction in consumption.

Thirdly companies need to be good corporate citizens and like individual citizens provide the infrastructure base that makes our society function. And this means paying taxes in full in the way individuals have to. At the moment tax minimisation is seen as one of the main goals of company directors as that protects the revenue of shareholders. At the moment billions of pounds are lost through tax avoidance and in a private survey by Deloitte and Touche in the year 2000, 85% of companies surveyed admitted to using tax avoidance schemes that often went unchallenged. For many countries and especially underdeveloped ones then tax revenue is important but they know if they enforce the paying of taxes then companies will just leave. A socially responsible company would be transparent in terms of the levels of taxes it is paying in every country. It would see paying tax as part of its responsibility to society rather than seeking to avoid it.

Finally we have to encourage small companies that do less harm to the environment and show far more ecological efficiency. This means finding ways of directing capital away from the larger and more powerful corporations. But it is clear this cannot be done on the basis of the free market alone acting under the ideology of free trade. Smaller companies need support and some degree of protection if they are to take off and become successful so government has a role to regulate for their success. *At the moment,* companies, which claim to be socially responsible, can often put pressure on government that is against the public interest. They also often make donations to political parties to help entrench their position so that those parties often appear to represent big business more than they do individual citizens. Some of the major global companies also have access to international forums tackling global issues such as poverty, sustainable development and climate change and thus capturing the political agenda that undermines moves towards real change.

Without major restructuring then it will be difficult to operate in a finite world. We have lived too long in the fiction of the infinite economy and that has formed the basis of modern economics. As long as the ideology was one of infinite resources then companies could always produce at the margin until costs were too high and then a substitute would be found. In the world of plenty then there was always a harvest of substitutes and the free market was deigned to encourage constant growth. But today all the rules have changed and there is recognition that the world is finite as resources become scarce, population increases and climate change makes sustainability difficult. In these circumstances the larger corporations become the modern dinosaurs bent on protecting their position through their size and power rather than through their competitive edge. As the realities of the modern world descend on them they fear extinction and become increasingly devious. Today they may support "free trade" but tomorrow they may support their own "protection." The behaviour is what we should judge them by and not the ideology that they hold as that can be a moving feast.

Somehow we have to turn perceived reality upside down so that reality is based on substance and not fiction. Our present mode of economic activity is based upon a bubble that we hope will not burst and individual character and behaviour is based upon that. But it is fragile and more and more people are crying out that the emperor has no clothes. But as long as a fictitious market rules and voices go unheard then it is difficult to make the changes needed. And voices are often not heard because democracy itself is in crisis.

CHAPTER 11 - The Democratic Deficit

The Crisis of Democracy

Just as the global sustainability is under threat and the global economy threatened as the reality of a finite world encloses around us so our social institutions are also challenged in a way that they have rarely been for decades. Indeed one of the most endangered is that of democracy itself as the challenges to it grow with every impending crisis.

It is ironic that this challenge to the viability of democracy has happened when the Middle East erupted in 2011 with demands for democracy as thousands of people demonstrated from Egypt to Libya and from Barhain to Tunisia – sometimes with success but often with brutal suppression or near civil war as in Libya. They demand democracy at the same time as the very process they demand is in serious trouble in the West.

Just as demonstrations flaired over the Middle East and North Africa, young people in many parts of Europe began questioning their own democracy and took to the streets in protest at the wide public expenditure cuts being imposed upon them by a crisis that they perceieved having been caused by an out of control banking sector and the inadequate government response to it. Many felt that democracy could no longer deliver and wanted a new type of politics. In May of 2011 over 60,000 demonstrators rallied in Madrid's Puerta del Sol square in an event that almost appeared to have been transported from the Arab spring in north Africa. The demonstrators called themselves "the indignant ones" and one commented.

"We want real democracy. Not just freedom for bankers.[111]"

Another young demonstrator expressd her frustration with the established ssystem of party politics saying,

---

[111] The Observer May 22nd 2011 in article by Giles Tremlitt.

"There is nothing new or different, just two parties who take it in turn to govern because our electoral laws favour them."

It was a demonstration seen also in other Spanish Cities and had taken politicians by surprise as demonstrations had also done in London, Paris Athens and other parts of Europe. It was a new assymetric type of poltics that used social networks to mobilise and organise and traditional political structures were finding it difficult to understand what was happening.

The events in the Middle East and north Africa and the imposed cuts on Western economies had woken up a new generation to the inadequacies of their own democracies and yet the demise in the West has taken place over the 40 years or more and was now beginning the reap the whirlwind.

In 1959 researchers Gabriel Almond and Sidney Verba wrote about Britain:

'The participation role is highly developed. Exposure to politics, interest, involvement, and a sense of competence are relatively high....there is general system pride as well as satisfaction with specific government performance.[112]*"*

The two General Elections in the UK in 1950 and 1951 had high turnouts and people still felt that politics was credible and could deliver. And yet now almost 60 years later there is widespread cynicism about the effectiveness of our democracy. If that continues then it will end up being a cancer that eats away at the legitimacy of our democratic society and endanger it. The signs are not good.

From the peak of 1951, turnouts at elections have gone down and in 2001 the turnout was only 59% - the lowest since 1918! Although it increased to marginally above 60% in the 2005 election the winning party had only 22% of the total eligible vote. This compares with 34% in 1959 when it lost the general Election of that year and had fewer MPs. Low turnouts have also been the norm in European, local and regional elections. Party politics seems to be in disarray.

---

[112] Gabriel Almond & Sidney Verba, The Civic Culture, Princeton: Princeton University Press, 1963, p. 315

In 1964, 44% of the electorate described themselves as identifying very strongly with a political party but by 2001 this had declined to 14%.[113] This disinterest reflected in party membership, which fell from 10% of the UK population in 1950 to 1.9% at the turn of this century. Despite a brief increase under the new leadership of Tony Blair, disillusionment crept in again very quickly and membership slumped again.

The story is much the same in the USA where turnout at presidential elections has declined since the 1950's. It is true that in the 2004 Presidential elections the turnout went up. Turnout was 6.4 percent higher than in 2000, the largest increase in voter participation since the 1952 election. Yet even then more than 78 million Americans who were eligible to vote stayed home on Election Day. President Bush won with just 30.8 percent of the total eligible voters. In the US this is partly because there are many people of voting age who are not registered either because of disinterest or because they have had difficulties placed in their way over registration. It has been estimated that in 2004, the U.S. had about 17,500,000 people of voting age who were eligible to vote. Even though the 2008 election did bring new people in and provide hope it is too early to say whether this will be a long term trend or whether politics will return to its state of demise. The Presidential election of that year did galvanize people but politics goes much further than one Presidential election.

The political syatem includes politicians of all kinds and the trust people have in politicians has also declined at the same time. Over thirty years ago over 60 percent of Americans thought that the government generally would try to do the right thing. The proportion of those today that think that government would generally do the right thing is not much more than 10 percent. According to the polls, people believe that members of Congress are less honest today than they used to be.[114] In the UK it was similar.

---

[113] Paul Whiteley, 'The State of Participation in Britain', Parliamentary Affairs, 56(4), 2003, p. 611.

[114] Much of the data about trust in American government cameos from the Pew Research Centre - a nonpartisan "fact tank" that provides information on the issues, attitudes and trends shaping America and the world. It does not take positions on policy issues.

The percentage of people who had "great confidence" or "quite a lot of confidence" in parliament dropped from 54 per cent in 1983 to only 10 per cent in 1996; and 71 per cent of British 16- to 21-year-olds surveyed in 1998 believed that the way they vote will make little or no difference to their lives.[115]

There are two main reasons for this decline in support for democratic party politics. First there have been a series of structural changes across the globe that have had a negative impact on democratic discussion. Secondly there is the responsibility of politicians themselves. They have pretended that everything has gone on as usual when most people could see that it had not. We have the same party and tribal structures in an age where they are increasingly inappropriate; and because politician's career futures depend on that structure, they find it hard to break free and begin to imagine and promote new structures and processes.

The changes that have taken place across the globe that have had a negative impact on present day politics are varied. However democracy has grown up within nation states and became a popular form of government when those with growing economic power found themselves disenfranchised and without a vote. This happened during the 19th century first to the middle class and then at the end of the century to the working class. As each gained economic power then they demanded the vote. By the early 20th Century women also made the same demand. Probably the height of Parliamentary democracy was found after World War II when the tools of economic management (the fiscal tools of Keynesian economics) and Parliamentary activity went hand in hand and through the post war Labour Government in the UK and the Roosevelt New Deal in the USA began to bear fruition. This was the time of reconstruction and economic growth.

But after the 1980's, we saw power being taken away from the nation state as globalisation and consumerism gathered pace. Under

---

Its work is carried out by these seven projects. It can be found on http://pewresearch.org/
[115] Form Why consumer power is not enough by Noreena Hertz NewStatesman, Published 30 April 2001

the Thatcher Government in the UK and the Reagan presidency in the USA, the consumer now became king. Many argued that the true ballot box was not in a polling booth but in the shopping mall. People voted for the type of society they wanted with their wealth and not their electoral ballot paper. As the reward of rising incomes and wealth were dangled over people then they became less interested in being citizens and more interested in consuming. Why bother to debate the future when you could spend it.

As consumerism spread so did the liberalisation of financial markets leading to globalisation where international free trade was the new ideology. This again took power away from national legislatures and placed it in the hands of those who benefited most by the "free market" the powerful corporations. Regulation that was the hall mark of the nation state as a tool to protect the vulnerable in society was replaced by the anti regulation ethos of global and non accountable bodies like the International Monetary Fund, World Bank, and World Trade Organisation. They curbed the power of national legislatures to make a difference.

At the same time as these trends were happening, power became increasingly centralised as more power was transferred from local authorities to central governments and from central governments to regional bodies like the European Union. In these circumstances the power of the citizen was diminished as they found it impossible to understand that a vote could change anything. This was fine as long as economic growth and wealth creation continued. The lure of consumerism acted like a drug that made people oblivious to the power they were losing. However once consumerism came under threat with the credit crunch crisis of the mid to late first decade of the 21st century then the shallowness of it all became apparent. Both citizen power and consumer spending were disintegrating and in its place was a dangerous void that heralded a difficult time for modern democracies.

Stakeholder Society

If the world is changing around us in terms of the global economy, the sustainability of our planet and the absence of maps to make sense of it then what probably effects us most is our feeling that we are no longer a full part of all that is going on. We are no longer stakeholders in the world in which we live.

And yet politicians have advocated the idea of a stakeholder society now for the last twenty years. It was part and parcel of the Clinton "Third Way" and was taken up in 1997 by Tony Blair who as Prime Minister advocated the stakeholder society as the essential ingredient of the third way and also of New Labour. Such was the enthusiasm for this idea that it led commentators like David Marquand to write,

"Not for the first or the last time, the New Right and the Old Left are at one. Neither understands what Blair is saying, but both sense that he spells death to the old politics in which both are mired. Both are afraid of him; and both clothe their fears in world-weary superciliousness[116]."

The essence of the stakeholder society as perceived by Blair and Marquand was that of a society where free enterprise was the foundation of our economy but where individuals had some sort of stake in it. How that stake was to be held was never fully defined other than through training and education, which was hardly a new idea. It also involved companies understanding that they must discharge obligations to the wider community and not just their shareholders. This would lead to a revolution in socially responsible management that planned to work in partnership, with unions, employees, government and organised citizens. For Marquand the consequence of a stakeholder economy is that it would lead to "stakeholder politics" and by this he explained,

And stakeholder politics must be a politics of power-sharing, negotiation and mutual education - a politics that requires the transformation of the British constitution and the reconstruction of the British state.

But today people feel more powerless than ever and their perception of politicians is one the lowest recorded. Instead of being

---

[116] Written by David Marquand for Nexus and appearing on their web site at http://www.netnexus.org/library/papers/marquand.htm

stakeholders in society, people often feel excluded. So what happened and how did the dream of the stakeholder society go so wrong? It seems that at some point in recent years politicians became more interested in narrowing who the stakeholders were in society than expanding their numbers conducive to a democratic society. What we seem to have in recent years is a new elite that is held together by a wish for personal enrichment, rather than an interest in the common good. Money and wealth still dominate the ruling elites and have through the Thatcher/Blair years in the UK and the Regan/Clinton/Bush years in the USA. Long gone was the Tory Party concern about the "unacceptable face of capitalism" and both Tory and Labour governments were dominated by banking interests and capital movements. Indeed many businessmen felt very much at home with the Blair Government as that government became more dependent on private investment in our service industries and corporate donations made to the coffers of the Labour Party. Despite the decline in party membership, income of political parties rose by two-fifths (in real terms) between the 1960s and 1990s. Political parties are increasingly relying on large donations from organisations or wealthy individuals, some with questionable links to government activities. Anthony Sampson commented on it,

"The new Establishment was looking like one giant boardroom, linked by common interests and agreements[117]."

At the same time fewer people were expressing their democratic rights through voting at elections. In the UK, General election turnouts have fallen from 84 per cent in 1950 to just above, and just below, 60 per cent in 2005 and 2001 respectively. Participation in local polls is worse. Voting turnout only seem to rise when elections are adorned by celebrity status such as the London Mayoral elections in 2008 or the Democratic Primaries in the US in the same year. But it is personality that then attracts rather than policy.

And in the very homeland of democracy – the Parliamentary system in the UK and the Presidential one in the USA – there were signs

---

[117] Who Runs This Place?: The Anatomy of Britain in the 21st Century
Anthony Sampson Publisher: John Murray; Updated ed. edition (17 Jan 2005) ISBN-10: 0719565669

that the system was not quite what it was made out to be by politicians who insisted on exporting it to every corner of the world. The US Presidential Election of 2000 was fraught with questions about vote rigging and exclusion of key voters especially in Florida. And in the UK, the Joseph Rowntree Reform Trust[118], a foundation set up to promote social inclusion and constitutional change, issued a reminder of the parlous state of our democratic machinery. That report made it clear that the electoral process in the UK was vulnerable to large-scale fraud through incomplete and inaccurate registers and doubts about the integrity of postal voting. Indeed in 2007 it almost appeared that Britain could be the first western democracy to face monitoring over vote-rigging and electoral fraud by the European Commission.

A part of the problem is that government faced with falling turnout at the polls have desperately looked at ways of increasing that turnout by celebrity politics and gimmicks. In the absence of ideologies to motivate people, governments have been reduced to public relations and gimmickry trumpeting their interest in people participation whilst at the same time centralising decision-making. At the same time, campaign spending by political parties has replaced the truer battle of ideas in some closely run contests. Huge amounts of money are put into closely run American elections and in the UK where expenditure on elections is more rigorously controlled in each constituency, national spending outside the election period has increased. The electorate is treated like consumers and the more the Parties are alike, the more they spend to emphasise differences that just do not exist in reality. And yet people know what the reality is and it is often politicians and their advisers who live in fantasyland failing to understand that each new campaign advertising minimal differences between competing parties merely creates more disillusionment and distain.

As with the economic system, the political one is beginning to look increasingly threadbare. Politics is increasingly becoming a sideshow as people get on with their lives and look for other ways to effect change – some creative and some verging on the dangerous. It is not just social cohesion that is threatened in society but political

---

[118] The Joseph Rowntree Reform Trust's report, Purity of Elections in the UK: Causes for Concern 2008

cohesion as well as the art of politics is being turned into a sham - a show to be observed as if it were a political version of Big Brother but with all substance and gravitas missing.

Palliative Politics & The "General Will."

The danger when politics is held in so much disrepute is that Government will try to govern through either gimmicks or some mistaken notion of the "general will" based on the belief they know what people want even though the avenues of public participation are continuously closed.

Gimmicks are a kind of palliative democracy. Palliative care is often defined as a form of medical care or treatment that concentrates on reducing the severity of disease symptoms, rather than halting or delaying progression of the disease itself or providing a cure. Palliative democracy is similar. It is a form of government that concentrates on reducing the symptoms of discontent in society and the frustration with politics rather than finding a cure where people feel empowered once again. As long as economic growth went on at a rapid pace and wealth increased then disenchantment with political powerlessness was compensated by consumer power. In a growth environment, politics copied the economic model and real discussion was replaced with constant opinion polls and focus groups. Few noticed except a minority of commentators and enthusiasts that these were palliatives, that on one hand allowed government to avoid alienating the electorate too profoundly and on the other fooled some into thinking that their views were valued. But it was a shaking foundation that was as fragile as it was superficial.

Ancient Greece is regarded as the birthplace of democracy, in particular Athens (5th century BC). Small Greek city-states enabled direct political participation amongst its citizens. As states grew larger, direct democracy of this kind was not viable so forms of representative democracy began to emerge. In these systems, representatives were elected to legislatures and they made law through discussion. Forms of discipline began to emerge through Party systems that curtailed the power of the representatives but the concept of the "public place" of the Greek city-state was somehow maintained. In Ancient Greece "public space" was always considered far more important than "private space." Although homes could be bare and modest the city-state "public space" was valued because it was here where citizens would meet to discuss the issues of the day. Debate was considered an important skill and the exchange of views through debate the essence of participatory democracy.

As representative democracy emerged "public space" was still valued and the Party structure allowed members a stake in their Party. Local party meetings became "public space" where resolutions were discussed and voted on and referred up to the next level. This was particularly true in Parties like the Labour Party that began as an extra parliamentary force through the trade unions and socialist associations. Discussion was valued and the Party Conference became the showpiece where "public space" still had an important role to play. But in the second half of the 20th Century all this became endangered.

As politics became globalised and major decisions were taken across national boundaries local discussion began to lose its relevance as less and less people became involved. Party membership went into a spiral decline. By the use of polling and focus groups and some of the more participatory think tanks, Governments maintained the illusion that democratic participation was still alive but as the century came to an end public space was being eroded. Even Party members began to complain that politics were no longer discussed at party gatherings.

As participatory democracy declined then there has been more of a reliance on "general will" politics with politicians believing that they somehow express the will of the people better than others. It was Rousseau[119] who introduced the concept of the "general will" to political philosophy. The "general will" is not the will expressed by a majority but rather a holistic concept of the will of the people that somehow has a life of its own. It is a normative concept in that the *general will* is that which the sovereign assembly of citizens or

---

[119] The Social Contract by Jean-Jacques Rousseau Publisher: Wordsworth Editions Ltd; New Ed edition (1 Oct 1998) ISBN-10: 1853267813

leader representing them *ought* to decide. It is distinct from the majority will or the will of individuals. It is an organism endowed with goodness that surpasses that of any one individual or collection of people. It is what coordinates and holds society together.

The concept of the "general will" is an interesting one as it places in the hands of leaders the power to say that it is they who express the general will and that they somehow can deduce what it is. When elections become meaningless to many and cynicism sets into the political fabric then politics resorts to gimmickry though marketing techniques rather that participatory debate and this gives leaders the freedom to express the "general will." This is what the modernisation of politics in the late 20th Century seems to have been about – the replacement of participative democracy with "general will" politics.. Debate and discussion is old fashioned and assessing the will of the people through surveys and translating this into some sort of collective will is what modernity seems to mean. It is a new form of benevolent dictatorship, which can appear humanitarian but can end up with the crushing of dissent. Often today, politicians will talk about the common good, the aim of society or the will of the people but in doing so they often refer to their own will transfigured into the "general will". Tony Blair was often a "general will" politician in the UK in that he felt that he intuitively knew what was the common good even though it was not the will of the majority as in his decision to join in the invasion of Iraq.

But this form of mystical democracy can hardly replace real participatory debate and will in time become distorted either by corruption or disillusionment. In the 21st century this is what has exactly happened.

Politics The Master Science

In the long run that is dangerous for society because politics is important and when it is treated with contempt then society itself is in danger and in the fragile world of the early 21st century then that is critical because genuine and meaningful politics is needed more than ever.

It was Aristotle who described politics as the "master science." He saw the creation of what he called the state (different from the modern concept) as the organising principle of people who live together in any society from family to tribe and to cities. He argued that no man was self-sufficient unless a "beast or a god" and that community was therefore a basic instinct of survival. He argues,

"A social instinct is implanted in all men by nature, and yet he who first founded the state was the greatest of benefactors. For man, when perfected, is the best of animals, but, when separated from law and justice, he is the worst of all; since armed injustice is the more dangerous, and he is equipped at birth with arms, meant to be used by intelligence and virtue, which he may use for the worst ends[120]".

Politics is what separates men from war by substituting violence with discussion and using that discussion to create rules whereby people can live together without constant turmoil. Indeed it was Thomas Hobbes who stated in his book Leviathan[121] that without government, humans find themselves in a "war of all against all" where life would be "nasty, brutish and short!" For Hobbes, it was politics that provided the salvation from such a state. Of course he lived in time where the "world was turned upside down" by the civil war that had engulfed Europe and then England. He saw a mighty Leviathan as the means to achieve order and stability.

But in our present world mighty Leviathans are no guarantor of order and may cause more conflict. We live in a world that is not only diverse but also increasingly fragmented. The US has often been looked upon as two countries – the liberal East & West Coast on one hand and Middle America on the other. In reality it is much more diverse than that and is constantly changing with new waves of immigration much of it illegal. The United Kingdom like much of the rest of Europe is undergoing constant change and is becoming fragmented into different cultures as well as religions.

What is different in the post 9/11 world is that many of these fragmented sections of our society believe that they hold the truth –

---

[120] The Politics by Aristotle, Publisher: Prentice Hall; Revised edition edition (19 Nov 1981) ISBN-10: 0140444211
[121] Leviathan by Thomas Hobbes and C.B. Mac Pherson Publisher: Longman; New edition edition (24 Jul 2008) ISBN-10: 0140431950

and look for the victory of their deeply held faith. No longer do they look at their belief as a personal way of explaining a complicated world but as a blueprint for the entire human race. And many of these growing fundamentalist sects use the tools of the Enlightenment to argue their cause – human reason used for irrational ends. Even secularists and some humanists have a messianic zeal in their dislike of religion that exposes them as the mirror image of those they criticise. In their hands reason becomes rationality as they use reasoned arguments to advocate their own emotional mission in life. Reason becomes the servant to emotion rather than the guarantor of tolerance.

In this environment of turmoil and conflict politics as the "mater science" is needed more than ever. Instead of contracting the public space we have to find ways and means to expand it so that individuals again feel potent enough to affect the world they live in a way that also respects others. And that is the difficult problem.

It was John Buchan who is quoted as having said, *"Public life is regarded as the crown of a career, and to young men it is the worthiest ambition. Politics is still the greatest and the most honourable adventure."* But that is not a view shared today. The disillusionment with politicians has gone hand in hand with the decline of public space. Today politics has become privatised as with much else in life. Instead of championing the public good, politics is about the private acquisition of power, wealth and prestige. Until politics is restored to the public realm then it will always become marginalized and more extreme and violent forms of conflict resolution will fill the vacuum. In the 1950's an English Professor of Politics, Bernard Crick wrote what was then a widely read book – "In Defence of Politics[122]." In it he admitted that politics was a messy business but that in a diverse society it was the only way to hold back the dark forces of violent conflict. If we do not heed that lesson in the difficult times ahead of us then the future will be a very difficult one indeed.

---

[122] In Defence of Politics by Bernard Crick, Publisher: Continuum International Publishing Group Ltd.; New Ed edition (6 Oct 2005) ISBN-10: 0826487513

Change In Status – stakeholders to consumers

What has happened to politics to make it so despised by many as a worthy activity? One major reason for its decline is that stakeholders and citizens have been increasingly looked upon as consumers rather than actors in their own future. As the 1970's came to an end politics had reached a critical watershed. At the same time as an oil crisis in the early 1970's had caused a global depression there was a sense that the traditional way of solving problems both nationally through Government action and internationally through the existing channels were not working. Rather than look at reform, a number of academics and think tanks began to argue against politics and the intervention methods that had been forged through Keynesian economics in the post war period. Their view was that the world was growing too complex and that human intervention was always going to be imperfect. For them man could not be allowed to act as God through intervention. The only God that they could embrace was the market. If decisions where to be made, not by governments, but by the economic choices of millions of consumers then this would reflect what people want more than political discussion ever could. People would vote at the shopping Mall and the supermarket rather than at the ballot box. As Matt Connolly wrote in the new Consumer in 2008,

"So as individuals, what can they do to make a difference? Vote for some baby-kissing idiot in a bad suit (who's probably taking backhanders from the same corporations that are screwing their world)?

People have worked out there's a more direct way to change things. They can buy products from companies who have the same values as they do[123]."

This came from the voice of someone arguing against the major corporations and in favour of green consumerism and illustrated how far the anti politics movement had gone. As the 1970's turned into the 1980's the view of the voter as consumer entered mainstream politics through Ronald Reagan in the USA and Margaret Thatcher in the UK. By the 1990's this had become so

---

[123] Matt Connelly, New Consumer, April 22 2008

entrenched into the political fabric of society that it was taken on by the Blair Government in the UK and found its way into left and green movements through advocating a consumer revolt against the products of large corporations. What was being advocated was a revolt against large corporations not through massing on the street or government legislation but by consumer boycotts if they could be successfully organised at all.

In this new environment it is not governments and citizens that define the public realm but corporations and consumers. 51 of the 100 biggest economies in the world are corporations and the revenues of these massive economic companies often exceed many nation states. So although consumerism as the new democracy can be easily criticised it is not difficult to see how attention has shifted away from Government and towards markets and corporations. But corporations are not accountable to anyone but their shareholders and even then those with the largest bloc of shares have the most votes. Money determines all. Consequently many pressure groups have formed to keep a watch on corporations as well as to protest against their market behaviour. Companies like Tesco and Primark have been taken to task for allegedly using cheap labour in the underdeveloped world to produce the products sold in their shops. Indeed a Panorama programme in the UK highlighted the use of cheap labour by Primark by showing images of small children in a refugee camp sewing clothes marked with the Primark label and this led to demonstrations outside of their store in Oxford circus. These companies quickly rectified the situation and Primark even ask customers to report any abuses they came across in their production line. So there is a changing social responsibility that is growing even in the largest corporations.

Sites and organisations have now proliferated to keep a watch on major corporations – like CorpWatch for example. This was started originally because,

" it seemed then that a few hundred transnational companies were intent on remaking the earth in their image. As we saw it, the corporate version of globalisation undermined community, ecology and democracy."

Those who formed it saw the Internet as a

"vehicle through which to build an alternative – a form of grassroots globalisation that fostered human rights and environmental rights, and that helped hold corporations accountable across the globe[124]."

At the same time that pressure mounted on corporations externally sharholder action groups began to emerge in countless companies either to defend those shareholders who had lost money or to confront the policies of corporations over their record for example on the arms trade or the environment. Friends Of The Earth have looked at many of these shareholder actions groups and have noted that shareholder campaigns can be issue-oriented, or community-oriented. Although each type of shareholder campaign is informed by different concerns, processes and strategies, successful shareholder campaigns have certain elements in common, such as[125]:

- Alliances with social movements or public interest groups, where shareholder concerns and activity mesh with and play a part in a larger, multi-faceted campaign

- Grassroots pressure, such as letter-writings or phone-ins to public investors to generate support for the resolution

- Communications: media outreach, public and shareholder education, etc.

- High-level negotiations with senior decision makers

- Support and active involvement from large institutional investors

- A climate that makes it difficult for the company not to make the "right decision." For example, if you have plainly compelling financial argument, you have a better chance of

---

[124] From CorpWatch website - http://www.greenlearning.ca/
[125] From FOE website at
http://www.foe.org/international/shareholder/characteristics.html

getting company management and other shareholders on board with your proposal.

- Persistence. Shareholders don't go away. They own the company and have a right to be heard. Often shareholder activists stick with issues for years.

So consumerism with the emphasis on buying rather than voting has led to a response through direct action by communities and shareholders. In a world where confidence in government has declined this is a sign of hope but it still leaves huge gaps in accountability that has widened as globalisation has progressed at great pace.

The Impact Of Globalisation.

It is the pace of globalisation that has also had an adverse impact on democracy. It is clearly wrong to be critical of all forms of globalisation. The growth of the Internet has allowed people to make contact with each other across the globe and to set up communities that cross national boundaries. Also many of the problems now facing our increasingly finite planet are global in scope. No nation state can tackle the problems of global warming, pollution and global poverty alone. There has to be global action and this needs global institutions and processes to achieve this.

But this raises a major problem. It is true that many of the organisations that have become International like the World Bank and the International Monetary Fund have been often criticised because they are "forces in their own right" and lack accountability to electorates. But even those that do somehow link to national delegations or assemblies like the European Union or the United Nations itself, seem so remote from citizens that individual citizens feel disenfranchised. In the days of the Greek City State it was argued that democracy was at its best in communities of no more than 5,000 people. This was no longer possible when nation states began to adapt the principles of democracy to millions of people. There had to be another model – the representative one with elected members of parliaments or assemblies. But as we have already discussed this system itself is one that has been criticised as the

Twentieth Century came to a close. But global democracy in the world of 6 to 7 billion people is almost impossible to imagine even if the decisions that increasingly have to be made must by their nature be global ones.

Representative Democracy was built on the nation state and every power removed from the nation state without a compensating international power for the citizens appears anti democratic. Accountability becomes diminished. Some argue the primary tool, which we require at the international level, is to plug this gap with forms of global democracy. Yet how we do this whilst keeping the principle of accountability alive is a central question and one of the major issues of the 21st century.

Crisis For Politicians & Citizens

If politics is to be the" master science" then politicians are the craftsmen and women of that science but today they are as disillusioned as citizens and have a sense of impotence that is shared by all. They may find it hard to admit it but that frustration is there and they find it more and more difficult to define their role in the 21st Century. And indeed that role has changed through erosion.

This change began to gather pace in the 1980s when both Congress in the USA and Parliament in the UK began to loose oversight of many of the functions that were taken over by the Executive – by the President and the Prime Minister.

At the same time the tide of privatisation hived out service delivery to bodies that were not scrutinized as they were before by legislators. Deregulation also added to this. In the USA what used to be discussed and debated through Congress got marginalized as the President increased his powers by administrative interpretations of existing laws to fill gaps that once required legislation. And of course deregulation increased the power of many organisations and quangos outside of Congress such as the Treasury and the Federal Reserve. So negotiation between the Executive and these bodies became more important than either legislation or Congressional scrutiny.

When you add to this the growth of supranational organisations like the IMF, the World Bank and the WTO that deal only with the Executive branch of government then there is a real deficit of democratic accountability. And legislators have felt this worldwide. Suddenly the legislative cupboard has begun to feel a little bare

Although the changes have marginalized and reduced the role of legislators they have only partly themselves to blame. By sticking closely to the tribal party systems they have been willing contributors to their own fate. 21st Century politics has to somehow go beyond the Party system as it has grown up in the past two centuries. It is no longer "fit for purpose" as it is being used to support executives rather than hold them to account. In the final analysis mistaken loyalty and job security overrides the need for common sense and vision. The Forum for A New World Governance has argued that,

"The distance between concept and reality is often wider than we think. Establishing suitable governance structures that correspond to 21st century conditions requires a veritable revolution for our existing concepts, mentalities, institutions, and methods, a revolution that can only take place if we can mobilize determination, a firm will, and a clear vision of the objectives to be met and of the paths to be taken over the long term.[126] "

Politicians have to begin transcending their party structure and form alliances with civil society and other politicians across the globe not to reinforce their own Executives but to hold them more to account. This requires not just action but a change in mindset that politicians find hard to do in the circumstances of day-to-day politics.

But because citizens also feel frustrated because of the diminished accountability of global institutions and national Executives there is a growing synergy with politicians. It is the synergy of despair that can be turned into a positive future agenda. But to do that will mean that citizens must overcome their distrust of politicians and politicians must form new alliances with citizens globally outside of

---

[126] FNWH website at http://www.world-governance.org/spip.php?page=accueil

their party framework and begin to forge a new politics for a new century.

Recreating A New Democracy

It is easy to defend democracy and to advocate exporting it around the world as the ideal system. That is clearly the American mission of the neo conservatives and the desired mission in Francis Fukayama's book "The End of History." For him all the battles of ideology had been won at the end of the 20th century and all that is left is for the world to understand it and sign into the American dream. But of course not all the battles have been won. Many countries do not want to sign into that dream, as it appears to have major blemishes. The model that has grown up over centuries is now inadequate. Power is gradually moving away from not only local citizens and government but also from nation states and national politicians. Trying to reverse that trend would not improve the health of democracy in a globalised world where issues like poverty, trade and global warming need international solutions.

Nor in this complex world of diversity where national identity is changing and citizenship an ever-moving concept will government by the majority ever be sufficient to restore confidence again. We need a new form of global democracy that reflects diversity, freedom and involvement. But that is not an easy task and politicians raised on the basic foodstuff of party politics are ill equipped to tackle it. They have been socialised into the cut and thrust of party politics and this has shaped their view of the world. Particularly in the USA and the UK this view has been an adversarial one where every minute difference is magnified to a state of principle. The politics of accommodation seen in countries like the Netherlands is foreign to those who face each other across the dispatch box of minimal differences.

We have seen the growth of democracy over centuries grow from a direct form in the Greek city-state to a representative one in nation states involving millions of people. Now in this global environment of ever changing diversity we need to move on yet again to "active democracy" that crosses national boundaries and transcends party politics.

What is daily becoming clear is that we have to extend our democracy out from Parliaments to communities, civil society and business organisations through a network of involvement and engagement. This is not to replace the existing system of representative democracy but rather to enhance it. The concept of accountability enshrined in periodic elections is vital and to change that would undermine the basis of our freedoms but it is clearly not enough.

One of the greatest critics of democracy was Alexis de Tocqueville and in his famous book "Democracy In America" raised a number of criticisms of the infant form of American democracy in the early 19th century. He could seen how it attracted the mediocre and greedy, how it often discriminated against minorities and how it can stifle freedom. As he said,

"In America the majority raises formidable barriers around the liberty of opinion; within these barriers an author may write what he pleases, but woe to him if he goes beyond them[127]."

These deficits of democracy that de Tocqueville shrewdly observed in its infant state are even more glaring in a society that is increasingly diverse and where intolerance is growing. In such a state freedom is threatened in the name of democracy. In those circumstances it is no good defending democracy as it is, but rather finding forms of democracy that enhance freedom and protect diversity. That is one of the major tasks of the 21st Century. It was de Tocqueville who also said,

"The health of a democratic society may be measured by the quality of functions performed by private citizens."

Our task in the 21st Century is to find new ways and means where private citizens are engaged in the functions of governance again rather being dismissed to the margins by global forces. The failure

---

127 Democracy in America by Alexis de Tocqueville Publisher: Wordsworth Editions Ltd; New Ed edition (19 Feb 1998) ISBN-10: 1853264806

to do that in times of social and planetary turbulence is too dire to sometimes contemplate.

Part 4 – Making Sense Of Our Future

In the previous sections we have looked at how we get to know our environment and ourselves and what we mean by that. However it is the interaction between our environment and us that is critical. In much of this book we have looked at the relationship between individual change and social change. Much of the debate has been about the concept of individual and that of environment. How does one impact on the other? Often little attempt is made to look at the energy between the environment and the individual - the relationship itself.

In this final section we begin to look at this relationship and how it can be channelled through the growth of networks. The power of networks is that although it values both the individual and the external environment as agents in shifting paradigms and culture, it considers the most important element as being the relationship itself as the effective agent of change.

So we look at the growing networks centred on civic society as well as the growth of social businesses and how through global networks they are beginning to shape a new culture that can be the powerhouse of change. What is the nature of these networks and how can they help us form a new worldview?

Of course the growth of diverse and multitudinous networks present us with an anarchy of global energy that often it appears to have little focus. So we also address the issues of the focus and co-ordination of network activity and the necessity to create global forums of public space where discussion and debate can generate both ideas and direction. There is a great need to reintroduce public space back into life where people can meet again and talk about the pressing issues of the 21st Century – issues that are so important that they can impact on our very survival.

The concept of a 'public' – a whole polity that cares about the common good and has the capacity to deliberate about it democratically – is central to civil society thinking. It is here where shared interests are developed, where the cut and thrust of debate takes place and meaningful compromises reached so that people can work together more effectively. It is here where new ideas are examined and the thrill of what is possible explored. Without an effective public space then there can be no real governance or any peaceful resolution of differences.

So this last section is about the energy of networks and the focus that the global public square can bring to that energy. It is about creating a new democracy at a global level that is holistic in that is about not just representation but involvement as well. It also considers how the connections created by a "network" society can help to develop the "right action" necessary for our survival in the 21st Century.

CHAPTER 12 – Recreating Our Future

World On An Edge

September 29th 2008 saw the American stock market suffer its greatest fall in its history in one single day. The world was facing a financial crisis that looked like infecting the entire economy and leading us into the worst depression since before the Second World War.

The term **financial crisis** usually refers to situations in which some financial institutions or assets suddenly lose a large part of their value. The crisis facing the global economy in the autumn of 2008 was not merely that some assets were losing their value but that some had become what was widely being described as toxic.

The assets that had become toxic were "mortgage papers" held by banks that can be sold from institution to institution as a part of the bank's efforts to raise money. But by late 2008 banks had stopped selling to each other, and lending money to each other so that assets could be liquid. This was precipitated by the credit crunch whereby credit was no longer readily available. House prices were in free fall and people were unable to repay their mortgages or raise the money to do so. Consequently the "mortgage papers" owned by banks were no longer marketable and had become "toxic assets."

Much of this had been precipitated by the "buy to let" market. Buy to let was devised to encourage private investors to take advantage of highly competitive interest rates in the hope of sustained capital growth in future years. It was the engine to increase the amount of privately rented property on the housing market. By providing an opportunity for investors and linking this with professional management agents, the aim was to make more housing available to more people whilst providing a return on investment to those who sought mortgages to finance properties to let.

The "Buy To Let" market has seen an incredible growth in popularity from the mid 1990's and landlords have sought to ignore warnings on a possible downturn. This drive towards "buy to let" saw a restructuring of our financial institutions. Long established Building Societies like the Bradford & Bingley in the UK rushed to turn themselves into banks so that they could get involved in what they thought a lucrative market. So they became demutualised in order to expand and raise profits. This led them to move into the more vulnerable areas of the market like self-certified mortgages and the "buy to let" market. In order to finance this they no longer depended on deposits alone but sought finance in the international wholesale money markets. In the case of the Bradford & Bingley, they were heavily dependent on this market. This worked as long as the market remained liquid but as it began to contract it became increasingly difficult to raise money in this way. The money was no longer there to finance bonds and provide liquidity for the mortgage market. This was made worst for the those like Bradley & Bingley who took on packages of mortgages from the vulnerable American market such as General Motors Finance – a market with a higher default rate than the UK market.

And of course that vulnerable American market made the US the "sick man of the globe" with a huge problem of liquidity and debt. Since 1864, American banking had been split into commercial banks and investment banks; but that began to change. -- Overnight, some of the biggest names on Wall Street collapsed - Bear Stearns, Lehman Brothers, Merrill Lynch. The only giants left standing were Goldman Sachs and Morgan Stanley but even they have been hurt by mysterious slumps in prices and -- at least in Morgan Stanley's case -- have prepared themselves for the end. Many were drawing comparisons with the Great Depression, the national trauma that has been the benchmark for everything since. It was beginning to look as if the foundations of American capitalism were being shaken and the only thing certain is that the era of the unbridled free-market economy in the US had passed for the foreseeable future.

The financial crisis more than climate change, resource depletion or international security had impacted on so many people. For a moment they could see the whole economic edifice come tumbling down and their homes, jobs and pensions all at risk. Nothing is more galvanising than events to make a sea change in how we view the world.

Events & Perception

How we view the world we discussed in previous chapters – and the interaction between ourselves and the environment around us is an essential dynamic equation. If the world around us defines our status as reflecting what we have rather than what we are then a world of prosperity and growth generates within us an acquisitive character and it is that character that has been the dominant culture since the Second World War. Within that time there has been a number of countervailing counter cultures such as the youth cultures of the 1960's but none prevailed over the acquisitive energy of the post war years of unbridled growth. The counter culture failed partly because the desired change in individuals was not reflected in the economic circumstances of the outside world. The inner and the outer had little synergy for most people. The rapid economic growth of the post war world ensured that probably a majority of the citizens of the developed world sought after a share of that growth through increased wealth. Even the baby boomers that made up the youthful counter culture of the 1960's often joined in this world of wealth creation once the world of employment loomed.

However events can change all that. When the then British Prime Minister, Harold Macmillan was once asked by a journalist what is most likely to blow governments off course his answer was " events dear boy, events." Of course he was referring to political events that could so easily drive a government off course. In the late twentieth century we were faced with events after events that should have driven all of us off the course of the acquisitive society but our desire for status through wealth remained strong, as the economy appeared stable at the surface. As we noted in a previous chapter the advent of global warming and the growing shortages of important resources required that we reassess the world we are in and make fundamental changes in the infrastructure of our growth based economies. Increasing numbers of people began to argue this but they were faced with the impasse of a majority culture enjoying wealth creation and a social and economic infrastructure that supported that. For the counter culture to become mainstream then events would have to impact on human consciousness and perception.

And the financial crisis of the autumn of 2008 was an event that did begin to change perception. That crisis in world financial markets illustrated that we had built our economies on a foundation of monetary sand and that when met by a hurricane then those foundations shake. Essentially the weak foundation had been that of greed and the dubious pleasure of instant gratification at the expense of our planet and our long-term security.

This crisis should now give us time to reassess and attempt to create an economic system that is sustainable. The culture of credit, unregulated lending, share options and large bonuses with minimal regulation had produced confetti economies that relate only in fantasy to the real world of resources and actuality.

In the last few years we have seen a crisis of resources as oil peaked, food became more expensive, water became scarce and our climate warmed up. This should have been enough to reshape our attitudes and push us into creating a world based on actual needs rather than unlimited growth and wealth. However the last 20 or 30 years has seen a world build up where personal gain is what has been valued and both companies and individuals were determined to maximise their gain or profit. The rational cold water that poured on us from environmental and resource crises was not enough to dent the dream that countless wealth was possible and that it would trickle down from the wealthy to the poor.

But the crisis of 2008 not only ensured that wealth would not trickle down from the rich to the poor. The middle class began to suffer as well. They were faced with the inability to get loans or to remortgage their homes and repossession took pace as negative equity set in. The middle class was facing a sharp drop in their living standards and in some cases destitution. In this environment then fear became the prevailing mood. The issue facing the globe in the midst of such a crisis is whether the fear generated would make people more aware of the true nature of their planet and its finite nature or whether they would look for blame and seek revenge. When in September 2008 the President of the USA with the support of Congressional leaders sought to pass through the House of Representative a $700 billion rescue package to ease the crisis then it was rejected on the first vote. Many Congressmen voted against it because public opinion was hostile – and their mailbags and email reflected this. People were angry at the banks and Wall Street and wanted revenge. They shouted the slogan "no bail for Wall Street and the Banks but jail!" This was fear turning into anger and the demand for revenge.

So the change in culture that could be hoped for as the finite planet becomes ever more apparent did not occur as voter after voter sought blame. The middle class were angry and sought retribution. It was like the situation in the depression in Germany between the Wars that led to the rise of the Nazi Party as we examined earlier. When that depression happened the middle class who suddenly found themselves impoverished instead of turning to the working class in solidarity as classical Marxism would suggest they instead chose the Nazi Party because although they were objectively now the "proletariat, they did not subjectively perceive themselves that way. In their minds they were different. It was this point between what class is objectively and what it is perceived subjectively that became the fascination of Wilhelm Reich when he sought to explain the rise of Fascism. Psychology gets in the way of economics and one-dimensional theories stop working.

The crisis of the late first decade of the 21st century saw this again – status perception getting in the way of what was happening all around. Small town middle class America had lived through several decades where their hatred of the liberal cosmopolitan establishment had grown. Joel Dyer in his book "Harvest of Rage" says,

"What is left in the 90% of the landmass that is designated "rural" is massive poverty and despair.. For decades, men, women and children in our small towns and farms have cried out for help. But their pleas for assistance have gone unanswered, as if they couldn't be heard over the noise of the city. Rural residents are drowning in a tumultuous sea of circumstance beyond their control. The millions of rural Americans still trying to tread water are being pulled under by the callous decisions emanating from corporate boardrooms and the nation's capital. Unable to be heard or to rescue themselves, they've grown angry[128]."

---

[128] Harvest of Rage: Why Oklahoma City is Only the Beginning by Joel Dyer, Publisher: Basic Books; New edition edition (14 Aug 1998) ISBN-10: 0813332931

Joel Dyer wrote this in 1997 after two decades when Middle America saw their lives torn apart. Between 700,000 and 1 million small to medium sized farms had been lost since 1980. This sea change in the lives of Middle and small town America caused anger that culminated in the 1995 bombing of the federal building in Oklahoma City that killed nearly 200 innocent people. Federal government represented corporate America and in the eyes of the rural dispossessed this was equated with the liberal establishment. Their material world was being torn asunder.

Materialism & Scientism

The Enlightenment had shaped much of our view of the world after the 18th century and the philosophy of materialism had become a dominant force. Materialism holds that the only thing that can be truly proven to exist is matter. The universe is seen as one huge device held together by pieces of matter functioning according to classical laws of physics. The world is thus reduced to material phenomena and everything including consciousness itself is the result of material interaction. It is this view that led Schopenhauer to once exclaim,

"..materialism is the philosophy of the subject who forgets to take account of himself.[129]"

In materialism there is a form of reductionism in that all things are reduced to material substances. It was a paradigm that suited a growth economy where things as opposed to thoughts or feelings dominated the changing world. Technology was utilised to encourage growth and to construct a material world. It was also a viewpoint that suited the growing acquisitive society of the consumer era. If we live in a world surrounded by matter then it is a simple step to become obsessed by material possessions and to

---

[129] World as Will and Representation - Volume 2: v. 2 by Arthur Schopenhauer Publisher: Dover Publications Inc.; New edition edition (Jul 1967) ISBN-10: 0486217620

dismiss spiritual or intellectual considerations. Material goods become more important than anything else and this shapes our social character and the way we interact with others.

This material view of the world that dominated our thoughts and behaviour was reinforced by scientism – a view that emphasises that the methods of the natural sciences based upon empiricism were the only avenue of enquiry for progress. The view that true knowledge of the world only arises from perceptual experience is the one that emanates from the Enlightenment and August Comte. This view dominated the 19th and early twentieth centuries stating that natural science was more important than any other line of enquiry whether philosophical, emotional or spiritual.

The atomistic and gravitational universe came from the classical physics of Newton and the work of Galileo and formed the basis for a material based world. It also led to a particular form of scientism that emphasised science as the only means of enquiry dismissing all else as peripheral. The Romantic movement of the early 19th century was a reaction against this perceived world and although important and with lasting effect this movement never became mainstream when confronted with a world of growth and increasing wealth.

This was a view that began to shape all enquiry and other disciplines began to adopt scientific method in order to be credible including history and social science. Behaviouralism in social science and historicism in history were the results of this material concept of our world. At the extreme history was about looking for dynamic forces that created a pattern of development in the past and led to a form of historical materialism. Karl Popper the great critic of historicism stated,

"We now find that the historicist method implies a strangely similar sociological theory - the theory that society will necessarily change but along a predetermined path that cannot change, through stages predetermined by inexorable necessity.[130]"

---

[130] "The Poverty of Historicism" by Karl Raimund Popper (Originally published in book form 1957) (Edition extracts taken

Even the critics of industrial capitalism used materialism as their weapon to critique the world of capital and most Marxists were as much a part of the "material" paradigm as were those they criticised. But this was a view that came under attack as the twentieth century began to dawn. New scientific discoveries in the areas of biological complexity, cosmological design, quantum physics, and information theory brought these materialistic assumptions into doubt. Systems theories, chaos, networks became the subject of study and the world suddenly became much more than merely matter. There was a growing scientific base for challenging the material world and in consequence challenging as well the world of material consumption.

But as the financial crisis of 2008 began to create fear and panic globally the question is whether these new paradigms were strong enough to prevent both citizens and decision makers falling back into recreating business as usual or whether they would begin to construct a new world that reflected the realities of our finite planet. The materialism of the post Newtonian world had great philosophers who created maps to help us guide our way through the maze of material industrialisation. Yet the present world has seen the intellectual foundation of that world undermined but there is no grand design to make sense of it all. We are muddling through. What signs of hope are there to believe that we will not revert to old paradigms when the changing world of the 21st century confuses rather than enlightens?

Alternative Structures

The maps that were drawn up in the nineteenth century and laid the basis for liberalism, nationalism, conservatism and socialism did not happen overnight. They followed social movements that gave philosophers and other thinkers some evidence of the social forces at work. The Communist Manifesto was not written until after half a century of utopian experiment and barricades. In the world of finite resources we do not have a half-century to spare. What signs are there that change can happen in time?

---

from version published by Routledge and Kegan Paul, 1974 reprint, ISBN 0 7100 4616 2)

At first the financial crash of 2008 reinforced the perception of the corporate elite as perpetrators of a crime and increased the anger. It seemed at first that the change in personal attitudes that was necessary for adjusting to a finite planet would be lost under a sea of anger. And of course, saving the planet means much more than the cumulative change of individual behaviour; it also requires significant and fundamental change in the infrastructure of our energy system and this will mean rethinking almost everything around us, how we live, our transport, the way our cities work and our agricultural system. It will mean changing the very behaviour and goals of government and corporations. This is a bridge far beyond the assault of changed individual behaviour. So as 2008 came to an end there appeared little hope that the financial crisis feared by many to be as serious as the crash of the 1930's would change either perception or structure in a meaningful way. There was no New Deal in site or an economist like John Maynard Keynes with a way forward.

And yet it was not all despair. There were signs that changes were taking place that might yet lead to some fundamental reassessment both in how we viewed the world and how we structure it as well. Once the House of Representatives rejected the rescue plan negotiated by the president and leaders of Congress in September 2008 the markets began to fall. Suddenly a new fear began to appear – the fear that there was a real economic crisis and that the economy might collapse. Now people lobbied Congress because they feared for their bank deposits, their homes, their jobs and their children's education. Cosmopolitan America and Middle America had the same fear and it appeared that now they would all be losers unless there was action and change.

In Europe there was chaos at first in the approach to the crisis but a commitment that the problem needed not just an immediate fix but a long term solution that confronted the underlying dynamic forces impacting on the economy in an age of globalisation and increasing energy prices. There was a glint that politicians at last were beginning to think long term and be more honest and upfront with their electorates than was usual. However there was a long way to go in moving from the fear generated by crisis to the solution created by insight; and on the way there were many hurdles that fear generates including anger, revenge and the all too human response to find convenient scapegoats! The challenge was how to harness this fear to positive outcomes and not descend into negative passions that could lead to political and religious extremism and the politics of despair.

One voice of optimism during the 2008 crisis was Lord Stern of Brentford who suggested the credit crunch might provide an opportunity to invest in measures to tackle global warming as a way of stimulating economic growth. Lord Stern was the author of the government's influential 700-page report on climate change. It was this report that concluded that one percent of global gross domestic product per annum needs to be invested in order to avoid the worst effects of climate change, and that failure to do so could risk global GDP being up to twenty percent lower than it otherwise might be. His argument was that what we do now can have only a limited effect on the climate over the next 40 or 50 years, but what we do in the next 10-20 years could have a profound effect on the climate in the second half of this century.

Lord Stern argues that tackling climate change such as spending on renewable and other low-carbon industries could boost investment at a time of financial crisis and also increase international cooperation. In an interview with the Guardian in the UK in October 2008 Stern said,

"We're going to have to grow out of this ... and this is an area which looks as though it could well grow strongly and with the right support could be one of the major engines of growth."

Creating opportunities out of crisis is a skill necessary for the 21st century and that skill is what Lord Stern argues governments should be practicing. If they were to do that then they would be following what countless people are doing in the global community already. Today we see one of the largest social movements the world has ever seen. The last few decades has seen a huge growth of groups globally concerned with the environment and social justice and at the same time there has also been a flowering of social businesses where there is a strong motive to do good and not merely to maximise profit. Together this is probably the biggest grassroots movement the world has ever seen. The world is changing and if we can take advantage of a crisis to make this socially concerned social movement become ever more mainstream then the world can build itself again on stronger foundations. And if on top of this, Governments can work with this movement and invest in the future then there is positive hope.

On one hand the late first decade of the 21st century saw the pinnacle of the world of "to have" rather than "to be" where what you own defines who you are. This was the age of high salaries, share options and bonuses, the time when executive salaries went through the roof. It was the age when many felt that riches were there for the taking – a feeling that grew gradually through the post war growth years and became a mainstream ambition from the 1980's on. This was the age of house owning wealth and when the "buy to let" market created opportunities, the age of the four-wheel drive and the lure of foreign holidays. It was a time when if wealth did not trickle down then the fantasy that all could share this exotic life did. People's motivation was driven not just by what they had but the dream of what they could get. This was the age of the lottery built on the false foundations that the world offered prizes for all.

Yet it was also the age that saw the growth of a counter culture – not the one that sprang up in the 1960's as an expression of repressed youth rebellion but the one that probably can be dated from the publication of Rachel Carsons "Silent Spring" in 1962 and that offered us a vision of the perils of a world based on the blind faith that technology can solve every problem by providing an appropriate fix. Gary Kroll, a professor of History argued,

"Rachel Carson's *Silent Spring* played a large role in articulating ecology as a 'subversive subject'— as a perspective that cut against the grain of materialism, scientism, and the technologically engineered control of nature.[131]"

Slowly but gradually many began to question the world of materialism that had been offered to us since the Industrial Revolution and this made many reassess that world and the foundations on which it had been built. The Paradigm that the world

---

[131] Gary Kroll, "Rachel Carson-*Silent Spring* A Brief History of Ecology as a Subversive Subject". Onlineethics.org: National Academy of Engineering. Retrieved 2007-11-04.

was not just material that could be shaped by technology and science was seeping down to the consciousness of communities as they faced the unintended consequences of progress.

Civil Society & Social Concern

Since the publication of "Silent Spring" a whole movement has grown up around protecting the environment and many large non-government organisations such as Greenpeace, Friends of the Earth and The Sierra Club have become champions of a more sustainable world. In the late 20th century far more people were joining these groups than political parties. Trust had moved from the party political arena to those who championed causes. However as the end of the century drew near many of these organisations began to change their structures and became think tanks, non-membership organisations or became part of the "contract culture" thus diluting their original campaigning enthusiasm. But of course the larger organisations were but a part of what was becoming a much wider movement and one that was revitalising civil society. Civil society has been defined as an

"arena of uncoerced collective action around shared interests, purposes and values..... Civil societies are often populated by organisations such as registered charities, development non-governmental organisations, community groups, women's organisations, faith-based organisations, professional associations, trades unions, self-help groups, social movements, business associations, coalitions and advocacy groups[132] ".

The importance of voluntary organisations in any society has often been taken as one of the litmus paper tests of a free society. A totalitarian regime can be viewed as one where the society and family are less important than the individual and the state and if voluntary organisations and families can be weakened then there is always the capacity for more control by the state over the individual. A vibrant civil society is vital for an open society.

---

[132] What is Civil Society from the LSE website at
http://www.lse.ac.uk/collections/CCS/what_is_civil_society.htm

Yet as the twentieth century drew to a close civil society became much more than the larger established organisations. It almost became to some an alternative structure of governance in society. As formal governance became devalued in the eyes of electorates globally then either the free market or civil society provided an alternative. The 1980's saw the heyday of the free market as deregulation took pace and as politicians like Ronald Regan and Margaret Thatcher extolled the virtue of a free market economy. Indeed Margaret Thatcher dismissed civil society, as she saw no such thing as society. There was the state and then individuals in atomistic competition with each other – the very epitome of the materialistic model. The crash of 2008 raised serious questions about the free market and its effectiveness as an alternative mainstream way of governance through the market. The massive interventions by governments across the world heralded in a new era of partnership and regulation. Both Government and the free market had lost credibility over the years and in 2008 both struggled to survive and create new confidence.

However during this time civil society was rapidly growing on a global scale and became an alternative focal point for citizens to express their allegiance. What began as a number of distinctive NGO's that emerged from the 1960's blossomed into countless groups and organisations dedicated to preserving the environment, tackling the threat of global warming, seeking social justice and fighting for the rights of indigenous peoples. Such was the growth that Paul Hawken[133] in his book "Blessed Unrest" estimates that there are between one and two million of these groups globally. In that book he comments,

" This movement, however, doesn't fit the standard model. It is dispersed, inchoate, and fiercely independent. It has no manifesto or doctrine, no overriding authority to check with. It is taking shape in schoolrooms, farms, jungles, villages, companies, deserts, fisheries, slums – and yes, even fancy New York hotels. One of its distinctive features is that it is tentatively emerging as a global humanitarian movement arising from bottom up."

---

[133] Blessed Unrest by Paul Hawken, published by Penguin Books 2007 - ISBN 978-0-14-311365-2

These groups are different in kind from the well-established non-government organisations like Oxfam or The Sierra Club, which politicians often associate with civil society. It is less permanent and often less well structured. But the sheer scale of the movement makes it a massive network that probably represents the greatest social movement in history in terms of its size and scale. What is so unique about this movement is that it is almost organic in its growth. There is no central direction. It is the continuous spontaneous uprising of humanity against the insanity of politicians and corporations that treat our planet and its people with contempt by plundering our future. Like nature itself, it is organising from the bottom up, in every city, town, and culture, and is emerging to be an extraordinary and creative expression of people's needs worldwide.

It is not structured or institutionalised like government and corporate organisations but it is a network with a web of extremely good communications. The age of the Internet has made this possible. When in November 1999 700 groups and forty to sixty thousand people descended on Seattle to protest against the World Trade Organisation's Third Ministerial Conference then the power of this movement became apparent. The demonstrators were protesting that the WTO had set rules for global trade that considered only the needs of giant multinational corporations at the expense of protecting the environment and workers' rights.

Digital technology proved a more powerful weapon for protest than anyone could ever have imagined. The WTO's allegedly corporate globalisation agenda was placed at the top of newsroom running orders around the world and were coordinated on the Net and by mobile phone.

For thinkers like Paul Hawken, this movement represents an organic protest. How he describes it makes it difficult for many to identify with as his description is almost mystical. Just as James Lovelock described the world as a self-regulating mechanism so Hawken sees the world as a social organism with the flowering protest movement being the immune system reasserting itself against a disease in the body politic. That is probably taking anti materialism a little too far. However the movement he describes is massive. The problem for many is that it is not focussed in the way that 19th century movements were where groups coalesced under specific ideological banners. Of course this is both its strength and its weakness. Its strength lies in the fact it represents a world that is multi dimensional and diverse and to turn this varied movement into the tailored jacket of an ideological movement would destroy its true nature and the world it reflects. Its weakness is that because it is dispersed and spontaneous it can often be ignored and hidden except at moments of crisis or high activity. Never the less it is a vast movement and provides a basis for deep cultural change within society. At times of crisis when people are turning away from corporate capitalism through distrust of the market then this social movement provides an alternative vision of a sustainable future.

The Social Business Revolution

If the social movement that has emerged within civil society is one branch of hope in a world dedicated to irresponsible corporate behaviour and consumer greed then the other branch of hope is the growing social business movement. A social business is one, which aims to be financially self-sufficient, and profitable, whilst at the same time pursuing a social, ethical or environmental goals.

Much of the work about social businesses has been done by Professor Mohammed Yunus[134]. He has argued that social businesses are of two types. The first is one where there is clearly a social goal for example producing renewable energy or creating a fair trade business that benefits producers in developing countries. These have clear ethical and social goals that are as important as making a profit. For example in UK Divine Chocolate is such a social business. On their website[135] they tell us,

In the early 1990's, the structural adjustment program involved the liberalisation of the cocoa market in Ghana. A number of leading farmers, including a visionary farmer representative on the Ghana Cocoa Board, Nana Frimpong Abrebrese, came to realise that they

---

[134] Creating a World Without Poverty: How Social Business Can Transform Our Lives: Social Business and the Future of Capitalism by Muhammad Yunus Publisher: PublicAffairs; illustrated edition edition (3 Jan 2008) ISBN-10: 1586484931
[135] Divine Chocolate website at
http://www.divinechocolate.com/about/story.aspx

had the opportunity to organize farmers, to take on the internal marketing function. This would mean that they could set up a company, to sell their own cocoa to the Cocoa Marketing Company (CMC), the state-owned company that would continue to be the single exporter of Ghana cocoa.

These farmers pooled resources to set up Kuapa Kokoo, a farmers' co-op, which would trade its own cocoa, and thus manage the selling process more efficiently than the government cocoa agents. Kuapa Kokoo - which means good cocoa growers - has a mission to empower farmers in their efforts to gain a dignified livelihood, to increase women's participation in all of Kuapa's activities, and to develop environmentally friendly cultivation of cocoa. The farmers who set up Kuapa Kokoo, were supported by Twin Trading, the fair trade company that puts the coffee into Cafédirect and SNV a Dutch NGO.

The cocoa farmers, who were already getting a Fairtrade price from some international customers, voted at their 1997 AGM to invest in a chocolate bar of their own. They decided that rather than aiming for the niche market where most Fairtrade products were placed, they would aim to produce a mainstream chocolate bar to compete with other major brands in UK.

In autumn 1998, Divine, the first ever Fairtrade chocolate bar aimed at the mass market was launched onto the UK confectionery market. In an exciting new business model, the co-operative of cocoa farmers in Ghana own shares in the company making the chocolate bar.

The company Good Energy is also a social business in this category and they tell us on their website[136]

Recognising that climate change is a threat, that carbon dioxide is the primary gas responsible for climate change, that power stations are the biggest source of CO_2 emissions, and that individuals can make a real difference, we were established in late 1999 to help empower you to make this change.

---

[136] From Good Energy Website at http://www.goodenergy.co.uk/

All the electricity we supply comes from wind, small-scale hydro and solar power generators from all over Britain. They are either small or medium sized sites and many of them are the result of diversification from areas such as farming and other family businesses. Our Home Generation scheme supports the smaller generator and homeowner..

The second type of social business described by Professor Yanus is one where a company makes a profit but employs people who themselves are deprived so that their economic prospects are enhanced. Here the aim of the business is not to pursue a specific social goal but rather to work with those who benefit by economic investment. Indeed Professor Yanus says,

"Even profit maximizing companies can be designed as social businesses by giving full or majority ownership to the poor."

So for example if a company builds a bridge for the poor or a recipient gives a loan then they could create a "bridge company" that is owned by local people. Then a management company could have the responsibility of running that company whilst some of the profit goes to the local poor for building more infrastructure.. Yanus argues that,

"Many infrastructure projects, like roads, highways, airports, seaports, utility companies could all be built in this manner."

 Professor Yanus describes social business as,

" a new kind of business introduced in the market place with the objective of making a difference in the world. Investors in the social business could get back their investment, but will not take any dividend from the company. Profit would be ploughed back into the company to expand its outreach and improve the quality of its product or service. **A social business will be a non-loss, non-dividend company**.

In a way it is a profit minimisation company rather than one that maximises profit, and that is a different model to the one we normally understand. Indeed Yanus argues for a social stock market where money can be raised to enable social businesses. Certainly a number of investment and banking institutions are emerging to finance this new dawn of social businesses.

The Grameen Bank founded by Professor Yanus was the pioneer of this in Bangladesh. The Grameen Bank operates 1,092 branches in 36,000 rural Bangladesh villages, providing credit to over two million of the country's poorest people in Bangladesh. Since its inception, Grameen has loaned more than US$2 billion. This new banking system of providing unsecured credit to the poorest of the poor began as an action- research project at Chittagong University, and later grew into a full-fledged bank. Grameen Bank's patrons are 94% women who have an unparalleled repayment rate of 98%.

Tembeka in South Africa is another organisation that enables investment to be redirected to areas where it is socially needed. It mobilises investors to become involved in sustainable development through soft loans, institutional building grants and the purchase of Tembeka shares. This investment is then used to make relevant and affordable finance accessible to service providers such as NGO's, Trusts, CBO's Credit Unions and Development companies and, by extension their clients from disadvantaged communities.

In France, a network of 150 local savings clubs called CIGALES support socially innovative entrepreneurship. They have helped to capitalize over 100 small businesses. Another French cooperative, GARRIGUE, provides risk capital to socially responsible small businesses. The first GARRIGUE helped to finance over 35 enterprises, and has just opened a branch office in the northern part of France near Belgium.

A New Dawn?

For many, movements like the growth of social action groups and social businesses are signals of a new dawn that outlines the future in the ashes of the wreckage of our existing financial institutions. The collapse of large financial players has seriously called into question the nature of free-flowing financial markets. These have grown up particularly since the 1980's and both corporate business and government have been responsible for them. They did not happen by chance. They were manufactured. Free markets were often fuelled by a culture of debt and when this became unsustainable then there was a collapse. And when such a collapse takes place then social programmes are under threat as corporations and banks retrench. Against this challenge social business and investment has a big role to play. Yet our whole investment infrastructure is geared towards the existing dinosaur corporations and institutions that have created the world we live in.

Yet there is some evidence that SRI Funds are becoming more popular and are having a place in the whole area of "ethical investment." A Guide for Pensions Funds and Institutional Investors, defines SRI as

"investment where social, environmental or ethical considerations are taken into account in the selection, retention and realisation of investment, and the responsible use of rights (such as voting rights) attaching to investments."

Responsible investors wish to achieve financial and non-financial objectives although how successful this is has become a widely debated issue with some arguing that their portfolios essentially mirror those of mainstream funds. Never the less this is part of a growing movement to shift the focus of investment from the arena of corporate greed to social business and those with corporate responsibility. There are a number of organisations that are trying to take this redirection of focus further and companies are finding ways of raising capital even though they are not strictly profit maxamisers. For example, UK-based Adili has secured further funding for its own expansion, while Divine raised funding in the USA for expansion into that market and companies like the Ethical Property Company expects to raise up to £10 million of share capital in the near future from UK and European investors, to fund future property purchases. Also, the Netherlands-based Noaber Foundation, has been recycling capital earned in mainstream activities into social businesses. These steps are only small beginnings but it is the beginning of a movement and the financial crisis of 2008 and beyond make these alternatives ones that make an attractive alternative to the conventional wisdom of debt based economies.

Other organisations are beginning to spring up like "The Global Sustainability Challenge" and its subsidary "Transform Capital Management" which are new ventures with the goal of driving massive action to bridge gaps between economic necessity and environmental responsibility. GSC is particularly interested in climate change and argues,

"Our aim it to dramatically accelerate the start up of enterprise whose business is tackling climate change. As a result, untold numbers of people will need training in the many areas that can have an impact. New Industries will come about. Scientists in renewable energy development, deployment, and pollution control need driving. Businesses that can banish inefficiencies from the manufacturing or logistics cycle need launching, and we all need to be aware and adjust how we live and work.[137]"

Its founder Steve Podmore cites that in the developed world, the fact that less than 0.1% of institutional capital is invested into start ups and small, medium enterprises (SME's), which are responsible for over 60% of employment is evidence of just of how distorted things have become. His aim is to redirect capital to these more efficient and sustainable smaller businesses.

How successful these companies will be in redirecting investment is something only the future will tell us. However the year 2008 was a watershed year in creating a culture change that might lead to both more responsible business and also investment. Not only did the financial crash change how people saw the world but the election of a new President in the United States also provided hope that change might happen. Certainly Barrack Obama has championed social business in the past. His mother helped found Microcredit in Indonesia and women's world banking. His senate area in Chicago is one where microcredit's Shorebank is strong. And when visiting Kenya's slum area of Kibera - Obama praised the role of micro lending and saw it as a way of ending poverty.

In many developing countries, the self-employed comprise more than 50 percent of the labour force. Access to small amounts of credit—with reasonable interest rates instead of the exorbitant costs often charged by traditional moneylenders—allows poor people to move from initial, perhaps tiny, income-generating activities to small microenterprises.

---

[137] GSC website at http://www.globalsustainabilitychallenge.com/

So the change now taking place economically has also been mirrored by the change that is taking place in civil society with the growth of countless numbers of voluntary groups campaigning for sustainability and social justice. Together they reflect the view that classical economics with its view that motivation was based on greed was no longer true, (if it had ever been true in the first place) and was certainly not viable in the fragile world of the 21st century.

Re-examining Motivation

When we behave in a particular way then the reason that we do so is the basis of our motivation. In the classical view of business there are not several reasons but usually one – the maximisation of profit. This one-dimensional model of what motivates us makes it simpler to build up an economic model that forms the commercial dynamics of our society. When you reduce motivation that way then the result is theoretical simplicity in the systems we construct.

Yunus, the founder Grameen Bank, argues that the fact that people live in poverty all around the world, including in the United States, is not a sign that capitalism doesn't work, but that it is interpreted too narrowly. He believes that Adam Smith's idea of a profit motivated market as too limited and does not reflect what truly motivates people. He argues,

*"I am in favour of strengthening the freedom of the market. At the same time, I am very unhappy about the **conceptual restrictions imposed on the players in the market**. This originates from the **assumption that entrepreneurs are one-dimensional human beings**, who are dedicated to one mission in their business lives – to **maximize profit**. This interpretation of capitalism insulates the entrepreneurs from all political, emotional, social, spiritual, environmental dimensions of their lives. This was done perhaps as a reasonable simplification, but it stripped away the very essentials of human life. Human beings are a wonderful creation embodied with limitless human qualities and capabilities. Our theoretical constructs should make room for the blossoming of those qualities, not assume them away."*

He believes that by defining what we mean by an "entrepreneur" then the very nature of capitalism can itself change. The fact that capitalism is as it is today has to do with the structure of capitalism and the impact that this has on people's motivation. It is a vicious circle and breaking out of that is essential according to Yunus. If an entrepreneur has several sources of motivation instead of one then the structure of capitalism would change. Many people involved in social business are there to both make a profit and to do good. Also because entrepreneurs are also family members with children and possibly grandchildren then they are also concerned about the fate of our planet and the survival of our species because of the challenge of climate change. So there is a mixture of motives. If profit is all that matters then profit maximisation is the sole motive and our economy of financial speculation and consumer debt has been based on that premise. However if other motives come into play then business can become social.

Adam Smith himself, the great champion of early 19th century capitalism understood that what determines whether the profit motive leads to good results are the institutions through which human action is played out. The institutions we create, the laws we make and the policies we follow all affect which activities are profitable and which are not. If we create institutions that are geared only to profit then that will reinforce the profit motive in us but if we create institutions and develop law and policy that reflect the value of social good them other motives come to the fore within us.

So a society that values socially responsible business as well as civil society could be one where the ethos of greed that has plundered our planet could change to one that sustains it. Creating structures based on the single dimensional motivation that all people seek to maximise their economic gain does not reflect the complexity of human nature nor is it sustainable. If one has a one-dimensional view of what motivates people then the danger is that you create a society that is based upon reward and punishment. Many studies have shown that this restricted view can damage the other drives that are in people and that are not grounded in personal aggrandisement. Also once you direct people through the mechanisms of external reward and punishment then it impacts on the mosaic of inner dives that exist within us all. Once you assign a pay check as a reward to an activity then it changes its very nature. What was once a vocation or a pleasure suddenly become work and people begin to perform less well than when motivation was based on commitment rather than reward.

So the task of the 21st century is to create structures and processes that reflect that humans are not just programmed towards self interest and that they can be also motivated to sustain our planet and do good to others. But how do we do this? When our society has been dominated by possessive individualism for many years and the structures that we have set up have rewarded power and wealth then how do we move towards a different world where community is valued over competition and sustainability over gluttony?

Making Connections

It is clear that there is much happening that gives us hope for the future. The massive development of groups concerned with social justice and the environment is almost unprecedented in our history. Also the growth of a business environment that is concerned with "social good" and not just with profits is another huge development that is only just beginning to take off. Whether these will have sufficient momentum and structure to make the difference that is needed in the 21st century is another question. Many argue that they are not yet really a movement and that there is no unifying force. However some who argue this do so from the old blueprints and maps of the 19th and 20th centuries where change had to take place through revolution or huge waves of social protest. The growth of the unions, the suffragette movement, the civil rights movement and the demand for democracy are all given as examples of movements where there were sufficient unifying factors to make them successful. Gender, race and class were all factors that cemented these movements and gave them their unifying force.

But in the 21st century these are no longer sufficient. Most of the movements that have grown up at the dawn of the 21st century contain people from all classes, races and genders and are often issue orientated. People are fighting to save one indigenous group or another, to protect the rainforest, to extend the human rights of migrants, to expose the evil of corporations and so on. It is an amorphous sea of protest and to reduce it all to a gender, race or class focussed movement would diminish it and reduce its effect. And that is the dilemma. To apply the unifying dynamics of the previous centuries to the flowering progressive movements of the 21st would undermine the strength of its very diversity: and yet not to have focus will also reduce its impact. Its diversity is both its strength and its weakness. The unifying factors of the present century must be something else and that something is the ever-growing web of networks. It is the growth of global networks that is giving focus and momentum to the movements of the new century. They provide communication, contact, community and direction to a motley yet energetic crew of change agents in the world. It is to networks that we devote our next chapter.

Chapter 13 - The Dynamics Of Networks

Power of Networks

In much of this book we have looked at the relationship between individual change and social change. Much of the debate has been about the concept of individual and that of environment. How does one impact on the other? Often little attempt is made to look at the energy between the environment and the individual - the relationship itself. The power of networks is that although it values both the individual and the external environment as agents in shifting paradigms and culture, it considers the most important element the relationship between the two.

Social network theory views social relationships in terms of nodes and ties. Nodes are the individual actors within the networks, and ties are the relationships between the actors. What these ties are and how they affect us is what is the unique characteristic of network theory and it is this that makes social network theory different from traditional sociological studies, which assume that it is the attributes of individual actors that matter. Here you have an alternate view, where the attributes of individuals are less important than their relationships and ties with other actors within the network.

So in network theory reality is far more about the properties and relations between and within units or nodes rather than the properties of these units themselves. Network theory is a relational approach that examines social units in terms of their interaction and the energy link that acts as the lifeblood of the system. Social network theory can be applied not only to relationships between two people but to larger units or groups and indeed to society itself.

Communication theory also looks at relationships to some extent as well. Rogers characterizes a communication network as consisting of "interconnected individuals who are linked by patterned communication flows." [138] The pattern of these flows is the energy

---

[138] Rogers, E.M. & Kincaid, D.L. (1981). *Communication Networks: Toward a New Paradigm for Research*. Publisher: Macmillan USA (1 Jan 1981) ISBN-10: 0029267404

between actors and can affect outcomes. Social network theory takes this further and looks at this pattern of flows as different forms of ties that can have profound impacts on the actors (or nodes) involved.

A whole new discipline of social network theory has grown up around this. Although the interaction between individuals goes back as far as Durkheim, the phrase social network was coined by the sociologist J.A. Barnes in 1954 to explain the friend-of-a-friend-of-a-friend connections that cut across traditional groupings of family or ethnic groups. These relationships form the path to getting on in life, finding jobs, homes and indeed partners too. In the UK there has always seen the term the "old boy network" and that portrays a network that reinforces a distinct social class; but network theory applies that to us all and examines its impact on results and attitudes.

The problem with concentrating on "relationships" or the ties that bind units together is that it can take on an intangible form and sometimes have a somewhat mystical or neo religious property. It has something of the Jungian "collective unconscious" to it. Indeed some modern gurus have defined this "relationship" as "consciousness." For example Andrew Cohen is an American guru who has developed what he characterizes as a unique path of spiritual transformation, called Evolutionary Enlightenment. His movement is about awakening what he describes as the "ground of our being" (shades of Paul Tillich) and in doing so enabling human beings to liberate themselves from selfish motives and discover their "authentic self." What is interesting about Cohen's work is that he teaches that enlightenment is no longer the possession of individuals but instead becomes the ground of the "relationship" upon which a new culture can be based. It is the relationship that creates the consciousness and it is through such relationships that such consciousness will evolve to a new level.

Changing consciousness of course is not the prerogative of neo religious movements but is also grounded in materialism. Marxists argue that changes in the material substructure of society can change consciousness from what is false to what is true. So although the change agent is the material world, the consciousness is never the less a state of mind that comes from this and is usually enabled by the interactions or relationships of class solidarity.

Network analysis (social network theory) is the study of how the social structure of relationships around a person, group, or organization affects beliefs or behaviours. And in a world where the material base of our society is a shifting sand and where the agents of solidarity such as class, race and gender no longer hold firm then social network theory takes on a new interest. Can networks be the new focus that can create the sort of solidarity experience that once class, gender or race evoked? Can it be the instrument for personal and social change through the new relationships it creates? This is the crucial question that needs an understanding of what networks can do and need to do to affect change and to do so in the time we have left for that change to be effective. Can it change our material world as the materialists would demand and can it cause a shift in our consciousness as the gurus of a new age hope for?

The Social Media World

Only in the 21st century could people display their social commitment, join causes, virtually hug and sexually poke everyone in sight and still call for the slow euthanasia of the over 65's as part of a population strategy to save the planet. Unbelievable yes but true! Such characters exist and they are found roaming the new communication hub of the 21st century – social networking sites. In a way they reflect the symbolic confusion of the 21st century when all the maps of what to believe and how to behave have vanished. For centuries, people had religions, ideologies, shared national and international beliefs to help them navigate the world and give it meaning. Now many of these have collapsed or have been found wanting and there is a gaping vacuum that is being filled by cults, fundamentalism, hedonism, tokenism and sexy ass shoes!

Yes really sexy ass shoes! There is or was such a group on one site and people are creating them everyday. Some people create them all the time. There are also many social action groups and many join and get involved but others join and by doing so, believe they have made a difference merely by joining and wearing the badge. Many after a casual chat believe they have found their very best friend and others fall in love after the whiff of a mere whisper. People are frenetically trying to create community because the older communities are fading away and the web allows people in a hurry to have their day.

The average Internet user now spends three hours a week on social networking sites, according to the research organisation YouGov. That adds up to six days a year, and makes social networking more popular than online banking, shopping or music downloads. This does mean that large fractions of people's existence online are often invested in rival realities. For example, with Second Life, the Internet-based virtual-world, its "Residents" interact as avatars in group activities, and in trading items with one another. A virtual world can be created that takes over from the real.

Virtual worlds are also becoming the suburbia of the present century. They provide an unreal world as the Suburbia of the mid 20th century did for many and as was so strikingly described in Richard Yates novel "Revolutionary Road[139]." And just as in suburbia people took on a character that reflected a competitive, status seeking and acquisitive attitude to life so the new suburbia of the Internet is creating new character traits. Much research still needs to be done on it but it represents a growing reality of the present century.

The problem of an age without direction is that many people become arbitrary, dogmatic, obstinate, and fill their web profiles with empty ego. They call it having fun, or not taking life too seriously but at root it is a directionless leap into nothingness. Instead of coming to terms with the "nothingness" of our existence described by many philosophers and mystics, they fill their personalities with empty activity. From this can come a social character that shuts out reality and dismisses the imperatives of the real world!

In a frenzy of constant surface activity they prevent the reflection that Confucius described two and a half thousand years ago as a way of opening ourselves up to communicate with others and behave to others through "right action." But for many people the web of

---

[139] Revolutionary Road by Richard Yates, Publisher: Vintage Classics (13 Dec 2007) ISBN-10: 0099518627

social contact has created a new world of the collective imagination that hides the essence of the real world that is changing fast. And just as the acquisitive society of the past half-century or more has created social character that insulates people from both themselves and their world so the silly ass shoe world does the same in the present. It can be a camouflage to make sense of a confused world without help or guidance that gives some meaning however artificial.

From Media To Action

But the new world of the social media is not just about sexy pokes and silly ass shoes. There is also a growing swell of social action network sites and sites that discuss ideas and invite debate.

Even politics has been quick to see the force of social networks. One man to use the Internet as a method of political and social action was one of the democrat runners for president in the 2005 elections, Howard Dean. Dean never became the candidate but was for a time its front runner. His campaign slowly gained steam, and by autumn of 2003, Dean had become the apparent frontrunner for the Democratic nomination, performing strongly in most polls and outpacing his rivals in fundraising.

Dean achieved this with the help of Meetup.com and hundreds of bloggers,

"We fell into this by accident," Dean admits. "I wish I could tell you we were smart enough to figure this out. But the community taught us. They seized the initiative through Meetup. They built our organization for us before we had an organization.[140]"

Using meetup this way found new audiences that politicians had not thought possible. In early 2003, Dean himself was lured to an early New York City meetup where he found more than 300 enthusiastic supporters waiting to greet him. Meetup quickly became the engine of Dean's Internet campaign.

---

[140] Quoted on the "Wired" website at
http://www.wired.com/wired/archive/12.01/dean.html

By 2008 this approach to politics had become essential for success but not all politicians understood this – but Barack Obama certainly did as he fought for the Democratic nomination and then the Presidency in 2009. Obama has both used and been used widely by the Internet. He used all sorts of people to make connections through social networks. He was also been successful at converting online clicks into real world currency – through action and donations.

His main website, at **www.MyBarackObama.com,** is ostensibly about signing up so that "you" could join in his campaign or even be an organiser. The website also invites users to *display* who they are so they are not there just to add a name to a data base of volunteers; they also have the opportunity to create a personal profile, share their story on a blog, list all of thier campaign activities as they complete them, get in touch with their neighbours, add a photograph, and more. This is part of the success of social networking. You do not sign up as an anonymous supporter. You declare yourself a supporter with your own online identity. Others who also have affirmed an identity online can then see others and interact with them.

The essence of social networking is that you begin by creating a web identity and then make connections from there. Influence then flows from the connection and it is the connection that creates the relationship. For politicians, using this tool can be very powerful and was in the 2009 Presidential race. But all this comes at a price as Eellen McGirt in an article on the campaign noted.

"*Traditional top-down messages don't often work in an ecosystem where the masses are in charge. Marketers must cede a certain degree of control over their brands. And that can be terrifying.*[141] "

The power of social action networks is that can take on a life of their own and are not merely fodder for politicians or those who think they can use them for personal ends. One of the sites used by Obama successfully in his campaign and also later to cast transparency on the transition period between election and office is

---

[141] Fastcompany.com . The Brand Called Obama by Ellen McGirt, http://www.fastcompany.com/node/754505/print

"change.org" Although "change.org" has been closely aligned to the Obama campaign it makes clear in its blog

"But the world still turns, and our bloggers are already busy directing their attention to governance, pushing the coming Obama administration to take heed of their issues[142]."

Social networkers are not like party members. They actually discuss politics, make connections with each other and often take action. A whole host of social action networks are now appearing online that connect people and make relationships. Some also make relations not just with individuals but also with non-government organisations or companies. Some exist to develop social enterprise or social business whilst others are specific concentrating on the environment or holistic living and much more. Even the giants like facebook and myspace are engaging in causes and social action. Millions of people globally either online or from the countless array of existing groups and organisations are making new contacts, developing new ideas and forging a variety of forms of social action.

These networks have often been responsible for organising huge petitions, calling people across the globe to direct action demonstrations, engaging in mass lobbies of decision makers and creating and enabling new ways of achieving ends from social business to environmental protection and from changing personal consciousness to just creating Internet noise through volume and scale that is then noticed.

But we still have to ask the questions as to whether such networks can first create the focus that class, gender or race once did to develop concerted action that is sustainable and secondly whether this mass of activity can change consciousness itself through the relational nature of social media networks. And these are big questions.

What Needs to Be Done?

---

[142] Quoted on the blog of http://www.change.org/my_change/home

Social networks are not enough and often we put too much faith in them but they are important and can act as a major catalyst for change. They are forging new alliances everyday and these can have tremendous potential. However to effect change so that it can really make a difference we need to act on several fronts that will help to both change consciousness and reshape our world.

First social networks need to develop so that they create real relationships rather than many of the ephemeral ones that are the essence of so much social networking today. And they need to be autonomous and independent.

Secondly we need to encourage and expand the work of civil society by encouraging more action groups and then find ways of linking them together for common action including use of social media.

Thirdly we have to find ways of connecting these growing action groups to decision makers and through doing create a new type of politics and leadership than we have at present.

Fourthly we have to consider how all this reflects on our own lives and how we relate to the world in a meaningful and sustainable way.

Finally we have to recognise the importance of ideas as a force for change and recreate public space – the square where people meet and exchange these ideas. There has to be a coming together of minds where synergies and energy are freely released and alliances continuously forged anew.

Let us look at each of these in turn as they can help us create the engine that revitalises our hope and makes a difference.

Meaningful Social Networks

Social networking does help people to get together, make new friends and get a sense of recognition that humans so often crave. At this very basic level they fulfil an important role. It can also help with a wide variety of philanthropic activities including activism, education, donor and volunteer development, and direct fundraising.

But some argue that social networks can also create cavernous echo chambers where people reiterate what their friends posted so that many within those networks hear the same thing over and over until they believe it to be true. Constant repetition on different sites can turn an illusion into a perceived reality. Politicians like Obama understood that creating the illusion first was important if the reality was ever to be realised ultimately. Illusion creates momentum and momentum can be a force for change.

But it can also remain an illusion. Sites like facebook are full of groups that people join thinking that by joining they have actually done something. Often it progresses little from there. Meaningful social networking is about turning the joiners into doers and ensuring that supporting a cause requires some degree of action. Groups then become no longer a hobby but rather an opportunity. Communities and individuals associate their online activities with interests, character and personality. When it comes to social causes, the cause must inspire the individual on personal level, and then activate that person to engage in the larger community and corresponding conversations. Such engagement and dissemination of cause-based ideas by the community represents the life energy of civic-minded social media.

Yet it is not enough that such conversations take place unless the social media platform develops pathways to action. Some are beginning to do this. For example, Change.org is beginning to make this change by hiring expert bloggers who will act as daily guides, or curators, around each topic. The reason is that with so many groups emerging and vanishing, those who join more often than not, need more directing. Too many people believe that if you set up a network then you can sit back and just watch it all happen. It is like the Deist view of God back in the 18th century – the clockwork view of the universe. God just wound the clock up and then sat back and let the clockwork globe tick away. Networks do not work successfully like that. The word network has two syllables and each is important to its meaning. First there has to be the "net" and social media networks are excellent for that and then you have to "work" it and many platforms are certainly not good at that.

So Change.org is trying to do more than set up networks. Through their blogs, they want to aggregate and filter and provide context. So if someone is interested in human rights or fair trade for example then people want to know how can they connect to others in a meaningful way so Change. org is looking into how they can point out the most compelling content on the web or the most useful actions. They are trying to turn a social network into a hub for social action. With Change.org you will still have a profile that tracks the money you've raised, the actions you've taken and the number of people you've recruited to your causes. Like Facebook, the site will still allow you to befriend other users and track their activities. And Change.org still draws on a huge database of more than 1 million non-profits, so participants have a lot of latitude to use the site to rally support for groups they like. But it will also direct the committed; those who really want change to the places where it is happening.

Other sites are doing similar things. Meetup is one site that understands the importance of the cyber and the real life interface and has set up a site where people can actually meet and is actually designed for just that purpose. Justmeans brings companies into touch with individuals and encourages its site to become a focal point for social action groups. There is still a long way to go on this but the social network revolution is beginning to become more focussed and is bringing the "work" back into the "net" so that people are not left feeling empty and frustrated.

But throughout all this it is vital to realise that people can collaborate and coordinate their activities at scale, without requiring much of the imposed hierarchy of large organisations. The danger is that large corporations and even government will try to take over social networks. Myspace is already owned by the Fox organisation and this trend could continue. Social networks have to remain free and autonomous and open source. So the question for the future is will social networks evolve beyond 'connect' to 'collaborate' autonomously or will there develop a network-centric collective drive to control the actions of networks and thus ultimately undermine them? For the world to change then networks have to be free.

Extending Civil Society

Establishing connections and groups online is an important development of the last decade but it cannot stand alone as the engine for social change. It can help immensely and also change the nature of both thought and action. But we also need to focus on the causes of alienation and disillusionment that stop people from participating in communal and civic life. We need to break down the barriers that prevent a healthy civil society. We need to activate unmotivated groups, so they can engage their own networks and convince others to participate. Social media can certainly help with this and organisations like NetSquared and the Social Innovation Camp are helping with this. NetSquared for example state their mission as " to jumpstart the leading edge of online technological change -- and to help nonprofits use that edge to change the world![143]" They argue that Non-profits and NGOs thrive on relationships. They believe that the social media offers tremendous potential to have an impact on this process. So they exist to build the strategic capacity, knowledge and skills needed to put these powerful new online social media tools to work to achieve positive change. They can thus enable civil society. The Internet can be an important tool in the community and voluntary sector. It can assist citizens to be more informed, improve access to information and allow individuals to publish alternative viewpoints. It can also have the ability to influence decision makers.

A healthy civil society is vital in any society as the very base of our survival. The great 19th century Russian anarchist Peter Kropotkin[144] argued that it was through mutual aid that our species survived and evolved and that it was indeed a natural state of our being and much more so than competition. The co-operative and self help society has had a long tradition and has often been the way that the poor and dispossessed have survived long before any form of state intervention. Friendly Societies grew up as mutual aid organisations from the simple premise that if a group of people contributed to a mutual fund, then they could receive benefits at a time of need. The early meetings were often held as a social gathering when the subscriptions would be paid. Prior to the Welfare State they were often the only way a working person had to receive help in times of ill health, or old age. Whether civil society is successful or not in the 21st century will partly depend on the relation of civil society to the state. The history of the last few decades is that the state has tried to

---

[143] NetSquared website at http://www.netsquared.org/
[144] Mutual Aid: A Factor of Evolutio, Peter Kropotkin, Publisher: Dover Publications (7 April 2006) ISBN-10: 0486449130

take over civil society rather than enable it as an autonomous force in its own right. This has been done through creating a contract or commissioning culture and straight jacketing civil society organisations into a targeting environment in order to obtain financial aid. They have also done this by redefining citizenship in terms of duty to the state and also by relating to the major not for profit organisations in a manner that has changed the very nature of those organisations. Many of these organisations have moved from being member based to becoming think tank and delivery organisations dependent on state and corporate funds. Their organisational structure begins to reflect the state culture and they often end up more hierarchical in their organisation and less network organised and bottom up in their inspiration. This has often been a threat to the vast array of smaller and locally focussed organisations. For example Steve Johnson of AdviceUK has argued that the commissioning culture when applied to the third sector to be " a recipe for extinction" and has warned that the 90% of the UK's 20,000 voluntary sector advice agencies could close as a result of it[145]. The problem as Johnson sees it is that public service reform has largely been based around the commissioning of services and the voluntary sector is being caught up in it with the result that the smaller organisations will vanish leaving some much larger organisations in tact and dependent on funding through the commissioning process – a recipe for control.

For civil society to be vibrant and alive then it must have a high degree of autonomy. The debate about civil society ultimately is about how culture, market and state relate to each other. Today we have a growing interdependence of state and a globalisation of markets. And as we have already noted there is also an explosion of groups, networks and organisations that engage in discussion and action across national boundaries. This brings into question at times the legitimacy of states. One of the reasons behind the state seeking to set the programme for the voluntary sector through citizen programmes and commissioning is to try to create social cohesion both in culture and in service delivery. And yet it is doing this when cohesion and states are both under challenge and the results can often be counter productive. Civil societies arise from the increasing

---

[145] Champagne Philanthropy, Guardian Society Supplement September 2008

complexity of social and economic life and the proliferation of interests, identities, and causes. A particular civil society is thus the result of a unique combination of structures, cultures and values, and of notions of public versus private spheres. And in the 21st Century all these spheres are confused. The public sphere is both national and global. Nation states try to defend their boundaries as global institutions and governance become increasingly important. The private sphere is also becoming more global as well. Civil society has partly reflected this and has taken on a global presence in the world. Many civil society groups now form global alliances and launch global demonstrations. Nation states often fight rearguard actions to contain civil society within the nation state framework and this causes many stress points within our growingly diverse cultures.

So when we think of enabling, extending and encouraging civil society then we have to begin to understand the complex nature of such a society and the fact that it grows organically from the changing world culture at any one time. When that happens the state should be an enabler to civil society rather than establish procedures and structures that conflict with the real world of our increasingly inter dependent globe. Anything else would be counterproductive.

New Politics

We have looked at how politics in the last century has changed and how it has created disillusionment for so many people. The election of Barrack Obama in the US in late 2008 did provide a window of hope in an otherwise period of decline for the legitimacy of politics as a noble activity. Whether that will last remains to be seen.

Discussing what is meant by "new politics" in the 21st century is a moot point as it has been used so often. Franklin D Roosevelt talked about the "New Deal" and offered a new approach to the economy in an America that was in depression. Oswald Mosley in the 1930's created the "New Party" when he became disillusioned with the Labour Party's approach to that same depression but this gradually evolved into the blackshirts of the British Union of Fascists. In the 1950's Adlai Stevenson offered a "new politics" that embraced civil rights and rapprochement with the Soviet Union. The term New

Politics became used in Britain in 1990's onwards as a way of describing a more participatory and democratic politics. It has now mainly become associated with the New Politics Network, which was founded in 1999 but merged later with Charter 88 to become the Unlock Democracy Organisation[146] – which it says "campaigns for a vibrant, inclusive democracy that puts power in the hands of the people."

So "new politics" tells us little other than there is a disenchantment with what has gone before. When disenchantment sets in then there is the danger that democracy will be undermined unless there is some form of renewal. Mosley wanted to undermine democracy with his concept of new politics. We need to strengthen democracy not destroy it. Strengthen means more than just the campaigns of organisations like Unlock Democracy. Their demands for stronger Parliaments and more accountability are important but the demise of our democracy goes further than this. Accountability in local government or of national executives is all very well but if many decisions are made globally and across national boundaries then it is not enough. We need to renew politics on several fronts apart from just national institutional change.

First we need to establish a concept of global citizenship where people can connect across national boundaries and take action. Institutional accountability at a global level is fraught with problems and is some way off. Until we develop global institutions that are accountable or create sustainable cosmopolitan democracy then the main hope for renewal is the development of our own consciousness as global citizens. December 2008 marked the 60th anniversary of the Declaration of Human Rights. This was a declaration, not a set of rules or international law. It was a declaration to the people's rather than the institutions of the world. Because of that it has been a benchmark to peoples around the globe and is an instrument of hope. The strength of global democracy partly depends on how we keep hope alive. The growth of new forms of social media has helped this considerably. People can be mobilised for petitions, letter writing and demonstrations. They can organise locally,

---

[146] Unlock Democracy website can be found at http://www.unlockdemocracy.org.uk/

nationally or globally and do so very quickly. This is beginning to produce a new worldview as citizens interact around common goals wherever they live. We need a declaration of global citizenship that gives hope to people across the world that they matter and are important.

Secondly we need politicians that will engage not just across national boundaries but also across their own party tribal boundaries as well. Many politicians that serve in legislatures across the globe feel that they are losing power to increasingly centralised executives and also to global organisations. They feel as impotent as most of us as they seek to find a new role. That new role can be found locally and globally. If politicians were catalysts and networkers both in their local communities and globally then they would have a very positive role. They can help develop civil society in their own areas as well as engage in creating alliances across the globe – alliances of people and of other legislators. As they do this then their Party ties will loosen because those ties will not relate to the new and changing alliances that form. The litmus paper test for politicians is how they are able to cope with this. At the moment, politicians are far too tribal and not local or global enough. Their Party is their church, which they follow in either blind faith or in the belief that promotion is found through party patronage. Somehow this tie has to be broken so that politicians and particularly legislators are free to be creative and imaginative in the work that they do.

Thirdly we need a new politics and politicians that understand that our existing institutions are ill equipped to tackle the problems of the 21st Century. Often they are too narrow or nationally focussed in a global world. As Krzysztof Rybinski argues in OpenDemocracy what we have at the moment is

"No leadership; no shared global vision; no shared values; bad incentives which favour short-termism, red-tape, and corruption - all have impeded global strategic thinking since the 1980s[147]."

---

[147] A new world order by Krzysztof Rybinski on OpenDemocracy at http://www.opendemocracy.net/article/a-new-world-order

Rybinski argues that with the power of the USA in relative decline the world faces two options,

- Design the new world order, the new vision
- Let the market and non-coordinated political processes determine the new world order.

The problem with the market approach is that it could have dire effects for all of us and for some areas of the world particularly. At the moment market development has seen growth in Asia but increasing problems and little progress in sub-Saharan Africa. This progress is based upon market based economic growth. This has two major impacts. First it can increase inequalities and that is dangerous in the world of the 21st century. The wealth of the West and the growing wealth of parts of Asia is not trickling down to Africa. Secondly market based growth has seen the growth of greenhouse gas emissions. East Asia doubled the amount of CO_2 emissions and China has now exceeded the United States on the list of biggest polluters. Growth reduces poverty but increases the amount of greenhouse gases with disastrous results for the future of our planet.

There are of course many international organisations but they often engage in contradictory activities leading to a waste in resources. Again, Rybinski argues,

"Global governance is collapsing and there are no signs of a process which could lead to the creation of a new world order."

What Rybinski advocates is a Global Strategic Council that reflects the new and growing reality of power in the 21st century. So many of our global institutions were forged in the power structure of the post Second World War 20th century. Whether that is a realistic suggestion remains to be seen but what is needed are institutions that can tackle poverty and climate change at a global level. And we need politicians that can see further than both their party and their national horizons and lead the way to creating a new concept and reality of global governance.

A Systems Approach

We have spent much of this book talking about change and whether a good society makes a good person or vice versa and argued that it is the interaction of the two that is critical for effective change. Those whose environment and constructs are that of the era of mass consumption and growth will create a social character that reflects this. Being effective change agents means understanding the new environment of the 21st Century and forging a character that is in synergy with that. This means integrating the personal with the social or put another way, the internal with the external.

The concept of integral thinking is becoming a new concept in the early 21st century and it means a comprehensive and inclusive approach to our place in the world that includes as many perspectives, styles, and methodologies as possible within a coherent view of the topic. It has been often described as a "meta-paradigm," or method to draw together an already existing number of separate paradigms into an interrelated network of approaches that are mutually enriching."

As the twentieth century progressed there was a growing disillusionment with Cartesian science. Mechanistic science concentrated on reducing things to basic material building blocks. What began to emerge was a new holistic paradigm recognising that systems are integrated wholes whose properties cannot be reduced to those of smaller units. The new paradigm produced a new approach called "systems theory" that studies the nature of complex systems in nature, society, and science. Ludwig von Bertalanffy[148] - an Austrian biologist, formulated general systems theory in the 1940s. He set out to replace the mechanistic foundations of science with a holistic vision. Like other organismic biologists, Bertalanffy believed that biological phenomena required a new way of thinking. His goal was to construct a "general science of wholeness" as a formal mathematical discipline. Systems theory provides a

---

[148] General System Theory by Ludwig von Bertalanffy, Publisher: Braziller (George) Inc.,U.S.; Revised edition edition (Dec 1968) ISBN-10: 0807604534

framework for describing the behaviour of a group of objects as they work in concert as part of a whole.

Fritjof Capra has been one of the main advocates of systems theory. Capra pushes for western society to abandon conventional linear thought and the mechanistic views of Descartes. In his book "The Web of Life[149]" He writes,

"The new paradigm may be called a holistic worldview seeing the world as an integrated whole rather than a dissociated collection of parts. It may also be called an ecological view, if the term 'ecological' is used in a much broader and deeper sense than usual. Deep ecological awareness recognizes the fundamental interdependence of all phenomena and the fact that, as individuals and societies, we are all embedded in (and ultimately dependent on) the cyclical processes of nature."

Systems theory offers a new perception of reality that has profound implications not only for science and philosophy but also for business, politics, health care, education, and everyday life. As Capra writes,

"Reconnecting with the web of life means building and nurturing sustainable communities in which we can satisfy our needs and aspirations without diminishing the chances of further generations. For this task we can learn valuable lessons from the study of ecosystems, which are sustainable communities of plants, animals and microorganisms. To understand these lessons, we need to learn the basic principles of ecology. We need to become, as it were, ecologically literate. Being ecologically literate, or "ecoliterate," means understanding the principles of organization of ecological communities (ecosystems) and using those principles creating sustainable human communities. We need to revitalize our communities – including our educational communities, business communities, and political communities – so that the principles of ecology become manifest in them as principles of education, management, and politics."

---

[149] The Web of Life: A New Synthesis of Mind and Matter by Fritjof Capra Publisher: Flamingo; New Ed edition (1 Jul 1997) ISBN-10: 0006547516

Integral thinking has emerged as a consequence of systems theory. It is an attempt to go beyond rationalism and materialism and incorporate all of human experience into a larger synthesis. Integral thinking incorporates what advocates consider the four domains of human experience - the psychological, cultural, behavioural and the social and to synthesise them into a new paradigm. Clearly some of this can verge on the mystical and the integral movement does have proponents of integrating both the reasoned world and the spiritual world into a new worldview. However when integral thinking is considered as part of a new paradigm for thought and action then it is a significant shift from the linear thinking of the post enlightenment period. As Capra says a systems approach can impact on all of our lives and politics is certainly one of them.

For example Ken Wilbur in his book " A Theory of Everything" he adapts the idea behind string theory (the notion that all of physics can be united under a single theory explaining the behaviour of matter) and applies it to social science, spirituality and even medicine. He rejects the dualist split of the Enlightenment between religion and science and argues that overlap between thought systems is the key to the universe. He applies this to politics. He looks at three areas that traditional political theories have attempted to tackle but failed to integrate into a whole system of thought – these being the tension between,

- The individual and the collective;
- The source of the cause of human suffering: is the individual primarily to blame or is the society primarily to blame? And
- The different levels of development that the different political parties tend to represent: any truly integral politics would include and represent all of them, and yet how on earth do you do that?

Wilbur has come under criticism from many for a too simplistic view of political dynamics and for neglecting what the representative system does already. It is also criticised because it seems to say let's get the best out of all parties whatever their basic ideology and for some this is considered absurdly simple.

Yet there is a truth in the idea however simple it may seem. The truth is that we have created a party system that has grown up in the

19th and 20th centuries and it has now outgrown its usefulness. There has to be some type of realignment and new structures and processes of politics to reflect the new 21st century. Rather than create this through the old linear systems of forces opposing each other (the world view of atomistic and gravitational sciences) we should try to create a politics that reflects the systems approach and holistic nature of our world.

Holistic Democracy

Our structures of representative and party democracy leave huge deficits that need to be addressed as we move through the 21st century. It has become too rigid and divorced from people and their needs. And at a time when it is undergoing such stress many advocate it as a system worthy of exporting around the world. Many of our international problems stem from this missionary zeal to export a discredited system around the globe. If democracy is to survive then it has to be grounded in local culture rather than be seen as a challenge to that culture. The strength of the notion of "holistic democracy" is that is does just that! Sergio Vieira de Mello the United Nations High Commissioner for Human Rights in 2002 stated in a Seminar on the Interdependence between Democracy and Human Rights,

"*Holistic Democracy does not seek to export or promote any particular national or regional model of democracy or of democratic institutions. To the contrary, a key strength of this approach is its recognition that each society and every context has its own indigenous and relevant democratic institutional traditions. From the village council to the diwaniya, from the loya jirga to the circle of elders, popular consultation has many faces. And while no single institution can claim democratic perfection, the combination of domestic democratic structures with universal democratic norms is a formidable tool in our quest to strengthen the roots of democracy*[150]"

---

[150] From opening speech by Sergio Vieira de Mello at http://74.125.77.132/search?q=cache:LwXte9nDBaAJ:www.unhchr. ch/democracy/hcfinal.doc+holistic+democracy&hl=en&ct=clnk&cd =1&gl=uk

The essence of his argument is that the heart of democracy is not to be found in national institutions, legislatures and executives but in a "free and active civil society, including NGOs and trade unions, women's groups and minority organizations, professional societies and community groups, social movements and watchdog associations."

Holistic democracy recognises the Achilles heal of majority democracy that De Toqueville pointed out in his "Democracy In America" that the tyranny of a majority can be as great as that of any one dictator. The early US Founding Fathers tried to tackle this through a separation of powers between the legislative, judiciary and executive branches of government on one hand and between Federal and State Government on the other. This failed to work as the African American minority can testify as their civil rights were trampled on for decades.

It is important that we develop a democracy that engages the aspirations and rights of all sectors of society whether they are minority or majority as this is the only way to get that important balance between democracy and freedom. Again as Sergio Vieira de Mello states,

"This means incorporating appropriate safeguards to hear and protect the less numerous, less powerful, less wealthy and less popular. It also means that every member of the polity must accept and embrace his or her civic responsibilities in protecting the rights and freedoms of others, and in meeting the just requirements of the democratic society, as explicitly required by the Universal Declaration of Human Rights. "

Of course there is the other dimensions that we have discussed that democracy today is also being challenged by global changes when many decisions are being taken across national borders and where there has been a shift from public to private spheres. These changes make it necessary for democracy in the 21st century to be centred around four simultaneous approaches.

First at the global sphere it is important for global positions to be debated and discussed and for there to be global declarations – and here the United Nations is still centre stage. The Universal

Declaration of Human Rights is surely a model for this as it was a declaration to peoples and not governments and thus makes a crucial link between global visions and civil society.

Secondly our representative institutions such as our Parliaments and Legislatures are important as they are guarantors of our freedoms but they also need to be radically reformed. We have to find new ways of holding our Executives (Cabinets and Administrations) to account and also creating forms of integral politics that radicalises the party political structure that exists at the moments and that is no longer fit for purpose. We have to find some way to concentrate on issues and not on structures and somehow this means de-institutionalising politics.

Thirdly we have to encourage, facilitate and enable the growing realm of holistic democracy that has sprung up in the late 20th and early 21st century and find ways to focus its energy so that its hopes do not turn to frustration. The social media revolution has a significant role in this but so do our politicians and leaders.

Finally we have to make links and relationships between all the three above. Politicians are often accused of being too much centred on the "Westminster Village" or on "Capital Hill," and that their focus is thus narrow and confined. The same is true of people working internationally in that they often forget local issues and those engaged in the process of holistic democracy often fail to engage politicians. We need to build relationships and create dialogue. We need to new Public Squares where people can meet and forge out the new directions and alliances of the 21st century.

All four areas are equally important. For two centuries or more the major focus has been on the second area – the growth of representative democracy. The 21st Century has to place this in the context of the other two and to make all three areas of democratic development of equal importance. This will require dialogue and will also mean a fundamental mind shift for all of us brought up within the confines of nation state politics. We have to become both local and global citizens all at once if we are to positively shape the world to come.

21st Century Citizens

In sections of this book we have looked at how social character is influenced by both individual potency and environmental considerations. We gave the example of Wilhem Reich's work cited in his book "The Mass Psychology Of Fascism" where in analysing class he identified both "objective" and "subjective" class. He argued that although external factors like economic depression can change objectively the class of groups of citizens, their subjective perception might well be different. How you perceive what you are is just as important an agent of change and action as what you are. Indeed the two interact continuously.

As we move from a mass consumption society based on cheap carbon fuel towards a world faced with global crises due to climate change and resource shortages then our external circumstance will surely change. How we perceive ourselves during that change period will be critical. Of course how we perceive ourselves now is also critical. At the time Reich was writing then there were clear-cut class divisions as industrial capitalism developed. In a post industrial society then those class demarcations become blurred and people perceive themselves in much more diverse ways that are defined by gender, race, community as well as class. As Toffler argues in his "Third Wave" in postindustrial societies then like Heinz we have 57 different varieties of families from single parent to communal with much in between. And so the groups that we identify with are no longer just determined by class but are based upon a host of factors from location, nation, virtual and much more. We are far more diverse than we were before and our subjective perception of ourselves thus more complex.

It was much easier to identify social character types in the period when Reich was writing than it is now and because of that it is more difficult to know how people will today react to changes in the external environment. The 21st century citizen is often confused and has a sense of hopelessness without the strong community that bound people together in the past. Certainly in the expanding urban areas there is a growing feeling of alienation and the atomisation of individuals. Writers like Michel Houellebecq[151] have bemoaned that such a society can only fall into a senseless hedonism. And yet the experience of the growing social networks has given the hope that people do want to connect again – not necessarily through class or even gender or race but through issues. Of course the new social media is full of triviality and froth but there is also a growing need to engage.

The 21st century citizen wants to engage at both a global and local level around issues that they think are vital for social justice or to save the planet from our own excess. It is this process that needs enabling and encouraging most of all. The great need is to help facilitate this process so that connections become meaningful and that issue driven relationships take on some sustainability. What is good about the social network revolution is that it is allowing this to happen at a global scale and the importance of that should never be underestimated. However what is missing is the local connections and a way to provide a public forum for ideas and connections to grow and have focus.

Local politics is suffering the decline that national politics is and there is often a huge effort to get volunteers involved. This is partly because those volunteers no longer feel stakeholders in what they are being asked to do. The same malaise effects local groups committed to change and as national campaigns like Amnesty International and Friends Of the Earth become part of the circulating elites of established politics then membership activity seems less important. But these groups still exist and others through social networking are beginning to form – from the movement for transitional towns, to fair trade groups and much more – and all are forming at local level. Gradually the social networking platforms are beginning to understand that actual meetings are as important as virtual ones and connections are being made at local level that result in action groups. This can only grow and be more successful as social network platforms become more advanced and imaginative.

---

[151] Atomised by *Michel Houellebecq* Publisher: Vintage; New edition edition (1 Mar 2001) ISBN-10: 0099283360

Once there is a link between local action and global platforms then the base is laid for a new kind of local/global citizenship that can focus the growing social movements and this will form the essence of 21st century citizenship. Just as social character has been based in the past on acquisitive consumption and wealth creation so the new local/global axis will create new perceptions and character that reflect the growing real world of the 21st century and when subjective and objective are in synch then there is a praxis that is very powerful.

But there is much to do to get to that point and little time to do it. To achieve the synthesis of individual motivation and external reality then we not only need to continue to make connections through the virtual and real communities of the 21st century. We also need to build those connections into relationships and understanding and thus develop potency – so that aspiration can be realised in results. We need to encourage dialogue and discussion at every level and for this we need to recreate public space – the public square where opinion matters and ideas are shaped. We need to recreate ourselves as political animals where politics is seen no longer as a route to personal power and gain but as an art that can transform and change our lives for the better in a time of critical change and turbulence.

Chapter 14 – The 21st Century Public Square

Public Space

In ancient Greek cities, an open space serving as an assembly area and backdrop for commercial, civic, social, and religious activities was an essential part of life. It is where citizens did business, talked philosophy and politics and where debate and rhetoric became important skills. It was called the agora and situated in the middle of the city or near a harbour. In effect The Agora was the Public Square. Public space was valued much more than private space. Well off and worthy citizens might live in humble dwellings but the public space was far from humble. This is where the energy and flow of citizenship took place.

There is a great need to reintroduce public space back into life where people can meet again and talk about the pressing issues of the 21st Century – issues that are so important that they can impact on our very survival.

The concept of a 'public' – a whole polity that cares about the common good and has the capacity to deliberate about it democratically – is central to civil society thinking. It is here where shared interests are developed, where the cut and thrust of debate takes place and meaningful compromises reached so that people can work together more effectively. It is here where new ideas are examined and the thrill of what is possible explored. Without an effective public space then there can be no real governance or any peaceful resolution of differences.

The modern public sphere began to emerge in the 18th century. through the growth of coffee houses, literary and other societies, voluntary associations, and the growth of the press. In their efforts to discipline the state, parliament and other agencies of representative government sought to manage this public sphere.

The Contraction Of Public Space

Today that management has gone to extremes and we have a contraction of public space in our society despite the massive growth of civil organisations. The state itself and its agents certainly have contracted its discursive role. Political parties are election winning machines rather than forums for citizen debate. Even our legislatures no longer debate the great issues of today outside the confines of strict Party politics. There are still individuals left in legislatures that stand out as independent thinkers but most politicians depend on their party machine for election and promotion or upon corporate interests for finance and this means that their independence as leaders of thought is seriously constrained. It is often the case that politicians exercise this freedom only when they retire from the battles for office but when we really need them to speak out they are silenced by the nosy engines of their party machines. Dissent can so often be frowned upon if it undermines the drive to electoral victory. When all politics is polarized, public policy problems become embedded, even frozen, in polities that cannot solve them. There is no integral politics where politicians try to look for common agreement as they are caught up in the theatre of the absurd.

Also what was once public has over the last thirty years or so become privatised and governments are abdicating responsibility for the survival of public space. Much that was once public has been taken over by private corporations. Increasingly the private sector is moving into schools, health care and social security and accountability is defined by private and corporate interest rather than public concern. As the private sector grows then private corporations take over from public institutions as the repository of trust, legitimacy and communal identity in our society. Consumer values take over from citizen values and voting by currency is the substitute for public involvement. This drowns the debate that once took place when the public sphere was valued

Recreating Public Space

Just as there is a need for social action around the critical issues facing us in the 21st century so there is the need to recreate public space and once again to turn it into a modern agora that becomes centre stage in our lives. Today we have a much more diverse society than ever before but this means a more fragmented one as well. Many cities have become a series of racially and economically segregated private enclaves whilst at the same time the privatisation of much of our lives has transformed the forums of public life into corporate silos. And although, as we have described, a massive social movement has emerged globally around a whole series of social justice and environmental issues many work in isolation and come together only sporadically. What is needed are greater connections between the diverse strands of our global activity or else we end up in social action ghettos. We need constant dialogue where common interests are identified, compromise achieved and ideas developed. We need to recreate public space and make the public square once more the social engine of coherent change.

In doing this, we need to change the way we think about politics and political culture, as this will certainly have lasting effects on the future and sustainability of democratic politics. What is now important is to find a new role for elected representatives and to find new ways to reconnect them to their communities. Also there is a need to find solutions to democracy at a global level and to develop forms of cosmopolitan democracy that crosses cultural and national boundaries. Public space has to be both local and global.

In the centuries when generations fought for democratic rights then they did so to defend parliaments and legislatures against the arbitrary powers of a monarch and thus all their efforts were to create the Public Square in those legislatures. Today those very legislatures exercise powers that often conflict with citizen's interests, as they become the captive of party whips, corporate interests and personal ambitions. This can lead to a distancing from citizen groups at the least and corruption at the worse. Of course the legislatures of our modern world are important, as they are essential in any form of representative democracy but they need reform but it is unlikely that reform will take place within the legislatures themselves. Decades of inward looking political activity have led to a form of narcissism that is hard to break. With fragmented social movements and ineffective legislatures then twenty first century democratic politics is in crisis.

In the 21st century there is a growing deficit between what citizens expect and what existing political institutions can deliver. What is now needed is change through democratic renewal. We need to bring citizens closer to decision makers and politicians closer to decisions. At the moment both politicians and citizens feel powerless to effect change. And yet it is at the citizen level that change is happening. The flowering of civil society organisations across the globe gives us confidence that renewal can happen. As Sergio Vieira de Mello quoted in the previous chapter stated they are the heartbeat of democracy in the modern global environment of the 21st century.

It is in civil society where you find the arena or Public Square for argument and deliberation as well as for association and institutional collaboration. How successful this is, of course, is crucial to democracy. It is here where new ideas are discussed, alternative viewpoints expressed and if this is ever constrained then the 'public' interest inevitably suffers. So it is in enabling the diversity of civil society to flourish and grow that a rebirth of democracy is possible.

The Public Sphere & Democracy

It was Jürgen Habermas.who asked some central questions about what the public was and how the public related to both the state and the economy. What is "the public" and does it really have power in a representative democracy? How does "public opinion" shape political power and policy? How is the system of political power maintained in a democracy?

Habermas defined the public sphere as a virtual or imaginary community, which does not necessarily exist in any identifiable space. He describes it as "made up of private people gathered together as a public and articulating the needs of society with the state"

In his later work, Habermas made a distinction between "lifeworld" and "system." That is quite an interesting distinction given what we have covered in this book – the difference between illusion and reality, the growth of social character based on non-sustainable environments and external processes and the need to find a way of harmonising the social characters that we develop with the world as it is fast becoming in the 21st Century.

For Habermas the public sphere is an extension of the "lifeworld" in many respects whereas the "system" refers to the market economy and the state apparatus. The lifeworld is the collection of individuals who debate out their real life with others in the environment of the system dominated by market forces and the state. The public sphere or square is where negotiations take place between the lifeworld and the system to create new paradigms and action. Habermas believed that it was thus a mistake to see the system as dominating the whole of society. The goal of democratic societies is to "erect a democratic dam against the colonizing encroachment of system imperatives on areas of the lifeworld"

For Habermas, the supreme communication skill is the power or argument provided that there were the conditions for equal participation. It was important that there was present,

- **Disregard of status:** that is the people engaged in discourse had a status of equality within the process of argument.
- **Domain of common concern:** that is there had to be a common concern between the participants with no manipulation or hidden agendas introduced by for example representatives there of state organisations and
- **Inclusivity:** that is the public sphere should be an open network where no one is excluded or there is any danger of it becoming a clique.

Habermas believed the public sphere can be most effective through dialogue, acts of speech, through debate and discussion. He also understood the importance of "opinion-forming associations"-- voluntary associations, social organizations, churches, sports clubs, groups of concerned citizens, grassroots movements, trade unions-- to counter or refashion the messages of authority.

Public Space & Diversity

However we have seen that the groups that Habermas refers to often have problems being as assertive and independent of market forces and the state as they would wish and this can adversely impact on the ideal of the public square.

For example Nancy Fraser[152] believes that marginalized groups are excluded from the universal public sphere, and thus it is impossible to claim that one group would in fact be inclusive. Rather than join the global public square they tend to create their own. They do this because the public sphere can often end up subject to crude majority rule. Fraser has argued that minority and repressed groups who form their own public sphere should look upon what they do as creating "parallel discursive arenas" where counterdiscourses" can be formulated and circulated.

This is a real problem, as civil society is not just made up of a growing social movement of environmental and social justice groups. It is also made up of a diverse complexity of existing organisations and a growing mosaic of cultures. As migration increases then so does the cultural diversity of civil society. Those cultures themselves are often under stress as they adapt to new environments and there is tension between generations, the new the old, the traditional and the modern. The public square has to accommodate this ever-changing dynamics in cultural awareness.

The complexity and multi-layered cultural diversity of modern societies challenges the ability of democratic systems to find a balance between integration and diversity. Preoccupation with notions of 'citizenship' is often a way of avoiding constructing this balance creatively on one hand or of favouring the forces of integration over diversity on the other.

Creating public space certainly has to be about understanding ideas of integration and cohesion. The 21st century public square is not the place of demagogues to harangue those there into notions of conformity.

In 2003 the Council of Europe produced a Declaration on Intercultural Dialogue and Conflict Prevention in which they emphasised "the vital importance of culture as a primary vehicle of meaning and tool for understanding, a democratic agent and instrument of individual and collective human development, and as

---

[152] Nancy Fraser (1990). "Rethinking the Public Sphere: A Contribution to the Critique of Actually Existing Democracy". *Social Text* (Duke University Press)

a forum for rapprochement and dialogue between all men and women.[153]"

They went on to assert "the rich nature of cultural diversity in Europe both within and between Member States, the Ministers responsible for Cultural Affairs intend to concentrate on encouraging dialogue as one of the bases for conflict prevention. Accordingly, they agree to seek inspiration in the values upheld by the Council of Europe that offer scope for a range of converging measures capable of generating strong synergies."

However how this vision worked out in practice was much more difficult than the assertion of the principle itself. The difficulties could be seen across Europe and was highlighted graphically in the dispute in France over whether Muslim women should wear headscarves in schools.

In Joan Wallach Scott's book The Politics of the Veil (The Public Square)[154] she reveals a surprising degree of chauvinism in the political ideals of French universalism, which conflicted with the very liberalism that the pro ban lobby was championing. Instead of understanding the demands of Muslim women French individualism was criticised as being too abstract that tended towards " absolutist secularism." Such a trend was seen as almost as intolerant as the "global Islam" that many feared and hid within it an unhealthy clash of civilisation tendency in the French secularist mindset. In this debate there was little attempt to see that the "veil" actually serves a strategic, even empowering, purpose in everyday life: a way for young women to negotiate their gender, spiritual, and political identities in woefully underfunded schools in the poorest sections of major French cities."

The public square if it means anything must mean a forum where these understandings can emerge and that conventional knee jerk

---

[153] Found on the website
http://www.coe.int/T/E/Com/Files/Ministerial-Conferences/2003-Culture/declaration.asp
[154] The Politics of the Veil (The Public Square) by Joan Wallach Scott, Publisher: Princeton University Press (September 17, 2007) ISBN-10: 0691125430

responses are somehow held in check. The growth of a whole new civil society in the midst of the new diversity that is much of our modern world requires that we reassess our views on what is liberating and what is constraining and to understand this from a wide variety of cultural perspectives. How we do this without friction erupting from our pre existing mindsets is the difficult question. It is clear that the modern institutions and organisations that have for the past fifty years or so acted as the public sphere are now woefully inadequate.

The Demise of The Political Party

In democracies the way that such friction was avoided and the way that compromises were reached so that there was coherence within the framework of diversity was through political parties. Parties formed the public forums where debate took place and agendas agreed. One American political scientist once claimed "No America without democracy, no democracy without politics, no politics without parties.[155]"

In America particularly as primaries have become more important and referendums increasingly popular then political parties have become less important as the coherent force for selecting candidates and debating policy. Fareed Zakaria in his book The Future of Freedom states,

"Political parties have no real significance in America today. Over the last generation the parties have become so decentralised that nobody controls them. The machines and their bosses, the party organisation, the volunteer cadres, and party elders have all withered in significance. The party is, at most, a fund-raising vehicle for a telegenic candidate.[156]"

---

[155] The American Presidency by Clinton Rossiter, Publisher: Harcourt, Brace (1960) ISBN-10: 1125372591
[156] The Future of Freedom: Illiberal Democracy at Home and Abroad by Fareed Zakaria Publisher: W. W. Norton & Co.; Revised edition edition (16 Nov 2007) ISBN-10: 0393331520

Once Parties were either dominated by machine professionals or by the members who all felt that had a stake in the party they supported. A candidate was the candidate of the party. Now as Zakaria points out candidates become selected through primaries and the machine that helps is a personal one. So power has moved from party members and organiser to the fundraiser and public relation firm. Campaigns are centred on personalities and parties usually follow. Fund raising has become the fundamental activity of the political campaign in America. Many believe that the Obama campaign moved this on by involving hundreds of new and young people on web sites by helping to give them a stake holding role in the campaign. Yet this was done outside the Party framework thus diminishing its role as the public forum where issues could be debated.

Vernon Bogdanor in an article in the New Statesman argues the same case in the UK where he said,

"There are signs that the age of the mass party is coming to an end; that our political parties are dying on their feet -------- the consequences of the demise of the mass party are likely to prove very profound. [157]"

Modern political parties grew up in the industrial and collectivist age and their organisation and raison d'etre reflected the imperatives of that time. They developed positions on a wide range of topics or as with the Democratic Party in the US provided welfare for the new immigrant and thus ensured his or her support. Today as Bogdanor states parties are more concerned with "valance" issues where there has been forged a fundamental agreement on basic positions and disagreement is reduced to which party is best placed to achieve the same objectives. So now in the UK as elsewhere parties are dominated by career politicians who see politics and their Party as if it were a major corporation and they seek promotion as fast as they can to help manage UK Limited. Westminster thus is the arena for career ambitions and not the public space of party politicians divided and yet debating the great issues.

---

[157] On the New Statesman Website at
http://www.newstatesman.com/200610230057

This has major consequences for the health of our democracy. If politicians battle for promotion around objectives shared by all parties, then how can the voter achieve change? Much of the disillusionment of politics can be seen because there is a huge gulf between citizens and politicians? Mass parties are no longer the public forums they once were but what is there that can replace them?

Traditional Alternatives

Of course political parties were not the only forums for public debate. The 20th century saw the growth of other forums that could have provided some space for wide discussion to take place. Faith organisation, voluntary organisations and think tanks all provided an opportunity to engage in a wide debate but even these organisations have found themselves so changed that the public square that they once offered has contracted.

Faith Organisations

Faith organisations could be important contributors to the public space debate in the 21st century especially as there is a resurgence of religion into the political sphere. Yet Church attendance in Britain is declining fast. According to *Religious Trends,* a comprehensive statistical analysis of religious practice in Britain, published by Christian Research, even Hindus will come close to outnumbering churchgoers within a generation. The forecast to 2050 shows churchgoing in Britain declining to 899,000 while the active Hindu population, now at nearly 400,000, will have more than doubled to 855,000. By 2050 there will be 2,660,000 active Muslims in Britain - nearly three times the number of Sunday churchgoers. Only the large, evangelical churches of the Baptist and independent denominations show less of a decline but many of these churches also show some dwindling away. Many churches are overwhelmed by financial crisis and are focussed on decline, solvency and membership. There is little time for churches to think about religion and its relation to the new society of the 21st century and even less time to engage in cross faith discussion as well as engage the secular world in the issues facing us. Of course some still do and many individuals get involved in social campaigns but this is less significant than it used to be. Yet if they wanted churches could play an important role. Nick Spencer in a publication *"'Doing God': A Future for Faith in the Public Square*[158]*"* for Theos, the Public Theology Think Tank says,

"The fact of public reason, therefore, places two demands on those religious thinkers who wish to participate in the public square. They should be willing to 'accommodate' their language and reasoning to what is currently acknowledged as the norm in public discourse. But they should also be willing to challenge that norm, questioning axioms, confronting arguments and asking all parties, irrespective of their public identities, to justify their faith-based positions."

The growing religions of Hindus and Moslems do provide an opportunity to engage and debate and it is vital that civil society organisations engage them this way. But there is a long way to go and the catalyst will often have to be external to these religions if real cross boundary discussion is to take place. Bu there is a need for Muslims as well as others to forge a new identity that combines their faith with their place of residence There is a need to build a new consciousness that Muslims in the UK are not the same in the same condition as Muslims outside the Western world. Muslims living in the UK are British Muslims who definitely share the same faith with all fellows Muslims but also have to build community and bridges outside the Muslim world. So the public square has to be there and it has to cross the faith divide and there is a long way to go to achieve that in the same way as as there is with some of the more exclusive Christian communities.

But this provides opportunity if those bridges can be built – an opportunity to understand both human rights and faith within a multi dimensional society. This is what the public square can do but it has to bring people of different views together and that work is only beginning.

---

[158] See the Theos website at http://www.theosthinktank.co.uk/God_in_Public_Life_Tops_Faith_Agenda.aspx?ArticleID=103&PageID=12&RefPageID=51

Voluntary Organisations

The larger voluntary organisations also provide a forum where people can meet and engage but as we have seen many of the larger voluntary organisations are beginning to mimic the political structure in which they find themselves. Like political parties, they are becoming less member based and more centred on career orientated professionals with links to the circulating elites and the raising of funds being their prime incentives.

Even for the smaller organisations funding needs can compromise the independence that they could bring to the public square. A survey carried out by Compact Voice, based at the National Council for Voluntary Organisations (NCVO), shows that independence is far from a reality for many voluntary organisations in England.

Sixty-nine per cent of organisations surveyed said local groups were afraid to campaign in case their funding would be affected. This is despite voluntary organisations having their own 'declaration of independence', in the form of the Compact, whose first commitment is to 'recognise and support the independence of the sector.[159']

That independence is often compromised by the "commissioning culture." As Ben Wittenberg wrote in the Guardian[160],

"Commissioning services is about government deciding what is needed and who should be supported and prescribing exactly how that work should be carried out before inviting organisations to tender."

Wittenberg believes that the relationship between state and voluntary activity is changing and that without proper discussion and debate, the larger, more dangerous unintended consequences could have devastating implications for the sector. Of course it has unintended consequences on the voluntary sector being part of the

---

[159] As quoted in the One Voice Network website at
http://www.onevoice.co.uk/ovn/News0.nsf/LookupUNID/222D874
EFDC702848025730F003B9045?OpenDocument
[160] Society Guardian, Wednesday 6 June 2007 23.54 BST

public square as independent thinkers and actors on the part of their communities. To be an effective part then they need to link to others as mediators in the process of public debate.

Think Tanks

Think tanks once occupied a position in society that offered public space where new ideas could be examined and explored. When Robert Brookings first established his research institute in 1916 in the US it was to be a non-partisan organisation that went well beyond the confines of party politics. This was true of several of the earlier think tanks that were to emerge in the US like the National Bureau of Economic Research and the Council on Foreign Relations (CFR). These organisations became part of a method developed to increase civil discourse on public issues. They served as a public square that went beyond the narrow interests of political parties. Today most think tanks are decidedly partisan. As Burton Pines director of research at the Heritage Foundation admitted,

" We're not here as some kind of Ph.D committee giving equal time. Our role is to provide conservative public policy makers with arguments to bolster our side[161]."

Fareed Zakaria in The Future of Freedom: Illiberal Democracy at Home and Abroad goes further and argues that,

" Many of the new "institutes" and "foundations" in Washington are in fact, front groups for special interests: corporations, labour unions, even foreign governments. They produce a barrage of "research" to prove that their benefactors deserve government subsidies or other kinds of favouritism.[162]"

Once the organisation that could play the role of the mediator in American society, think tanks are now the captive servant of parties

---

[161] Quoted in *The Future of Freedom: Illiberal Democracy at Home and Abroad by Fareed Zakaria Publisher: W. W. Norton & Co.; Revised edition edition (16 Nov 2007) ISBN-10: 0393331520*
[162] Ibid

and corporations. The role needed in the public square to provide independent evaluation of public policy has seriously diminished.

In the UK there is beginning to also be doubt about the quality of think tanks as part of the public square. The think tank world began as a set of outsiders challenging the old establishment. Today it has largely become a part of the new establishment that has emerged and is part of an increasingly narrower world at a time when imagination and breadth of vision is needed. The influence of corporate funding, and how success is judged by insider access to politicians and media coverage determines the direction of so many think tanks and that in a way neutralises their impact as part of the public square.

They are also increasingly linked to political parties at a time when party politics is in decline. This makes the world of the new establishment think tanks an incestuous one full of "bright young things" tied to the professionalisation of the modern world of politics. They do not stand out as independent forces that can make a real difference. . Gerry Hassan writes in Open Democracy[163] that

"The think tank revolution in the UK is a story of the decline of party, which can be seen in the dilution of party research departments..... Nowadays, we can see across all the mainstream UK political parties the dislocation of party leaderships from their party structures, and their shift of attention towards the world of post-democratic elites, of which think tanks are a part. This leads towards the corporatisation of politics and the ultimate outsourcing: the privatisation of policy making. "

So with the decline of the political party itself the difficulties found in faith groups, the larger voluntary organisations and think tanks taking on the role of genuine and independent civil discourse the public square is beginning to look a little bare. Somehow this has to be revived if liberal democracy in the global world of our century is to remain alive

---

[163] See the Open Democracy article at http://www.opendemocracy.net/article/yes/the-limits-of-the-think-tank-revolution

False Dawns

Confining the public space to declining political parties and corporations in the world of the 21st century is to mute discussion and avoid the pressing issues that face us.

The whole idea of public space is that it is about the public – not the establishment. When the establishment restricts public space then it is no longer the space of the public. There is a crying need for new public spaces and squares that stand outside of the established institutions where people can engage and make connections.

In recent years there has been a move towards experiments and innovations in so-called "participation" as if somehow this engaged the public in the real cut and thrust of the public square. Forums and focus groups have abounded and we are told that this is the new way to engage people. But of course for the most part they are at the worst public relations exercises and at best a way of politicians finding out what people want as voting consumers so that they can maintain their popularity. They are superficial exercises in maintaining the status quo as painlessly as possible. They never delve deep into the issues that confront us in a way that engages people over the long term.

It is true that there has been a growth in recent years of the idea of deliberative democracy, also sometimes called discursive democracy and refers to any system of political decision making that is based on the implementation of some form of consensus decision making. Deliberative democracy theorists argue that legitimate lawmaking can only arise from the public deliberation of the citizenry. In the USA there is a deliberative democracy movement with its own website that states[164],

"Central to our work is the conviction that the outcomes of deliberation result in qualitatively better, more lasting decisions on policy matters. Participation in such forums is a central to democratic renewal. Essentially, our view is that democratic deliberation is a powerful, transformational experience for everyone

---

[164] Deliberative Democracy website at http://www.deliberative-democracy.net/index.php

involved--citizens and leaders alike--which can result in attitudinal shifts toward the institutions and practice of democracy overall."

Deliberative democracy has a real role to play in bringing citizens in to engagement with decision makers. The Deliberative Democracy website above gives many examples of local and state governments involving citizens in deliberations about issues. For example it cites that three evaluations of the CaliforniaSpeaks statewide effort on health care have been combined into one report on the project's impacts and lessons learned. CaliforniaSpeaks involved over 3,500 residents in eight cities, linked by satellite, in a day-long deliberation. But most of these cases are examples of state institutions using the processes of deliberative democracy for their own ends as they often set the agenda. They can be significant but the deliberative democracy movement is hardly the public sphere that many want.

In the UK there has been a growth of "citizens juries" and these are experiments in deliberative democracy. A Citizens' Jury is normally made up of 12-50 people called together to hear evidence and make a judgement on issues that are of a complex nature. They call and cross-examine witnesses, consider the evidence and then make a judgement. The Jury has the opportunity to explore an issue in detail and then make informed recommendations. Typically a citizens' jury lasts between one and three days. In 2007 Gordon Brown the UK prime Minister launched citizen's juries to discuss children's issues[165]. The first was in Bristol where a group of 12 to 20 people were picked to represent a community and they discussed issues affecting children like school discipline and internet pornography. They heard from a range of experts before reaching a conclusion, which will then be presented to ministers. But some questioned the validity of this and whether the state was taking over the tools of deliberative democracy for its own ends to demonstrate that is listens. Used this way critics argue it is no more than a public relations exercise. Indeed Ed Mayo, the National Consumer Council's chief executive, said: 'There has been a genuine surge of enthusiasm for citizens' juries and summits over the past year. However, they are only worth doing if they give people a genuine

---

[165] Reported in The Guardian September 6th 2007 at
http://news.bbc.co.uk/1/hi/uk_politics/6980747.stm

say. Otherwise they are, at best, glorified focus groups and, at worst, no more than a pale sham of democratic dialogue.' He said that people now identify 'fake listening' as one of their top gripes[166].

In a way these all presented us with false dawns of opening up the public sphere to real debate. They have thus far been an attempt by the state to engage the tools of public sphere debate to their own ends. It can only be self-defeating in the long run as it will merely add to the disillusionment with politics.

The Real Public Square

When writers like Jürgen Habermas wrote about the public sphere. they did not envisage it being taken over by the state as a method of compliance although they saw the dangers. For them the public square belongs to the citizens and not the state. Habermas was concerned with the social conditions necessary for a rational-critical debate about public issues conducted by citizens willing to let their arguments rather than their status determine the outcome. One thing he was clear about was that the public sphere must be independent from the state. As Craig Calhoun states in "Habermas and the Public Sphere"

"The importance of the public sphere lies in its potential as a mode of societal integration. Public discourse (and what Habermas later and more generally calls communicative action) is a possible mode of communication of human life, as are state power and market economies. But money and power are non-discursive forms of communication, as Habermas' later theory stresses; they offer no intrinsic openings to the identification of reason and will, and they suffer from tendencies toward domination and reification. State and economy are thus both crucial for and rivals of the democratic public sphere.[167]"

---

[166] The Observer September 30th 2007 at
http://www.guardian.co.uk/politics/2007/sep/30/immigrationpolicy.
observerpolitics
[167] *Habermas and the Public Sphere (Studies in Contemporary German Social Thought) by C Calhoun Publisher: MIT Press; New edition edition (5 April 1993) ISBN-10: 0262531143*

It is the independence of civil society in the public sphere that is crucial to a vibrant and free democracy. We have seen how both the economy and the state often shape social character so that it reflects the status quo. It is in the public sphere where space is created for change both in the individual and the environment. Yet we have seen how public space has contracted as individuals have been reduced to either economic consumers or state defined citizens. What is needed are channels for the public square to be reinvented that is reflective of civil society as it is growing in the 21st century.

The growing legions of social movements make up a new dimension to civil society but it is a civil society that is local, regional, global and national and often these spheres overlap. Groups co-operate for campaigns at a very local level, communicate about national issues and often link with others globally because many of their concerns only have global solutions. When there is such a mosaic of activity then identifying a public square where discussion can take place is an exercise in creative imagination. In some respects these spaces are multiple in character and variety and are part of a growing "global agora." These new arenas of discussion have to interact with what is a "pluralisation" of actors and multiple-authority structures. In the world we live in authority is more diffuse, decision-making, dispersed and sovereignty muddled.

The creation of a new public sphere or square is only beginning but it is essential if individuals are to break free from the social character that has been defined by economic consumerism and state defined citizenship. And it has to be both local and global because that reflects the imperatives of 21st century living. It is the "lifeworld" to use Habmas's term of the present century

There are signs that this is now beginning to happen as the growing movement for social change in civil society hold their own meetings and discussions but it is a diverse world out there and there is still a need to bring people together and to link up the dots. And this is not just happening in the world of the environmental and social justice movement. It is also happening with new forms of think tanks that are emerging that are not aligned with established corporations or political parties and who espouse4 the idea of "the do tank" moving away from merely just "thinking."

Tom Bentley the Director of Demos for example talks about "everyday democracy" and on its website Demos calls itself "a think-tank focused on power and politics. We search for and communicate ideas to give people more power to shape their own lives. Demos' vision is a democracy of free citizens, with an equal stake in society." Another is The New Economic Foundation who says of itself - "NEF is an independent think-and-do tank that inspires and demonstrates real economic well-being. We aim to improve quality of life by promoting innovative solutions that challenge mainstream thinking on economic, environment and social issues. We work in partnership and put people and the planet first."

There are others like this that are beginning to make a difference like the Young Foundation and the Centre for Social Justice. These are all very different from the conventional think tank organisation and combine doing with thinking and tries to open the public sphere up to a wider audience of people.

Also businesses are beginning to realise that there is increasing disenchantment with conventional public relation exercises and that this is fast turning into resentment and cynicism. As a result there is the beginning of the co-creation movement. Co-creation is the practice of product or service development that is collaboratively executed by developers and stakeholders together and where value is increasingly being co-created by the firm and the customer, rather than being created entirely inside the firm. Here the customer is given space to help design the future collaboratively rather than merely be market research fodder for competing professionals. For example Promise Communities in London UK say,

"At the centre of our technology sit an array of tools that allow us to co-create solutions with the community. These tools include Brainstorming Rooms, Idea Voting Sessions, Live Online workshops, quant and qual surveys, usability testing, diary keeping, multimedia exchange and 1-2-1 interviews. These tools are complimented with a mix of powerful features that have been designed to absorb participants in the process and build their engagement.[168]"

Because co-creation companies work with communities and stakeholders and involve them then they are beginning to work with a global and highly intelligent group of people who are increasingly concerned with the state of our planet. Co-creation has the possibilities of opening up space for communities with the corporate world as space is elsewhere being opened up with the state world.

However the most important role of the public sphere is the ability to bring together all of these endeavours by joining up the dots through discourse and discussion 21st Century Network[169] is one organisation looking at the public sphere from the widest of perspectives.

21st Century Network (GlobalNet21)

As the maps that navigated us through the last two centuries have been found wanting and the charts for our new century are only now being drafted it is difficult have a one-dimensional view abut change. Economic determinism, the importance of personal change, incremental approaches set against the rational approach all have their part to play. However we have a planet in a hurry faced with ecological disaster and technologic change so rapid and democratised that what was once the prerogative of the state and large corporations is becoming available to the many. These changes have opened up the media well beyond the lobbies of the political and business elites and have also placed weapons of destruction in the hands of dedicated minorities. And all of this has happened as our economic world is in crisis and global poverty continues unabated.

---

[168] From Promise Communities Website at
http://www.promisecommunities.com/
[169] 21st Century Network meetup site is at
http://www.meetup.com/21stCenturyNetwork/

Change has to be total in the individual, in the polity, in civil society and in the business world. We need a public square that will engage all of these segments of society in order to create a new consensus for action and change. We no longer have the luxury of thinking that it is only big business that will effect change or the masses on the street, or the electorate working through political parties. We have to address change in every dimension. We live in a multi dimensional world of thought and action and time is short. We need organisations that will address this need and engage all segments of society in what is the vital but mammoth task of saving our future by acting in the present and on all fronts. Past tribal loyalties and ideological and organisational barriers need to be replaced by the stark reality that faces us.

21st Century Network was set up partly as a way of re introducing public space back into our lives where people can again discuss the issues of our century. By bringing people together with decision makers, voluntary and business organisations 21st Century Network sought to encourage debate that could lead to social action and change. It was one of the many initiatives that were being developed globally to reintroduce the debate around ideas and to involve people and groups on a wide scale.

21st Century Network started up in April 2007. There was nothing remarkable about that as organisations come and go in this ever-changing world. But 21st Century Network was interesting for several reasons. First it was an attempt to look at the issues of the 21st century with the present and future in mind rather than the blueprints of a past century. At a time when global warming threatens our very survival, when inequalities are increasing world wide, when new forms of intolerance and extremism are emerging in a world of diversity then thinking through this new reality mosaic was essential.

But it was not just about thinking but discussing and action as well. When I was a young teenager I always thought that political parties were the place where debate and discussion took place and action would consequently result. Brought up on the post war model of organisational politics where organisations like the Labour Party, trade unions, CND, The Anti Apartheid Movement and much more had local groups discussing politics and passing resolutions it seemed this was the very model of modern democratic politics in a post war age. But the immediate post war period was one of denial for so many reasons. In an attempt to return to "normalcy" after a half century of wars and depression, people created an illusion about so much of life. This was the time when the war was not talked about, sex did not exist, respectability was the norm and families reasserted themselves as a form of nostalgic comfort. In this environment it was natural that politics appeared "civilised" and that people could meet in friendly debate, pass resolutions and firmly believe that by referring them up that they could make a difference. When the 1960's exploded on us then the deficiency of that model became apparent as a counter culture of frustration exploded amidst the turmoil of the Vietnam War and the rediscovery of poverty. But this was also a time of economic growth and this eventually became the driving force of the second half of the twentieth century shaping our behaviour and character. The problems this created were often of Frankenstein proportions in that we created an entity that we could no longer control. Frustration and cynicism became a common response.

Today it is not just that people are disillusioned with political parties but members of those parties often are as well. They are often heard complaining that political parties are the last place on earth where politics is discussed. 21st Century Network provided a forum where that discussion could take place with people from all parties and indeed religions and who shared a common humanistic perspective on life. It was a vehicle for people to jump on board and discuss the future. It was also a way of involving other groups and acting as a conduit to let people know what is happening there and indeed to provide a framework for those involved to start action groups themselves.

21st Century Network developed using the social network sites now made available through the Web 2 Internet technology. Through sites such as meetup, myspace, twitter, justmeans, linkedin and facebook a new audience of people keen to discuss the issues of this century began to emerge. Many were fed up with the existing political structure that tended to stifle debate and wanted a forum where issues could be engaged and people could get together for follow up action including mapping into existing networks and social action groups.

It involved working with businesses, politicians, community groups and individuals involved through the new social networks and to try to create a forum where as Habermass emphasised status was not important. That has been a difficult journey but one that is well worth travelling. What made it easier is that the confidence so often present in politicians and business people only 20 years ago is fast dissipating. Businesses know that their existing model is inadequate and are unsure of the future and politicians often have the same sense of hopelessness that others have and seek an alliance with those who still believe that change is possible.

21st Century Network has now developed into GlobalNet21 and has opened up to a global as well as national and local audiences using webinars as a way of creating a global public square to compliment local face to face meetings. It is one of the new network organisations that are fast developing that put people in touch with each other on both a local and a global basis. Using social network platforms like, for example meetup, it encourages face-to-face meetings as well as online contact and in the future this hybrid approach that combines traditional meetings with web networking will become a powerful force for change and a basis for the resurgence of democracy.

Jumping On Board

There is always the danger that the new social platforms will be used and to some extent taken over by the traditional organisations. Indeed traditional politics has been quick to see the force of social networks to further their own ambitions. We see that Howard Dean used it to further his ambitions to become President and Barack Obama certainly did as he fought for the Democratic nomination and then the Presidency. Obama has both used and been used widely by the Internet. He has used all sorts of people to make connections through social networks. Engaging Chris Hughes who four years previously had helped launch Facebook, Hughes brought with him a mastery of the human side of social networking that has translated into real results for the campaign. He has been successful at converting online clicks into real world currency – through action and donations. People joined the Obama campaign as stakeholders and became involved.

But as Ellen McGirt [170] commented in an article quoted earlier this can come at a price for politicians and anyone who attempts to use networks to control. They tend to have a life of their own and could eventually change the nature and culture of those trying to use them.

21st Century Network like many new organisations exists to make this terrifying experience a part of the norm so that it becomes accepted and change more easily takes place. The future is terrifying and the new media technologies add to that experience. The fear generated by both situation and technology now makes it a fertile time for real attitudes to change and paradigms to shift. After all business men like politicians are the same as all of us and have children and grand children who face the prospect of a dismal future unless we take action now. They want solutions as much as the rest of us so the need to engage is now greater than ever and the opportunities are there to take.

Through the connections that we now can make across organisational and belief barriers using both new and old technologies there is the possibility that both the individual and the environment can interact with synergy. Bridging the structural holes that divide these groups and organisations, communities and beliefs is just as challenging online as offline, if not more so. Offline, you know if a door has been slammed in your face; online, it is impossible to determine the response that the invisible audience is having to your message. But bridge it we must and it is that synergy between individual and environment that we must now work towards. Doing this effectively and in a sustainable way requires "right action."

Public Space & Right Action

Business as usual is not really an option for the 21st century. The decades of profligacy that have preceded this century have placed us all in a situation of turbulence and confusion. For much of their history and all of prehistory, humans did not see themselves as being any different from the other animals among which they lived.

---

[170] FastCompany.com . The Brand Called Obama by Ellen McGirt, http://www.fastcompany.com/node/754505/print

The Enlightenment that placed reason on a pedestal resulted in the 20th century rush for growth at all costs. Reason became reduced to quantifying output rather than reflecting on our condition as part of a whole. Modern religion and indeed humanism as well reflected this aberration. Once we placed reason as defined by the Enlightenment in prime position then we created ideologies and belief systems as competing scripts of reason that people were willing to die for. Now those past systems of belief and thought are under attack as never before and because of the turbulence of the 21st century we are in a position to reassess and think again but to think beyond reason alone.

It is no longer possible in our times to make political action the surrogate for salvation. My early days of mission driven effort either in religion or politics was the baggage that I brought with me because of my circumstances and the culture that I had inherited. I have long begun to realise that political programmes are expedients either to obtain power or to live in the illusion that we humans can create a world of our own making. The world already exists and will take care of itself. We have to learn what is the right action to live within it and survive. Our happiness and well-being has been seriously and adversely affected by the belief that we can save the world or live in one of our own making. It is a view that starts with hope and ends in despair.

Somehow we have to create a new political agenda that is in harmony with change that is possible and this necessitates a need to consciously experience ourselves as part of the unity of life. It is the separation of self from the planet we live in that has been the root cause of our demise. Instead of the belief that we can dominate our environment we have to learn to live with it and that means listening to our own inner voices, our intuitive self and the voices of our environment in a receptive manner. We have to develop the skills of using the intelligence of our whole body and not only our brain. This means valuing experience and that of others so that we can respond readily to the needs of the environment, which of course includes ourselves. Long before the growth of the world's monotheistic religions that lay the foundation for the Enlightenment in the Western World the ancient Chinese sage Lao Tzu wrote

"By listening carefully within, as well as to our surroundings, by remembering that we are part of an interconnected whole, by

remaining still until action is called forth, we can perform valuable, necessary, and long-lasting service in the world while cultivating our ability to be at one with the Tao"

The ability to be one with the universe means admitting our humility rather than asserting our dominance. This is the major change needed in the 21st century. It is not a formula for inaction as some suggest but one that requires right action and appropriate change that is real and responds to the universe in which we live.

Since the Enlightenment at least, we have shaped our social characters by the belief that we can do anything. The omnipotent God of the Judaic, Christian and Islamic world has been transferred to the omnipotent human being who through reason can solve all. Instead we are in danger of destroying all. It is the realisation of that danger that may at last bring us to our senses. Instead of creating an inner self that reflects growth, domination and self-aggrandisement we maybe on the beginning of a journey to develop an inner voice that reflects the planet on which we live with all its wonder and its fragility.

There is a long way to go on this journey and we have little time. Whatever we can do to achieve this, it is the most important political act of our age. If we can create the public space – the sphere to engage and connect - then through the energy of those connections we may succeed. As we said at the start, this is the challenge and it is a challenge for our survival.

Lightning Source UK Ltd.
Milton Keynes UK

177636UK00001B/8/P